T0345371

# Assessing Justin Trudeau's Liberal Government

## 353 PROMISES AND A MANDATE FOR CHANGE

# Assessing Justin Trudeau's Liberal Government

## 353 PROMISES AND A MANDATE FOR CHANGE

Edited by

Lisa Birch and François Pétry

Presses de
l'Université Laval

Financé par le gouvernement du Canada
Funded by the Government of Canada

Canada

Nous remercions le Conseil des arts du Canada de son soutien.
We acknowledge the support of the Canada Council for the Arts.

Conseil des arts    Canada Council
du Canada           for the Arts

Each year, Presses de l'Université Laval receives financial support from the Société de développement des entreprises culturelles du Québec for their publishing programs.

**SODEC**
Québec

Cover design: Laurie Patry
Layout: Diane Trottier

Legal Deposit 3rd quarter 2019

ISBN 978-2-7637-4443-8
PDF 9782763744445

Les Presses de l'Université Laval
www.pulaval.com

Printed in Canada

# Table of Contents

## CHAPTER 12
### Gender Equality, Diversity, and Inclusion: Between Real Change and Branding

*Karen Bird*

## CHAPTER 13
### Renewing the Relationship with Indigenous Peoples: An Ambitious Discourse, Limited Accomplishments

*Thierry Rodon and Martin Papillon*

# List of Figures

# List of Tables

# Acknowledgements

This book project assessing the record of the Liberal government of Justin Trudeau in French and English came to life following a suggestion from André Baril, then publisher at the Presses de l'Université Laval (PUL). André thought it would be interesting to produce a sequel to the successful book assessing the record of Quebec's Couillard government, which the PUL published in 2018. We acknowledge the support and work of Denis Dion, Director of the PUL, who picked up André's proposal and made it possible for us to rise to the challenge of publishing simultaneously in Canada's two official languages.

This book would not have been possible without the financial support of the PUL, the Center for Public Policy Analysis (CAPP) supported by the team grant from the Quebec *Fonds de recherche du Québec—Société et culture* (FRQSC), the Centre for the Study of Democratic Citizenship, and Université Laval's Department of Political Science. We express our immense gratitude for their generosity.

Several experts who collaborated on the book assessing the Couillard government in Quebec agreed to collaborate on this book. We thank them for their loyalty and trust. We would also like to express our gratitude to all the collaborators who joined us on this new project. We thank Marie-Hélène Boucher, publisher at the PUL, for her effective support. We are also grateful to our research assistants who contributed to this project, notably Antoine Baby-Bouchard (for the concordance between the tables and the Polimetre), Myriam Dumais-DesRosiers (for the production and formatting of the manuscripts), and Yann Minier (for the translation of chapters 3, 13, and 15, as well as the Introduction). We further acknowledge Debbie Blythe, who translated Chapter 14.

We also express our gratitude to the organizers of the 2019 Canadian Political Science Association Congress for enabling us to organize four panels where some of our contributors had the opportunity to present their chapter's analysis.

We thank the CAPP, who detains the Polimetre's intellectual property and trademark rights, for allowing us to use the data from the Trudeau Polimetre for this project. All data concerning the Trudeau government's election promises and the verdicts as to their fulfillment come from the Trudeau Polimetre.

We also express our gratitude to UBC Press and their marketing and sales staff who accepted enthusiastically to participate in the distribution of this book in English Canada.

Finally, we thank Jocelyne Naud and the PUL staff for editing and formatting and Diane Trottier for the graphic design.

Lisa Birch and François Pétry

# ⅃Polimetre

**Their promises.**
**Our analysis.**

*A question* — Do politicians keep their promises?

*A mission* — The Polimetre measures the fulfillment of election promises. The Polimetre's mission is to provide citizens, the media and researchers with objective, transparent and reliable political information about government actions.

*A rigorous methodology* — The Center for Public Policy Analysis (CAPP) at Université Laval developed the Polimetre's methodology to extract promises from election platforms, conduct research to document government action related to promises, assess the level of promise fulfillment, update reliable verdicts in real time, and render them available online directly.

Our analysis of the different levels of pledge fulfillment and our rules for classifying promises by level of fulfillment is based on the method elaborated by the Comparative Party Pledge Group (CPPG), a consortium of international researchers who are interested in the comparative study of election promise fulfillment and who have published numerous scientific articles and books on this subject.

*A registered trademark*—Polimetre = polyvalent and bilingual name that combines Poli [for politics or public policies] + metre [for neutral and independent analyses]

*A little history*—In 2013, inspired by similar tools that existed in the United States (Obameter) and in France (*Lui Président*), CAPP researchers created this tool to measure the fulfillment of election promises

Since, the Polimetre team has analysed pledge fulfillment by governments in Canada (Polimetre Harper and Polimetre Trudeau) and in Quebec (Polimetre Marois, Polimetre Couillard and Polimetre Legault). In 2019, researchers developed the Polimetre Higgs in New Brunswick thanks to a partnership between the Donald J. Savoie Institute (IDJS) and the CAPP.

*Independent financing*—Since its creation, the operations and development of the Polimetre have been supported directly by the CAPP through a research grant from the *Fonds de Recherche du Québec Société et Culture* and through the dedication of CAPP researchers. Recently, the Polimetre received punctual support from the Centre for the Study of Democratic Citizenship (McGill) and the Political Science department at Université Laval. The Polimetre Higgs project is financed by the Quebec *Secrétariat aux relations canadiennes*, l'IDJS and the CAPP.

*For more information about the Polimetre:* *polimetre@capp.ulaval.ca*

*Polimetre logo:* Phil Langlois

# Foreword

THE HONOURABLE THOMAS MULCAIR

I wish to salute in this foreword the admirable work by Lisa Birch and François Pétry and the researchers who collaborated in this edited volume. Caught in the turmoil of political events on a daily basis, political leaders, a community of which I was a member until recently, tend to focus on the priorities of the moment and give themselves too little opportunity to take the necessary step back to analyze objectively the performance of the outgoing government as a whole. This book will certainly be useful to them.

## RELIABLE VERDICTS

The volume analyzes 353 Liberal promises in the federal election of 2015. The Trudeau Polimetre, an online application whose objective is to track the fulfillment of Liberal promises over time, makes this analysis possible. The results in March 2019 indicate that the Liberal government fulfilled 50% of its pledges entirely, 40% in part and 10% broken. The perception of the fulfillment of party promises is tainted necessarily by subjective and partisan considerations. Liberal supporters are likely to accentuate the fact that they fulfilled 90% of their promises at least in part, while others will point out that only 50% of their promises were fulfilled entirely. To avoid sterile quarrels, perhaps the best and most transparent way to proceed is always to distinguish three verdicts: "kept," "kept in part," and "broken" promises.

The Trudeau Polimetre is not the only online application of its kind. Two other instruments, the TrudeauMeter and the Mandate Letter Tracker, also assess the fulfillment of campaign promises by the Liberal Party, but their methods and their results differ significantly from the method and results of the Polimetre. Polimetre data also differ in that they are analyzed and disseminated in peer-reviewed scientific publications.

## LIBERAL PROMISES AND NEO-DEMOCRATIC PROMISES

During the 2015 campaign, there was, according to some commentators, an inverted, ideological crossover between Liberals and New Democrats. The Liberals had overtaken the NDP on the left, while the NDP had overtaken the Liberals on the right such that it had become impossible to tell them apart ideologically speaking. Does this purported ideological crossover really correspond to reality? The analyses by several collaborators of the book seem to indicate the opposite. The argument used to justify the claim that the NDP has overtaken the Liberals on the right was that the NDP had pledged to balance the budget, while the Liberals had promised to run a budget deficit. However, the truth of the matter is that achieving a budget balance does not represent a shift to the right in the NDP ideology. There is a long-standing policy in the NDP to have electoral platforms that promise balanced budgets. Jack Layton campaigned in 2008 and 2011 with balanced budgets proposals. I continued in the same vein in 2015. In fact, the concern for balancing budgets reflects the prudence of the NDP's founders, particularly T. C. Douglas, who, after 17 years of balanced budgets in Saskatchewan, was able to create the first universal and free health insurance system in North America. The sustainability of ambitious social programs such as universal health coverage depends on the presence of sound fiscal balances in the first place. Historically, the NDP doctrine has been that massive government borrowing in the long run only helps lending banks. When it comes to the budget deficit, the Liberals have clearly changed their position by voluntarily overtaking the NDP on the left. The chapter by Geneviève Tellier and Cheick Traoré on the Liberal fiscal plan reminds us that making deficits is not part of the ideological legacy of the Liberal Party. The Liberals did not model their fiscal policies on those of the New Democrats. Nevertheless, they borrowed several other ideas for policy change from the NDP. The Trudeau government failed to go through all the way with some of these borrowed promises, which were eventually broken. This is true, for example, of the promise to "restore home mail delivery" in the communities where the Harper Conservatives had cut it.

This promise, found on page 5 of the NDP platform "Building the Country of Our Dreams," had the support of a good number of Canadians, particularly in the Montreal area. Imagine my surprise to see the Liberals copy this commitment on page 36 of their own platform "A New Plan for a Strong Middle Class" and announce it at a press conference with the mayor of Montreal (Provost 2015). The story could have ended there, but this episode had aroused my curiosity. I came back to this issue in the House of Commons during one of the first question periods following the election. My question was very simple: Would the Liberals keep their promise to restore home mail service where it had been cut? In response, Prime Minister Trudeau simply referred to the promise to end budget cuts, which did not commit to restoring mail service. I insisted so everyone could see that his very clear promise was on the record. In fact, I had the opportunity to ask different versions of this question over a period of several months and I received the same evasive response every time.

The promise to restore home mail delivery was a "transactional" promise designed to influence directly a specific population of constituents, considered more like customers, and to be achievable in the short term easily. Other promises modeled on the NDP, and eventually broken by the Liberal Party, were more "transformational." They were designed to have a deeper impact on society as a whole. Here I am thinking of the promise to adopt a proportional voting system, analyzed by Henry Milner in his chapter on electoral reform. This promise was well received among progressive voters—including NDP supporters—who wanted a more democratic voting system. Clearly, keeping this promise would have disrupted the electoral status quo that had allowed the Liberals and Conservatives to maintain historically their exclusive control of the executive power in Ottawa. Many observers, including myself, were not surprised when the Liberal government announced it was abandoning it.

Another transformative Liberal promise modeled on the NDP was the pledge to end subsidies for fossil fuel production. Justin Trudeau's government broke this promise when Canada bought Trans Mountain from Kinder Morgan, as Pierre-Olivier Pineau points out in his chapter on reconciling the environment and economy. On a related issue, Justin Trudeau's Liberal platform promised that if the Liberals formed the government, they would change the assessment system for major energy projects. This new process would apply to all projects, even those in progress, such as the Trans Mountain pipeline. The part of the pledge promising to modify the evaluation system was fulfilled, but not the part promising to apply the new system to all the projects because the system that was used for the Trans Mountain project was the one that had been put in place by the Stephen Harper Conservatives (Linnitt 2016). Prime Minister Trudeau now says that the purchase and expansion of the Trans Mountain pipeline was part of its strategy to meet Canada's international obligations to reduce our greenhouse gases. In fact, fulfilling the Liberal pledge to reduce greenhouse gases would have required a complete reorientation of our ways of doing things and would have upset the established order.

## CHANGES THAT DO NOT THREATEN THE ESTABLISHED ORDER

Were the Liberal promises of change just so many smokescreens intended to attract progressive votes with no real intention of keeping them? Alternatively, did the Liberals honestly intend to fulfill their promises of change? The Liberals have kept several promises of change that were also present in the NDP platform, such as the pledges to increase Canada's intake of Syrian refugees and to improve the Guaranteed Income Supplement for seniors. However, the impression one draws from the comparison is that most of the promises of change that the Liberals fulfilled do not threaten the established order, whereas some important promises of change that threaten the established order have indeed been broken.

Although the Liberal Party of Justin Trudeau has made many promises, the fact remains that it has not fully met the expectations of those who voted for it. The Liberal management of energy and climate change—one cornerstone of Justin Trudeau's promises—has disappointed many Canadians at precisely the time when the Intergovernmental Panel on Climate Change (IPCC 2019) and the Auditor General of Canada (2018) are sounding the alarm bell on the climate crisis and policy inadequacy. According to the Edelman Confidence Barometer (2019), even though confidence in our political institutions remains high among the informed public, that is to say the better off, it is at a low ebb in the rest of the population. The SNC-Lavalin affair has undoubtedly aggravated the erosion of popular trust in our institutions. Finally, in their chapter on economic policies, Marcelin Joanis and Stéphanie Lapierre emphasize that Liberal measures to help the middle classes have failed to stem the downward trend in the average real wage of the middle class. According to Angus Reid (2019), 77% of Canadians now fear that they will not achieve the same standard of living as their parents. These signs of popular dissatisfaction translate into a crumbling support of the electorate for the Liberal Party, which was receiving fewer voting intentions than Andrew Sheer's Conservative Party in the spring of 2019 (Léger 2019). The coming months will tell us whether the Liberal Party will succeed in restoring its top position in the polls or whether the current trend will continue until the election.

## REFERENCES

Angus Reid Institute. 2019. "As government presents election-year budget, Canadians are uneasy about economic fortunes." March 18, 2019. http://angusreid.org/economy-trudeau-budget-2019/

Auditor General of Canada. 2018. *Perspectives on Climate Change Action in Canada—A Collaborative Report from Auditors General—March 2018*. http://www.oag-bvg.gc.ca/internet/Francais/parl_otp_201803_f_42883.html

Edelman. 2019. *2019 Edelman Trust Barometer: Canada*. https://www.edelman.ca/trust.

IPPC. 2019. *The Intergovernmental Panel on Climate Change (IPCC)*. https://www.ipcc.ch/

Léger. 2019. *Federal Politics*. March 21, 2019. https://leger360.com/wp-content/uploads/2019/03/Federal-Politics-March-21-2019.pdf

Linnitt, Carol. 2016. "Trudeau Is 'Breaking the Promise He Made' By Allowing Trans Mountain Pipeline Review to Continue Under Old Rules." *The Narwhal* (blog), January 16, 2016. http://thenarwhal.ca/trudeau-breaking-promise-he-made-allowing-trans-mountain-pipeline-review-continue-under-old-rules/.

Provost, Anne-Marie. 2015. "Rencontre entre Trudeau et Coderre." *Le Journal de Montréal*. September 3, 2015. http://www.journaldemontreal.com/2015/09/03/rencontre-entre-trudeau-et-coderre.

# Introduction
## A Mandate for Change

FRANÇOIS PÉTRY AND LISA BIRCH

> More than 100 years ago, a great prime minister,
> Wilfrid Laurier, talked about sunny ways. He knew
> that politics can be a positive force, and that is
> the message Canadians sent today. Canadians
> chose change, real change...
>
> Translated Excerpt from Justin Trudeau's victory speech
> *Maclean's 2015.*

On October 19, 2015, Canadian voters gave the Liberal Party of Canada (LPC) a legitimate mandate to govern Canada for four years. With 39.5% of the popular vote translating into 54.4% of the seats in the Commons, the LPC formed a majority government. This unexpected Liberal victory marked the end of Stephen Harper's Conservative Party's nine years of governance, the ineffectiveness of the Conservative Party's negative advertising campaign[1], and the beginning of a new era of change. The LPC, even more than the New Democratic Party and the Conservative Party, promised many progressive changes for all Canadians. This victory signaled a shift in the federal government's policy direction that can be summed up in two key commitments of the Liberal Party of Canada: (1) to implement its plan to "strengthen the middle class"; and (2) to provide Canadians with an "open and transparent" government that reflects "our values and ambitions."

---

1.   To view these advertisements, see the CBC News article and videos (October 9, 2015).

On October 17, 2019, voters will be called to the polls and will have the opportunity to express their performance assessment of this government elected under the banner of change. This book proposes to make it easier for citizens by scrutinizing the Trudeau government's record in a neutral, independent, and non-partisan manner. It reveals the answers to a very simple question: Did this government keep its 353 platform promises and implement its Canadian policy transformation agenda?

On October 17, voters will use their power as citizens in a representative democracy to hold their government accountable for its actions (or inaction). They are free to reelect the Liberals, with or without majority status, or choose another political party. Their appreciation of the incumbent government's performance is one of the factors that can influence their choices in addition to the leaders' and candidates' personal characteristics, the ideology of the party they represent, and the election promises they will make during the next electoral campaign. This citizen's power comes with the citizen's duty to be well informed about the facts. In an era of "fake news," negative advertising campaigns, and conventional and social media information overload, voters face a daunting challenge in providing a neutral and objective assessment of the past four years under the Liberal government. This book provides them with tools based on real facts to enlighten their evaluation of Justin Trudeau's government's record and achievements.

## RESEARCH QUESTION

To meet the challenge of conducting such an evaluation, we have replicated the proven model used when producing similar assessments. This model consists of two essential components: (1) the recruitment of a wide range of collaborators, recognized for their expertise in relevant policy areas and their intellectual rigour; and (2) the structuring of their research through common research questions, methodology, and research framework. We ensured consistency between chapters by circulating several chapters among our collaborators during the preparatory stage of the book. We also held a workshop at the Canadian Political Science Association Convention at the University of British Columbia on June 6, 2019. The main research question that guided our collaborators is as follows: After four years in office, has the LPC achieved the transformational mandate for which it was elected with a majority government?

We then invited our collaborators to answer a number of specific questions, each intended to clarify the meaning of the main question. The

Liberal Party's mandate for change was twofold. First, Justin Trudeau's government had an "imperative mandate" to implement its action plan for the middle class, including the 353 specific commitments in his election platform, which explains the questions about these commitments' implementation. Second, it had a "representative mandate" under which it could pursue its agenda of governing differently by implementing transformational policies, which explains the questions about government actions that were not specifically promised in the election platform. From an imperative mandate perspective, the Liberal government's performance can be analyzed as one of a "promise keeper," whose role is limited to delivering faithfully on its commitments. From the representative mandate perspective, the government's performance should be seen more as one of an independent "agent" or "curator" who governs with flexibility under the leadership of a prime minister who is on the lookout for problems and their solutions.

We asked our collaborators to focus their analyses on the promises they felt were important in their area of public policy and to select from among them the five most significant promises; that is, those with significant potential for political transformation and/or significant fiscal impact. We also asked them to identify the factors that could influence the fulfillment of these promises, such as the division of powers between levels of government in a federal system, the role of the designated minister, the more or less difficult political climate depending on public policy areas, the conflicts between actors, and any support from actor networks and public opinion.

Several collaborators have also divided the promises into promised actions (outputs) as opposed to promised results (outcomes). Here, the term *output* refers to commitments that governments achieve by taking action (or not taking action, in the case of a promise to maintain the status quo). The action may be legislative or executive. Examples would be committing to file an investigation report, amending a section of the Criminal Code, or holding a consultation. "Result" commitments are promises to produce an effect (outcome). Examples would be a commitment to reduce unemployment or improve living conditions for the middle class, reduce the debt-to-income ratio to a specific level, or increase economic growth. Outputs are generally achievable in the short term because they often fall under the direct control of the government and can be achieved within one term. Outcomes are delivered in the medium to long term, well beyond an electoral mandate. They are the lasting and expected effects of government action (or inaction) that can be influenced by factors beyond the government's control. Therefore, it is expected that outputs will be seen as more achievable and observable during a mandate than outcomes (Naurin, Royed, and Thomson 2019, 32–33). The government's performance on outputs should therefore better reflect Canadians' expectations than its performance on outcomes.

In summary, our collaborators sought to answer five specific questions:

(1) Did the LPC fulfill the specific promises of its election platform and its promise of change? Which of those promises are the most important and why?

(2) What significant government initiatives were not promised in this platform?

(3) What political or administrative factors influenced the Liberal government's ability to "deliver the goods"?

(4) Do the analyzed promises and achievements fall under the category of "policy output" or "policy outcome"?

(5) Does the performance of Justin Trudeau's government meet the expectations of Canadians?

## COMMON METHODOLOGY AND DOCUMENTARY SOURCES

This book is, to our knowledge, the first book devoted to the evaluation of the fulfillment of specific promises by a federal party. However, it builds on previous works whose objective was to assess the fulfillment of specific party promises in Quebec (Pétry 2002; Pétry, Bélanger, and Imbeau 2006; Pétry and Birch 2018). Several collaborators from these previous works also contributed to this one. We invited experts of federal public policy to contribute to this book. All our collaborators conducted their analyses using the same body of text data and using the same method of time-series content analysis. As a first step, our collaborators consulted the 2015 LPC election platform and the Trudeau Polimetre data, including the wording of the promises, the verdicts of the Polimetre team on the fulfillment of the election promises, and the documentary sources justifying each verdict (see Chapter 1 for methodological details of the Polimetre). These data are freely accessible on the Poltext project site (2019) under the Texts-Electronic manifestos and Data and Analysis-Canada-Trudeau Polimetre sections of this website.

Our collaborators consulted official documents from the Liberal Party upstream of its 2015 platform and sources from the Liberal government upstream of it. The first relevant document upstream includes the 32 political resolutions adopted at the Liberal Biennial Convention in Montreal in February 2014 (Liberal Party of Canada 2014). These 32 resolutions fueled the election platform with 353 specific promises, a tenfold increase. The election platform promises provide detailed commitments, which are essentially a faithful reflection of the 32 Convention resolutions. For example, the platform promises to reform the electoral system are consistent with Resolution 31 of the 2014 Convention about "restoring confidence in democracy."

However, some resolutions from the 2014 Convention are not reflected in the Liberal platform. This is particularly true of Resolution 100 in which the LPC committed to establish a basic annual income. This commitment is absent from the Liberal platform, and no initiative has been taken by the Justin Trudeau government to establish a basic annual income at the federal level. Conversely, some of the Liberal platform promises are not reflected in any 2014 Convention resolutions. This is the case, for example, of some promises related to gun regulations.

The second documentary source is the party platform released by Justin Trudeau 15 days before polling day under the title "A New Plan for a Strong Middle Class." The platform is not the only documentary source of the party's promises, but it is the only one officially sanctioned by the party leadership and therefore the most reliable and trustworthy source. The platform also has the advantage of bringing all the promises together in a single document, unlike scattered election speeches. That is why it is our main documentary source for studying the Liberal Party's promises.

The third source is the set of documents produced by the Liberal government from the beginning of its mandate until now. In the days following the election, the newly designated prime minister repeated the platform's specific commitments in the personal mandate letters to each minister for the swearing-in of the cabinet. The Throne Speech of the 1st Session of the 42nd Parliament on December 4, 2015, and the budget speeches delivered by Finance Minister Bill Morneau are also useful documentary sources for analyzing the fulfillment of promises. This set of documents also includes government bills, consultation reports, policy statements, strategic plans and annual reports, press releases, and websites of the Canadian government, departments, and Parliament. These traces of government action are available to our readers.

The fourth type of documents consulted by our collaborators consists of several different sources. It includes relevant media coverage, public opinion data, other political parties' platforms, key players' websites in a given public policy area, and, last but not least, relevant scientific literature. By combining data from these four different types of sources, our collaborators ensure the reliability of their analyses.

Our approach aims to anchor evaluations within the analytical framework of a mandate and a structured methodological framework using a single body of data that is accessible to readers. This approach differentiates the Liberal government's record presented here from other assessments of the Liberal government's record, such as media retrospectives at the end of the government's mandate or the *How Ottawa Spends* collection, which disseminates high-quality, thematic policy analyses without necessarily placing them within a parliamentary democracy mandate framework.

## PRESENTATION OF CHAPTERS

The first two chapters of the book provide an overview of the Trudeau government's election promises and legislative action in Ottawa's Parliament. These chapters invite the reader to reflect on the meaning of a mandate given by voters and therefore on the criteria for evaluating how the government exercised its mandate. Chapter 1 by Lisa Birch and François Pétry discusses Trudeau's mandate as a "promise maker" with an imperative mandate. They compare the methodology and verdicts of the Trudeau Polimetre with those of the TrudeauMeter and the tool created by the Trudeau government called "Mandate Letter Tracker: Delivering Results for Canadians." They suggest possible explanations for the unusually high rate of promises kept in full or in part by revisiting the distinction between promises focused more on "government actions" (outputs) and promises focused on "effects" (outcomes) and considering Justin Trudeau's government's use of "deliverology."

Chapter 2 by Lisa Birch, Steve Jacob, and Antoine Baby-Bouchard examines the articulation of the "imperative" mandate to deliver promises with the "representative" mandate to govern through an examination of the government's legislative actions. They provide additional insight into the meaning of a mandate by looking at the Trudeau policy agenda in relation to three cycles, namely the budget cycle, the election cycle, and the public policy cycle, across three time horizons—the short, medium, and long term.

François Rocher (Chapter 3) ponders over the type of federalism, cooperative, collaborative, or competitive, put forward by Justin Trudeau's government and the implications for delivering on promises that involve relations between government levels. At the end of the day, it seems that the Liberal government has become more committed to the cooperative federalism model, in which the federal government is predominant in relation to the provinces and territories, than to the collaborative federalism model in which each government level is an equal partner. Justin Trudeau's government has often favoured unilateral initiatives that provinces and territories have been persuaded to embrace, sometimes at odds with Liberal platform commitments. On the other hand, given the numerous sources of friction with the provinces, it is likely that the cooperative approach has allowed the Liberal government to go further in delivering on some promises than it could have done by taking a more collaborative approach with the provinces.

Geneviève Tellier and Cheick Alassane Traoré (Chapter 4) compare the financial plan of the Liberal Party's election platform to budgets. They conclude that the Trudeau government has steered left. It stayed the course on its fiscal plan, which proposed a level of public spending that was significantly higher than the Conservatives' and the New Democrats' fiscal plans to fund its vision of sustained state engagement in society. To do so, it chose to tolerate a high deficit and therefore to break its promise to return to a balanced budget by the end of the mandate in order to better stimulate economic growth.

The theme of a federal government spending more than it promised in order to better invest in the economy, promote job creation, and "strengthen the middle class" is echoed in Chapter 5 by Marcelin Joanis and Stéphanie Lapierre. Their chapter provides an overview of the Liberal government's successes and failures in public financial management, trade, infrastructure investment, and innovation. While, on the one hand, it is easy to observe the implementation of many government actions (outputs) that coincide with the commitments of the Liberal platform, it is more difficult to determine the medium- and long-term effects (outcomes) on Canada's economy. As the authors point out, the objective of the government's economic policy throughout the Liberal mandate has been to support the middle class. However, at the end of this mandate, one question remains — How is the middle class doing four years later?

Alex Marland and Vincent Raynauld (Chapter 6) note that Canadian political leaders are increasingly engaged in a "permanent campaign" by using government resources and political communication to their own electoral advantage on an almost-daily basis. The chapter examines the steps taken by Justin Trudeau's government to limit certain advertising and government communications practices that could be harmful to the exercise of democracy. The chapter summarizes the Trudeau government's progress on each commitment and invites the reader to reflect on broader trends in digital political communication and social media.

Henry Milner (Chapter 7) discusses Liberal promises to improve the way we elect MPs, particularly those related to access to the ballot box, and to the roles of the Chief Electoral Officer and the Commissioner of Canada Elections. It also analyzes the circumstances surrounding the government's abandonment of the most visible and controversial platform pledge to make the 2015 federal election the last one to be conducted under the first-past-the-post electoral system.

Mireille Paquet's Chapter 8 examines the fulfillment of Justin Trudeau's immigration promises in an increasingly polarized context of immigration debates in Canada and beyond. In particular, the chapter analyzes Liberal promises on immigrant selection, refugee resettlement, and the integrity and efficiency of Canada's immigration system. Justin Trudeau's mandate coincided with the end of Canada's isolation in relation to the movement of immigrants and refugees' global crisis. The chapter concludes that the fulfillment of election promises is more fluid when the federal government acts within its exclusive jurisdiction and by executive decision than when interdepartmental, intergovernmental, or international collaboration is required.

Daniel Béland and Michael J. Prince (Chapter 9) discuss the Liberal government's achievements in social policy, with a focus on family policy, housing policy, income support, and poverty reduction policies. While austerity still dominates the social safety net debates in many Western countries, Canada is clearly moving toward a gradual improvement in social policy, as exemplified by the achievements of the Trudeau government.

In Chapter 10, Jared Wesley traces the origins of the Liberal Party's commitment to legalize recreational cannabis and, in particular, Justin Trudeau's attitude change in this regard. It explains how the Liberal government orchestrated the public consultation process around public health and public safety issues. The chapter concludes with a reflection on the meaning to be given to the accelerated approach taken by the Trudeau government in legalizing recreational cannabis. Policy changes implemented to date are clearly limited to actions (outputs) under direct government control. Hence, the question of whether the Trudeau government can be credited with achieving uncertain long-term-expected results (outcomes).

Amélie Quesnel-Vallée, Rachel McKay, and Antonia Maioni (Chapter 11) review the context surrounding health policy in 2015. They assess the fulfillment of the Liberal Party's specific health promises and then review some of the Liberal government's health policy initiatives that do not necessarily coincide with those promises. In general, the Liberal government's actions on health policy have shown a return to a more interventionist position of the federal government, involving a greater federal role in the provincial/territorial health and social service delivery. In particular, the Liberal government sought to expand the scope of the Canada Health Act to include new areas of home care, mental health, and pharmacare. The Liberal government has also focused on implementing nationally harmonized performance indicators, consistent with its commitment to deliver visible results in a timely manner ("deliverology").

In Chapter 12, Karen Bird outlines the many initiatives of Justin Trudeau's government related to gender equality, diversity, and inclusion. The chapter examines the extent to which gender, diversity, and inclusion policy developments have aligned with Liberal platform commitments or whether they have been pushed onto the government agenda by a configuration of external events and forces that could not have been anticipated during the 2015 campaign. The chapter also discusses the possibility that the strong and diverse female representation in the Trudeau cabinet was a key factor in expanding the government's agenda in terms of gender, diversity, and inclusion.

Chapter 13 by Thierry Rodon and Martin Papillon remarks that Liberal ambitions exceed their achievements in relations with Indigenous peoples. The Liberal platform stands in stark contrast to the Conservative platform of the previous government with a bold agenda focused on reconciliation with Indigenous peoples through nation-to-nation relationships. The promises discussed in this chapter fall under two separate headings: (1) promises to reinvest in services, which are output promises; and (2) renewing the relationship, which are medium- to long-term outcome promises. Despite the goodwill to implement the 94 recommendations of the Truth and Reconciliation Commission of Canada, it is difficult to imagine that in a four-year term it would be possible to revolutionize a 150-year-old system that is fundamentally colonial. The authors point out that several proposals were still in the works at the time of writing, and that the outcomes of structural reforms related to the renewal of relations with Indigenous peoples will only be felt in the medium to long term. A true assessment of its successful reforms will have to wait.

Pierre-Olivier Pineau's Chapter 14 outlines the fate of the LPC's promises on the environment and climate change. It analyzes the two major environmental issues that marked the mandate of the Justin Trudeau government: environmental assessments and climate change. It points out that the Trudeau government's purchase of Trans Mountain goes against its environmental promises and symbolizes the tension between the economic and environmental concerns of various groups and regions in Canada. Although the Liberal government has kept many environmental action promises, it has not really achieved its goal of reconciling the environment and the economy during its four years in office, as it had announced.

Julien Lauzon Chiasson and Stéphane Paquin (Chapter 15) present the Liberal Party's foreign policy promises and record of accomplishment, including those in international trade, security, and defence. As in the areas of the environment and relations with Indigenous peoples, the authors of this chapter find that despite the ambitions for change and the many promises kept by government actions, the Liberal record on foreign policy does not match expectations. In defence of Justin Trudeau, Canada has faced a changing international environment that has been particularly hostile to it.

In the concluding chapter, Lisa Birch and François Pétry discuss both aspects of Justin Trudeau's mandate—the "imperative mandate" of the promise keeper and the "representative mandate" of an independent elected agent to create change. They compare the rate of fulfillment of the promises identified as most important for change with the rate of fulfillment of other promises and find little difference. They observe that popular support for the incumbent party is dwindling at the time of the March 2019 budget (Fournier 2019) and they wonder about the fate of the Liberal government in the next federal election. Will Justin Trudeau be re-elected for his good performance at fulfilling his campaign promises for change? Or will he be defeated through a redistribution of party support among voters, including those disappointed by the SNC-Lavalin affair?

REFERENCES

CBC News. 2015. "Conservative attack ads aim to sway voters against Trudeau come decision time." *CBC News*, October 9, 2015. https://www.cbc.ca/news/politics/canada-election-2015-ad-hawk-conservative-target-trudeau-economy-1.3263482

Fournier, Philippe J. 2017. "Projection fédérale Qc125: les Conservateurs creusent l'écart". *Québec 125*, 17 mars 2019. http://blog.qc125.com/2019/03/projection-federale-qc125-les.html.

Maclean's. 2015. "Justin Trudeau, for the record: 'We beat fear with hope'" [transcript of Justin Trudeau's victory speech], October 20, 2015. https://www.macleans.ca/politics/ottawa/justin-trudeau-for-the-record-we-beat-fear-with-hope/.

Naurin, Elin, Terry Royed and Robert Thomson (eds.). 2019. *Party Mandates and Democracy. Making, Breaking and Keeping Election Pledges in Twelve Countries.* Ann Arbor: University of Michigan Press.

Liberal Party of Canada. 2014. Policy Resolutions, 2014. https://www.liberal.ca/policy-resolutions/

Liberal Party of Canada. 2015. Real Change: *A New Plan for a Strong Middle Class.* https://www.liberal.ca/wp-content/uploads/2015/10/New-plan-for-a-strong-middle-class.pdf.

Pétry, François (ed.). 2002. *Le Parti québécois: bilan des engagements électoraux, 1994-2000.* Québec: Presses de l'Université Laval.

Pétry, François, Éric Bélanger and Louis M. Imbeau (eds.). 2006. *Le Parti libéral: enquête sur les réalisations du gouvernement Charest.* Québec: Presses de l'Université Laval.

Pétry, François and Lisa Birch (eds.). 2018. *Bilan du gouvernement de Philippe Couillard. 158 promesses et un mandat contrasté.* Québec: Presses de l'Université Laval.

Polimètre Trudeau. 2019. https://www.poltext.org/en/trudeau-polimeter

# Chapter 1
## Assessing Justin Trudeau's Performance at Fulfilling Campaign Pledges

Lisa Birch and François Pétry

On November 4, 2015, in his open letter to Canadians, newly designated Prime Minister Justin Trudeau declared, "I am writing to you, today, to reaffirm my commitment to spend the next four years working hard to deliver on those promises" (Prime Minister of Canada 2015). In doing so, Justin Trudeau explicitly recognized pledge fulfillment as a legitimate expectation for citizens and implicitly suggested this would be an important criterion for citizens' assessments of his government's performance four years down the road.

The importance of campaign promises in the conduct of government policy was enshrined soon after Justin Trudeau's arrival in power through the creation of a Results and Delivery Unit within the Privy Council Office (PCO) to track departmental performance and to ensure that government ministers would be working effectively to fulfill the party's election pledges. This was part of a larger plan to implement "deliverology" in the federal government. According to Sir Michael Barber, its creator, "deliverology" is a method for running a government and delivering ambitious promises for change through three successive stages, namely (1) the development of a strategy with indicators and results targets, (2) the implementation down the delivery chain from the cabinet to the frontline public servants, and (3) the routine tracking of indicators and trajectories to ensure effective delivery (Barber 2016; Barber, Kihn, and Moffit 2011). Following in the footsteps of Tony Blair in the United Kingdom and Dalton McGuinty in

Ontario, Justin Trudeau hired Sir Michael Barber as a consultant to teach his cabinet ministers about "deliverology" and to implement his method in the federal government. Within eight months of assuming office, the Trudeau government started to apply "deliverology" through changes in policies, organizational structures, and institutional routines (Birch and Jacob, Forthcoming; Wherry 2016). These recent developments naturally invite us to question ourselves: Has the government of Justin Trudeau kept its campaign promises?

## 1.1  THREE TOOLS TO TRACK CAMPAIGN PROMISES — A COMPARISON

The Polimetre was the first online application to track in real time the fulfillment of campaign promises by governments in Canada. Researchers at the Center for Public Policy Analysis (CAPP) of Université Laval created this tool in 2013 to answer a simple question: Do governing parties keep their promises? The objective is to provide valid, reliable, fact-based information to citizens, journalists, and academics on election promises and their fulfillment.

The Polimetre's method consists in first identifying the promises in the party's electoral platform by separating them from statements that do not constitute promises. To be classified as such, a promise must commit the party to take action, not to take action or to achieve an explicit goal in the event that it is elected. Then the Polimetre team periodically conducts research and reviews the evidence or lack of evidence of pledge fulfillment. At the start of a new polimetre, all promises are classified as "not yet rated." The verdicts are changed to "kept," "kept in part or in the works," or "broken" as soon as evidence of government actions (or inaction) becomes available. Each verdict is supported by one or more quotes from government press releases, bills, budget reports, other official sources such as policy statements or Auditor General reports, and media sources. To be classified as "fulfilled" or "kept," a promise must be followed by an officially sanctioned government action (law, regulation, policy or strategic plan, budget allocation, etc.). A promise is classified as "in progress or partially fulfilled" if an action to achieve it has been formally undertaken. A government measure that is a compromise is also classified as "in progress or partially fulfilled" or "kept in part or in the works." A promise is classified as "broken" if the government has renounced explicitly to pursue it for the moment or it has undertaken actions that go in the opposite direction from the promise.

When the next elections are called, promises that have not yet been rated for which there is still no evidence of action are classified as "broken." Promises are expected to be kept during the legislature following the election in which they were made. The criteria for pledge fulfillment are established by the Comparative Party Pledge Group, an international consortium of researchers who produce and analyze data to enlighten our understanding of pledge fulfillment in Western democracies (Thomson et al. 2017; Naurin et al. 2019). This renders the polimetre data ready to be used not only by citizens and journalists but also by researchers working on cross-national comparisons of pledge fulfillment.

According to the Trudeau Polimetre as updated at the end of March 2019, 178 (50%) of the 353 pledges contained in the 2015 Liberal platform had been "fulfilled," 140 (40%) were "in progress or partially fulfilled," and 35 (10%) were "broken or not yet rated" (Trudeau Polimetre 2019). We find that 39 (85%) of the 46 promises in fiscal and budgetary policies were fulfilled at least in part (Chapter 4 by Geneviève Tellier and Cheick Alassane Traoré), while 47 (85%) of the 55 economic policy promises were also fulfilled at least in part (Chapter 5 by Marcelin Joanis and Stéphanie Lapierre). The four pledges (100%) in the area of political communication were kept at least in part (Chapter 6 by Alex Marland and Vincent Raynauld), while 9 (69%) of the 13 pledges about electoral reform were kept at least in part (Chapter 7 by Henry Milner). Of the 17 immigration promises studied by Mireille Paquet in Chapter 8, 15 (88%) were fulfilled at least in part, and out of the 49 social policy promises analyzed by Daniel Béland and Michael J. Prince in Chapter 9, 41 (84%) were fulfilled at least in part. In Chapter 10, Jared Wesley finds that all five (100%) Liberal pledges for the legalization of recreational cannabis have been kept in whole or in part. Amélie Quesnel-Vallée, Rachel McKay, and Antonia Maioni also find that all the 18 health care pledges that they analyze in Chapter 11 are fulfilled at least in part. Seventeen (94%) out of 18 promises are kept at least in part in the area of gender equality, diversity, and inclusion (Chapter 12 by Karen Bird), and 22 (88%) of the 25 promises on relations with Indigenous peoples are fulfilled at least in part (Chapter 13 by Thierry Rodon and Martin Papillon). We also find that 47 (98%) out of 48 promises in energy and sustainable development are achieved at least in part (Chapter 14 by

Pierre-Olivier Pineau), and 36 (84%) out of 43 promises in international affairs and defence are kept entirely or in part (Chapter 15 by Julien Lauzon Chiasson and Stéphane Paquin). It should be noted that the ratios of fulfillment of promises vary little from one policy field to another, indicating that the Liberal Party of Justin Trudeau was anxious to keep its campaign promises across all public policy sectors.

Another source of information on pledge fulfillment is the Trudeau-Meter, which was launched in 2015 (TrudeauMeter 2015). Like the Polimetre, the TrudeauMeter aspires to be a neutral, third-party application. As of March 31, 2019, the verdicts of the TrudeauMeter on 231 promises were as follows: 97 (42%) "achieved"; 57 (25%) "in progress"; 44 (19%) "broken"; and 33 (14%) "not started." The TrudeauMeter is limited by the absence of a formal, transparent, and shared methodology to identify pledges and to determine their subsequent classification. For this reason, this collaborative initiative results in uneven verdicts, erratic time frames for evaluating pledge fulfillment over the mandate, and sporadic commentary. Promises that retain the attentive public's appreciation receive more comments and more frequent updates than other promises. This inconsistency limits the validity and reliability of verdicts over time. The TrudeauMeter website self-defines itself as "just a platform for people to exchange ideas, and for the public at large to see what has been achieved by the government" (TrudeauMeter). In contrast, the Polimetre relies on a common, systematic methodology to assess all promises at regular intervals, generating data that can be used for comparative research internationally.

The third source of information on pledge fulfillment is the Mandate Letter Tracker that was launched by the PCO in November 2017 to track government commitments as stated in the mandate letters that are made public each time new cabinet ministers take office (Mandate Letter Tracker). A detailed comparison of their respective contents reveals that almost all the promises in the Liberal platform were repeated verbatim in the November 2015 mandate letters at the start of the Liberal government. However, as new mandate letters, with new commitments, were made public following subsequent cabinet shuffles, it became more and more difficult to compare their pledge content with that of the Liberal platform. As of March 31, 2019, the last available Tracker update before submitting this manuscript to the publisher, the 432 verdicts of the Mandate Tracker were as follows: 156 (36%) commitments "completed—fully met"; 5 commitments (less than 1%) "completed—modified"; 216 (50%)

"actions taken—progress made"; 35 (8%) "actions taken—progress made toward ongoing goal"; 20 (5%) "actions taken—progress made—facing challenges"; and 3 (less than 1%) "not being pursued." Note the absence of a category for commitments that are "broken", which is replaced by "not being pursued." In some regards, the Mandate Tracker responds to calls for transparent, open government; in others, it seems to be, and has been portrayed in the media as a self-serving masquerade (Clark 2017; Ling 2017). It is worth noting that the names of the ratings on the Mandate Letter Tracker varied between 2017 and 2019 with the addition of sub-categories and nuances, suggesting efforts to reframe the government's actions and results.

Table 1-1 summarizes the main differences between the three tools by comparing the method they each use to track two specific Liberal campaign promises. Whereas the Trudeau Polimetre explicitly identifies the three promises (one for the electoral system reform legislation, one to end the first-past-the-post system and the other to explore other reform options) using the exact same words as the Liberal platform, the Trudeau-Meter identifies only one promise containing two dimensions (ending the first-past-the-post system and exploring alternative electoral reform options) but no mention of the way the government promised to achieve this. The Mandate Letter Tracker only focuses on the creation of the parliamentary committee. Readers must click for additional information to find out that the decision to reform the electoral system was abandoned by the government. The Trudeau Polimetre is thus more precise and transparent compared to the other tools regarding pledges and their classification.

TABLE 1-1 – Comparison of Available Promise-Tracking Tools

| TRACKING TOOL AND METHOD | SOURCE | EXAMPLE OF VERDICTS AND ENGAGEMENT WORDING |
|---|---|---|
| Trudeau Polimetre (third-party assessment using expert judgement based on well-established methodology) | 353 promises from the Liberal Party platform (original wording) | 1) **Kept:** "We will convene an all-party Parliamentary committee to review a wide variety of reforms, such as ranked ballots, proportional representation, mandatory voting, and online voting. This committee will deliver its recommendations to Parliament." (p. 27) <br><br> 2) **Broken:** "Within 18 months of forming the government, we will introduce legislation to enact electoral reform." (p. 27) <br><br> 3) **Broken:** "We are committed to ensuring that 2015 will be the last federal election conducted under the first-past-the-post voting system." (p.27) |
| Mandate Letter Tracker (self-assessment) | Increasing number of commitments from Mandate letters updated at each cabinet shuffle (original wording) (366 in December 2018, 432 in March 2019) | 1) **Not being pursued:** "Establish a special parliamentary committee to consult on electoral reform." (Mandate Letter Tracker website) |
| TrudeauMeter (third-party assessment using crowdsourcing) | 231 promises from the Liberal Party platform (interpreted by contributors) (260 in October 2018, 231 in March 2019) | 1) **Broken:** End first-past-the-post voting system and explore alternative electoral reform options. |

## 1.2  COMPARISONS OF PLEDGE FULFILLMENT IN CANADA

The Polimetre team has applied its methodology retroactively to Canadian (and Quebec) governments to enable comparisons between the current government and previous ones. Figure 1-1 displays the results going back in time to the first government of Prime Minister Brian Mulroney. Immediately apparent is the fact that the Trudeau government and the third Harper government have fulfilled at least in part more campaign pledges than any earlier government since 1984.

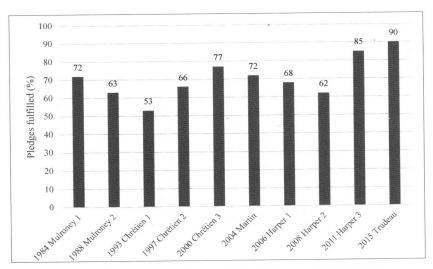

FIGURE 1-1 – Percentage of Promises Fulfilled in Canada 1984–2019
Source: Trudeau Polimetre 2019

The high rate of pledge fulfillment for Harper III and Trudeau could be coincidental, the spurious effect of factors unrelated to government efforts to fulfill their promises. For example, it could be attributed to the majority status of these governments. Majority governments fulfill larger percentages of campaign pledges than minority governments, mostly because they last longer (Pétry and Duval 2018a; Thomson et al. 2017). We also know that the likelihood of pledge fulfillment increases when the Gross Domestic Product is growing (Pétry, Duval, and Birch 2018). The high rate of pledge fulfillment could be a consequence of the relatively high rate of economic growth in recent years. The likelihood of fulfillment also depends on the amount of policy change that a pledge will produce if it is enacted. "Transactional" pledges focusing on services directly visible to citizens seen as customers (e.g., a promise to introduce a tax credit for a specific clientele) are more likely to be fulfilled precisely because they have limited effects beyond the clientele they target and consequently less "veto points" from which powerful organized interests can block their enactment. By contrast, "transformational" pledges such as the promise to change the electoral system are less likely to be enacted successfully before the end of the mandate because they have a potentially profound impact on society. It has been claimed that recent Canadian governments have proposed higher proportions of transactional pledges (Burgess 2014). This could be due to the rise of the permanent campaign that led parties to adopt political marketing strategies to target promises to specific voter market segments (see Chapter 6 by Alex Marland and Vincent Raynauld).

The Trudeau government has probably benefited from its majority status, sustained economic growth, and the kind of promises contained in the Liberal platform. In any event, Justin Trudeau's outstanding performance in fulfilling his promises is also because he was committed to keeping his word. Did the implementation of "deliverology" contribute to the high rate of promise fulfillment by the Trudeau government? It is difficult to say in the absence of solid evidence. Before drawing any conclusions, we need to consider the counterfactual case of the third Harper government, which fulfilled 84% of its promises without adopting Barber's "deliverology." This government enjoyed the same advantages as the Trudeau government in terms of majority support and relatively high economic growth rate[1]. On assuming office, both made honouring their words a high priority and a question of confidence and leadership. They and their ministers seemed to maintain this commitment to deliver throughout their mandates. Both were able to impose their agendas for change and to achieve high pledge fulfillment scores. Thus, it may be that just the status of their governments and their determination as leaders rather than their choice of delivery strategy accounts for their remarkable pledge fulfillment performance.

It might be the case that a causality loop exists between pledge fulfillment and our explanatory factors. This is what statisticians refer to as "endogeneity." In theory, a party expecting to win only a minority may want to lower its ambition during the campaign. Similarly, expectation of slow economic growth in the years ahead may lead a party to moderate its campaign promises. However, the fact that governments that do not enjoy majority support or high rate of economic growth fulfill significantly fewer campaign pledges suggests that parties do not adjust their campaign promises to expected conditions. Parties tend to "over-pledge," to promise things that they know to have a low probability of success (Pétry, Duval, and Birch 2018). Over-pledging makes sense in terms of creating negotiating space within the federal legislature or with other levels of government. In addition, pledges have an important signaling function indicating commitment to key supporters during the campaign and to prospective ruling partners inside or outside government in case a party is

---

1.   Unlike his predecessors, Stephen Harper personally insisted on reminding his cabinet ministers of the Conservative campaign promises in his mandate letters to them (Ibbitson 2015).

elected. As Thomson et al. (2017, 533) put it, "calculating fulfillment odds may well take a back seat to such concerns."

## 1.3  DISCUSSION

Conventional wisdom holds that politicians do not keep their campaign promises. According to a 2006 survey (International Social Survey Program 2006), only 26% of Canadians believe that "their elected representatives make the effort to keep their election promises." Citizens are not alone in their belief that politicians renege on their commitments. Elected representatives regularly accuse each other of lying to the electorate during parliamentary debates, and journalists frequently portray political leaders as promise breakers (Minsky 2017; Harris 2015; Visser 2012). Even political scientists are reluctant to accept the notion that candidates actually carry out their campaign promises. In their classic work *Absent Mandate*, Harold Clarke and collaborators (1996) affirm that "Absent mandates are likely to be the rule, not the exception. Elections decide who shall govern, but rarely the substance of public policy." For his part, Canadian-British political scientist Anthony King asserts that "party manifestos are empty and meaningless documents having a virtual random relationship to what a party will do in office" (cited by Rose 1994). The data presented in this chapter demonstrate that the conventional wisdom does not pass the test of empirical scrutiny.

Why do parties keep their campaign promises? The conventional interpretation is that governments behave as "promise deliverers" for fear of voters' retribution at the next election. The interpretation of government as "promise deliverer" assumes that voters are capable of retrospectively assessing whether pledges have been fulfilled or not. Duval and Pétry (2019) tested this assumption by checking whether respondents to the 2015 Canadian Election Study post-election survey were able to evaluate accurately the fulfillment of seven specific campaign promises made by the Harper Conservatives during the 2011 election. The results reveal that only half the respondents are able to tell correctly the difference between fulfilled and broken campaign pledges, roughly the same proportion that would be obtained by flipping coins. Pétry et al. (2018) report similar results in countries as varied as Ireland, Portugal, Sweden, the United Kingdom, and the United States. These findings strongly suggest that contrary to the conventional interpretation, the electorate has too little political information and is prejudiced too much by partisan considerations to hold governments accountable for their promises at the last election. These results are more in line with the realist interpretation that claims that democracy works not because citizens objectively monitor politicians' performance in office, but despite the fact that they do not (Achen and Bartels 2016; see also Pinker 2018, 206–207).

While pledge fulfillment is an important aspect of governance between elections, another limit of the conventional interpretation of governments as "promise deliverers" is that much legislative and policy action is not linked directly to election promises, but rather to agenda-setting dynamics for new issues and/or policy-cycle dynamics for existing policies and programs (Jacob et al. 2018). Government attention to pledge fulfillment tends to be high in the first part of a mandate after which other policy issues dominate the government's agenda. To illustrate, Figure 1-2 shows the cumulative change over time in the promises fulfilled by Justin Trudeau's government on a biannual basis. The Liberal government fulfilled 18 promises at least in part (5% of the total) in the first two months of its mandate. By June 2016, it had fulfilled at least in part 88 new promises, for a cumulative total of 106 promises (30% of the total). The subsequent pace of pledge fulfillment was significantly lower, with 54 new promises fulfilled at least in part on average each semester until December 2017. The pace of pledge fulfillment from January 2018 to March 2019 has been even slower, with 22 new promises (6% of the total) kept at least in part on average each semester.

Fulfilling campaign promises is not a uniform process over time: governments generally tend to run out of promises to fulfill in the last year of their mandate (Duval and Pétry 2018). This result is largely in line with findings from public policy experts, which show that most policy changes occur soon after an election and then things tend to stabilize (Jennings et al. 2011; Mortensen et al. 2011). However, this does not mean that governments are inactive in the last year of their mandate. On the contrary, government policy outputs tend to accelerate as the next election draws closer (see Campbell and Garand 2000 and Lewis-Beck and Stegmaier 2000 for reviews). The key to solve the apparent paradox is that government outputs in the latter period of a mandate tend to take the form of short-term, voter-oriented measures that do not correspond to promises made during the last election campaign.

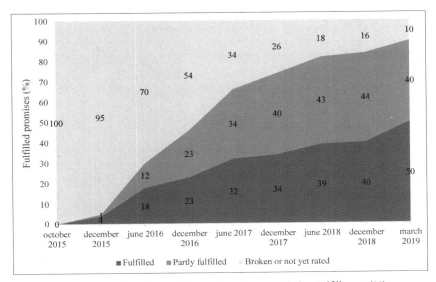

FIGURE 1-2 – Cumulative Change Over Time in Pledge Fulfillment (%)
Source: Trudeau Polimetre 2019

If important government decisions have not been announced by election promises, we cannot talk exclusively about government as a "promise deliverer"; we are more in a situation of government as a "trustee," whereby citizens hold government accountable by assessing the quality of representation and deliberation in policymaking during a term of office.[2] Lisa Birch and collaborators examine this question in the next chapter. We will see that the content of the majority of the bills passed by the Liberal government of Justin Trudeau is about issues that were not in the Liberal Party's election platform, a result more in keeping with the "trustee" model than the "promise deliverer" model.

---

2.    For a wonkish version of the views of government as a "promise deliverer" and as a "trustee," see Mansbridge's (2003) "promissory representation" and "anticipatory representation" models, respectively.

# References

Achen, Christopher, and Larry Bartels. 2016. *Democracy for Realists: Why Elections Do Not Produce Responsive Government.* Princeton: Princeton University Press.

Barber, Michael. 2016. *How to run a government so that citizens benefit and taxpayers don't go crazy.* London: Penguin Books.

Barber, Michael, P. Kihn and A. Moffit. 2011. *Deliverology: From Idea to Implementation.* Washington. DC: McKinsey and Co.

Birch Lisa, and Steve Jacob. 2019. Forthcoming. "'Deliverology' and Evaluation: A tale of two worlds," *Canadian Journal of Program Evaluation.*

Burgess, Mark. 2014. "Conservatives have kept 68 per cent of 2011 campaign promises study shows but many transactional," *The Hill Times,* July 27, 2014. https://www.hilltimes.com/2014/07/27/conservatives-have-kept-68-per-cent-of-2011-campaign-promises-study-shows-but-many-transactional/29171/39171

Campbell, James, and James Garand. 2000. *Before the Vote: Forecasting American National Elections.* Thousand Oaks, CA: Sage Publications.

Clark, Cambell. 2017. "Liberal government's promise tracker is a good idea that does not deliver," *The Globe and Mail,* November 14, 2017. https://www.theglobeandmail.com/opinion/liberal-governments-promise-tracker-is-a-good-idea-that-doesnt-deliver/article36983570/

Clarke, Harold, Lawrence LeDuc, Jane Jenson and John Pammett. 1996. *Absent Mandate: Canadian Electoral Politics in an Age of Restructuring.* 3d edition. Vancouver: Gage Publishing, 143.

Davis, Michael L., and Michael Ferrantino. 1996. "Towards a Positive Theory of Political Rhetoric: Why do Politicians Lie?," *Public Choice,* 88 (1): 1–13.

Duval, Dominic, and François Pétry. 2018a. "Citizens' evaluations of party pledge fulfillment in Canada," *Party Politics.* DOI: 10.1177/1354068818789968.

Duval, Dominic, and François Pétry. 2018b. "Time and the Fulfillment of Election Pledges," *Political Studies.* DOI: 10.1177/0032321718762882.

Harris, Micheal. 2015. "Harper's success part of a global network of lies ... and liars," *Ipolitics,* January 25, 2015. https://ipolitics.ca/2015/01/25/harpers-success-part-of-a-global-network-of-lies-and-liars/

Ibbitson, John. 2015. "Stephen Harper: The Making of a Prime Minister." *The Globe and Mail,* January 25, 2015. https://www.theglobeandmail.com/news/politics/stephen-harper-the-making-of-a-prime-minister/article25809825/

International Social Survey Program. Role of Government IV ZA4700 (v1.0.0),DOI:10.4232/1.4700https://www.gesis.org/issp/modules/issp-modules-by-topic/role-of-government/2006/

Jacob, Steve, Lisa Birch, François Pétry and Antoine Baby-Bouchard. 2018. "Le gouvernement Couillard en tant que 'mandataire indépendant'." In *Bilan des réalisations du gouvernement Couillard: 158 promesses et un mandat contrasté,* directed by François Pétry and Lisa Birch: 77-89. Québec: Presses de l'Université Laval.

Jennings, Will, Shaun Bevan, Arco Timmermans, Gerard Breeman, Sylvain Brouard, Laura Chaqués-Bonafont, Christoffer Green-Pedersen, Peter John, Peter Mortensen and Anna Palau. 2011. "Effects of the core functions of government on the diversity of executive agendas," *Comparative Political Studies*, 44 (8): 1001–1030.

Lewis-Beck, Michael, and Mary Stegmaier. 2000. "Economic determinants of electoral outcomes," *Annual Review of Political Science*, 3 (1): 183–219.

Ling, Justin. 2017. "The Intolerable Immodesty of Justin Trudeau," *The Walrus*, November 15, 2017. https://thewalrus.ca/the-intolerable-immodesty-of-justin-trudeau/

MandateLetterTracker.https://www.canada.ca/en/privy-council/campaigns/mandate-tracker-results-canadians.html

Mansbridge, Jane. 2003. "Rethinking Representation," *American Political Science Review*, 97 (4): 515-28.

Minsky, Amy. 2017. "Trudeau called a liar, the most cynical of politicians for ditching electoral reform promise," *Global News*, February 1, 2017. https://globalnews.ca/news/3220253/justin-trudeau-electoral-reform-broken-promise-backlash-criticism/

Mortensen, Peter, Christoffer Green-Pedersen, Gerard Breeman, Laura Chaqués-Bonafont, Will Jennings, Peter John, Anna Palau and Arco Timmermans. 2011. "Comparing government agendas: Executive speeches in the Netherlands, United Kingdom, and Denmark," *Comparative Political Studies*, 44 (8): 973-1000.

Naurin, Elin, Terry Toyed and Robert Thomson (eds.) 2019. *Party Mandates and Democracy. Making, Breaking, and Keeping Election Pledges in Twelves Countries*, Ann Arbor: The University of Michigan Press.

Pétry, François and Dominic Duval. 2019. "The Fulfillment of Government Pledges in Canada." In *The Fulfillment of Election Pledges: Campaign Promises and Government Actions in Twelve Democracies*, directed by E. Naurin, T. Royed and R. Thomson. 2019. Ann Arbor: University of Michigan Press: 123-138.

Pétry, François and Dominic Duval. 2018. "Electoral Promises and Single Party Governments: The Role of Party Ideology and Budget Balance in Pledge Fulfillment," *Canadian Journal of Political Science/ Revue canadienne de science politique*. DOI: 10.1017/S0008423918000379

Pétry, François, Dominic Duval and Lisa Birch. 2018. "Do regional governments fulfill fewer election promises than national governments? The case of Quebec in comparative perspective," *Party Politics* DOI: 10.1177/1354068818787353

Pétry, François, Robert Thomson, Erin Naurin, Ana Belchior, Heinz Brandenburg, Dominic Duval, Justin Leinaweaver and Henrick Oscarsson. 2018. *A Comparative Study of Citizens' Evaluations of Campaign Pledge Fulfillment in Six Countries*. Boston: Annual Congress of the American Political Science Association.

Pinker, Steven. 2018. *Enlightenment Now. The Case for Reason, Science, Humanism, and Progress*. New York: Viking.

Prime Minister of Canada. *Justin Trudeau Open Letter to Canadians*, November 4, 2015.https://pm.gc.ca/eng/news/2015/11/04/prime-minister-justin-trudeaus-open-letter-canadians

Rose, Richard. 1994. *Do parties Make a Difference?* Chatham: Chatham House Publishers.

Thomson, Robert, Terry Royed, Erin Naurin, Joaquin Artés, Rory Costello, Laurenz Ennser-Jedenastik, Mark Ferguson, Petia Kostadinova, Catherine Moury, François Pétry and Katrin Praprotnik. 2017. "The Fulfilment of Parties' Election Pledges: A Comparative Study of the Impact of Power Sharing," *American Journal of Political Science,* 61 (3): 527–542.

TrudeauMeter. 2018. https://trudeaumetre.polimeter.org/

Trudeau Polimetre. 2018. https://www.poltext.org/en/trudeau-polimeter

Visser, Josh. 2012. "'You're a bunch of lying liars and the media agrees' NDP to Tories in attack Ad," *National Post*, October 9, 2012. http://nationalpost.com/news/canada/tories-should-stop-attacking-us-ndp-says-in-new-attack-ad-against-tories

Wherry, Aaron. 2016. "How Justin Trudeau plans to deliver on 'deliverology'," *CBC News*, August 27, 2016. https://www.cbc.ca/news/politics/wherry-trudeau-deliverology-1.3735890

# Chapter 2
# The Trudeau Government's Legislative Agenda: Election Promises and a Dual Mandate

LISA BIRCH, STEVE JACOB AND ANTOINE BABY-BOUCHARD

> Canadians have spoken. You want a government with
> a vision and an agenda for this country that is
> positive and ambitious and hopeful. Well, my friends,
> I promise you tonight that I will lead that
> government. I will make that vision a reality.
>
> Justin Trudeau

This excerpt from Trudeau's victory speech on election night captures at once the dual dimensions of democratic mandates and election promises. Trudeau confirmed the newly elected Liberal government's general, overarching promise to deliver its vision of "real change". He confirmed his government would begin by implementing the Liberal plan with its 353 specific promises found in the platform entitled "Real Change: A New Plan for a Strong Middle Class". Thus, Trudeau embraced a vision of dual mandate.

In democracies, the electorate bestows upon the winning party two legitimate mandates: one to govern according to its vision for the common good of all citizens and another to implement its election promises. Each party's election platform contains specific promises that provide voters with a sampling of how the party's vision translates into government actions. Beyond the myriad of specific promises, each party makes a general promise to deliver good government according to its vision and to act responsibly regarding issues that were either not mentioned or unforeseen prior to the elections or that may have already been in the works within government departments.

Next fall, citizens will evaluate the government's performance relative to both mandates. Consequently, an assessment of pledge fulfillment must extend beyond analyzing the fate of specific platform promises to review how the government fulfilled its implicit, overarching promise to govern according to its vision. This chapter proposes to do just that by integrating key ideas about democratic mandates and public policy cycles, by situating the legislative agenda of the Trudeau government relative to these ideas, and by comparing the bills to the election promises. Our analysis reveals the articulation between government actions driven by an imperative mandate to fulfill specific pledges and those guided by an independent mandate to govern on matters not mentioned in the election platform or unforeseen at the time.

## 2.1   MANDATE MODELS AND PUBLIC POLICY CYCLES

The notions of democratic mandates and public policy cycles provide a useful conceptual framework for understanding what governments do during the four years between elections. These notions determine the ebb and flow of activity for the key institutions of government, which are the executive, the legislature, and the bureaucracy. On the one hand, the executive (prime minister and cabinet) and elected members of Parliament receive a four-year mandate through elections. On the other hand, the bureaucracy is a constant feature in continuous operation. While governments come and go, the public policies they implement and the bureaucracy that manages them assure continuity. For the bureaucracy, elections are interludes during which public administration continues to carry out government business as usual until the new government takes office and begins to provide policy directions according to its vision. As part of the usual business of government, public sector managers and workers ensure that existing policies and programs are implemented, administered, and evaluated. They perform these tasks according to the public management routines and obligations laid out by the Treasury Board of Canada in various policies and directives. They continue the preparatory work for new or revised policies and programs, which may involve activities such as completing stakeholder consultations, program evaluations, or regulatory impact assessments, all of which may be impervious to the election results.

However, with the rise of new political governance, new governments expect public sector managers to be more responsive to their vision and their pledge fulfillment efforts (Birch and Jacob 2019). Figure 2-1 shows the "deliverology" model followed by the Trudeau government. It illustrates how the new political governance dynamic plans pledge delivery over the four-year mandate (see Chapter 6 by Marland and Raynauld for the permanent campaign).

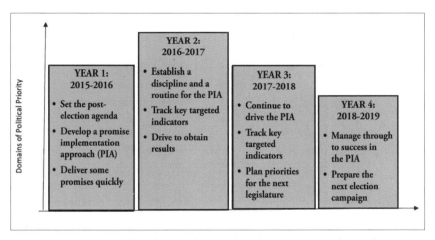

FIGURE 2-1 – "Deliverology" and New Political Governance under Trudeau
* Source: Adapted from an image presented by Michael Barber to the Trudeau cabinet during a cabinet retreat. (Canada School of Public Service, 2016a) and Birch & Jacob (2019 forthcoming).

Three different cycles with different timelines and different priorities regulate the rhythm of work and interactions between the elected government of the day and the bureaucracy (Jacob 2006). First, there is the election cycle that occurs once every four years to determine which political party will govern. The winning party's election promises set the government's initial policy priorities, especially for the early years (Fagan 2018; Flynn 2011; Panova 2017; Sulkin 2009). When the government acts to fulfill its election promises, it is pursuing its imperative mandate. Second, there is the budget cycle that occurs once a year. During its mandate, the governing party produces four budgets and, occasionally, budget updates according to its priorities and fiscal policy choices. The government fulfills its imperative mandate by allocating resources and modifying taxation to support its promised policy initiatives. When it allocates resources to pre-existing programs or to new ones about which it made no election promises, it exercises its independent or representative mandate. Last, there is the public policy cycle. This cycle involves five stages as follows:

(1) agenda setting to determine what issues require public action;

(2) problem definition to circumscribe the problem and possible solutions;

(3) decision making to choose the course of public action;

(4) implementation of the policy decision by the bureaucracy with oversight by the executive; and

(5) evaluation of the policy through program evaluations, courts, elections, and other feedback mechanisms.

Once the government implements a new policy, the bureaucracy integrates it into their administrative routines and government budgets. Policies and programs usually remain in place for very long periods, decades in fact, until there is a compelling need for policy change. The need for change may arise for one or a combination of the following reasons: (1) an election cycle brings in a new government with a new vision; (2) court decisions annul laws in whole or in part or reveal weaknesses in laws; (3) a routine program evaluation, a commission, or an Auditor General report formulates recommendations for change that the government accepts; (4) mediatized events (especially crises) focus attention on a problem and provoke a public call to action; and (5) lobbying efforts by businesses and civil society groups are successful in bringing forward a new policy idea. Due to the co-existence of these different cycles, the democratic mandate attributed to the winning party following a general election *de facto* entails two dimensions: an imperative mandate to deliver election promises and an independent mandate to govern according to its vision.

## 2.2 METHODOLOGY

In order to examine the impact of these three cycles on legislative activity, we conducted content analysis of government bills and the available legislative summaries in comparison to the analysis of election pledges found in the Trudeau Polimetre. We constituted a database comprised of the 93 government bills deposited from the start of the 42nd

Parliament in December 2015[1] as well as the Polimetre data. We retained government bills and excluded Private Members' bills since our goal is to examine the government's initiatives relative to the three cycles and to its election mandates.

We conducted content analysis of government bills and available legislative summaries in light of the wording and context of election promises. Coders classified government bills according to the presence or absence of a link to election promises, the policy domains, and the main *raison d'être* of the bill (i.e., policy modernization, miscellaneous policy initiatives, court decisions, and treaty implementation). We used the data from the Trudeau Polimetre for comparisons between government bills and election promises.

We note three caveats regarding these data. First, some laws enable governments to fulfill multiple pledges (e.g., the Bill C-22 on national security, intelligence and anti-terrorism addressed 10 promises) whereas some pledges may require new laws and modifications to existing ones. For example, Trudeau's promise to implement the Truth and Reconciliation Commission's 94 recommendations led to various government actions, including new legislation such as C-70 on Cree-Naskapi governance, C-91 on Indigenous languages, and C-92 on Indigenous family policy. Accordingly, readers cannot assume that there is a direct, single pledge-to-law or law-to-pledge linkage. Second, legislation is not required to fulfill certain types of pledges. Status-quo pledges require no action and others require changes to regulations only or executive decisions. For example, the promise to hold consultations on electoral reform only required the attribution of a mandate to the parliamentary commission on electoral reform. Similarly, the PLC promise regarding gender-based impact analyses of policies only required administrative measures initially. However, in 2018, the government decided to reinforce this policy by including it in a budget bill (see Chapter 12). Finally, changes to Polimetre verdicts frequently follow budgets. As such, we coded budgets as linked to promise fulfillment. However, budget bills serve a dual purpose: the ongoing funding of established programs at various stages in the policy cycle and the financing of new initiatives that arise from election promises.

Table 2.1 situates the overall legislative activity during periods when Parliament usually sits. Legislative activity started quickly with 23 government bills introduced between December 2015 and June 2016.

---

1.   Our analysis covers the bills presented up to mid-March when we finalized this chapter.

It peaked in the second year of Trudeau's mandate, with 36 new bills, and then began to taper off from 23 to 11 bills in the third and fourth years, respectively. By mid-March 2019, the Trudeau government had introduced 93 bills of which 57 (60%) had completed all steps in the legislative process and received royal assent.

TABLE 2-1 – Government Bills of the 42nd Parliament*

| SESSIONS** | GOVERNMENT BILLS | |
|---|---|---|
| | INTRODUCED (%, NUMBER) | ROYAL ASSENT (%, NUMBER) |
| 2015–2016 | 25% (23) | 16%  (9) |
| 2016–2017 | 39% (36) | 33% (19) |
| 2017–2018 | 25% (23) | 33% (19) |
| 2018–2019 | 12% (11) | 18% (10) |
| Total | 100% (93) | 100% (57) |

\* Data to mid-March 2019

\*\* Sessions cover the fall and winter with holidays in December and summer.

## 2.3   MANDATES, CYCLES, AND THE LEGISLATIVE AGENDA OF THE 42ND PARLIAMENT

Table 2-2 associates the government bills to the election, budget, and policy cycles. These data show that the election cycle generated more legislative activity compared to the policy and budget cycles. A similar analysis of Quebec's Couillard government (2014–2018) revealed that the policy cycle generated more legislative activity (Jacob et al. 2018). This may be a reflection of the Trudeau government's commitment to its change agenda and to promise keeping.

TABLE 2-2 – Policy Cycles and the Trudeau Government's Legislative Program

| CYCLE | GOVERNMENT BILLS (%, NUMBER) |
|---|---|
| Electoral Cycle | 41% (38) |
| Budget Cycle | 24% (22) |
| Policy Cycle | 35% (33) |
| Total | 100% (93) |

The legislative activities linked to the election cycle include a variety of bills in fulfillment of election promises regarding matters such as international trade, Indigenous peoples, election reform, and environment policy among others. For example, the Trudeau government introduced bills to implement new trade agreements, which are respectively the Canada-EU Comprehensive Free Trade Agreement (Bill C-30), the Canada-Ukraine Free Trade Agreement (Bill C-31), Comprehensive and Progressive Agreement for Trans-Pacific Partnership (Bill C-79), and the Canada-Israel Free Trade Agreement (Bill C-85) (see Chapter 15 by Lauzon Chiasson and Paquin). In keeping with promises to renew the relationship with Indigenous peoples, the Trudeau government presented Bills C-91 and C-92. With a view to undoing the Harper government's reforms, regulating party financing and expenditures, and ensuring fair and free elections, Karina Gould, the Minister of Democratic Institutions, introduced Bill C-50 and later Bill C-76 to amend the Canada Elections Act and other acts (see Chapter 7 by Milner).

The budget cycle generates two main types of legislation. The first is to implement the annual budget and the second concerns routine annual appropriations. Since the budgets finance existing and new measures, they are at the intersection of the government's imperative mandate to fulfill its election promises and its independent mandate to ensure good government by continuing to support policies and programs that work and by responding to needs for new policies when they arise. Much of the Trudeau government's change agenda involved budget measures to increase resources for social programs, for infrastructure projects, and for Indigenous reconciliation (see chapters 4, 5, 9, and 13), while reducing taxes for families and small- and medium-sized businesses, and increasing taxes or removing tax advantages for the wealthy.

Further analysis of the government bills linked to the policy cycle reveals the complexity of agenda-setting dynamics beyond election promises. It confirms the long duration of policy cycles. In 39% of the policy cycle cases (or 14% of all 93 bills), the government is modernizing existing laws, some of which went unchanged for decades. For example, Bill C-49, the Transportation Modernization Act, addresses issues such as air passengers' rights, airplane inspection and safety, and rail transportation and safety. This bill took into consideration a review of Canada's transportation legislation initiated in 2014 that was to propose the new rules for the next 20 to 30 years. Among other new measures, this bill imposes the installation of voice and video recorders in trains in the wake of the Lac-Mégantic train disaster. Another example is Bill C-77. This bill modernizes family and divorce law in Canada. It addresses the report of the Action Committee on Access to Justice in Civil and Family Matters (the "Cromwell Committee" struck in 2013), international obligations arising from Canada's adherence to the 1996 Hague Child Protection Convention and the 2007 Hague Child Support Convention, and a consensus that the 1985 legislation needed reform. In 2016, when the Trudeau government introduced Bill C-37, the justifications of changes to various drug and drug-related laws referred to the opioid crisis, the study of this issue by the House of Commons Commission on Health, international treaty obligations, and legislative changes proposed in Bill C-70 that died on the Order Papers before the 2015 elections.

Another 27% of the laws classified under initiatives led by the public policy cycle (or 10% of all bills) result from miscellaneous government decisions either linked to its vision, to conflict settlement, or to federal-provincial relations and the territories. The Liberal government implanted its vision of a diverse and inclusive Canada as well as its focus on human rights through legislative initiatives such as Bills C-16, C-25, C-38, and C-81 (see Chapter 12 by Bird). Bill C-16 amends the Canadian Human Rights Act to prohibit discrimination based on gender identity or expression and the Criminal Code to protect gender identity from hate propaganda. Bill C-25 seeks to encourage the democratic, transparent governance of businesses, cooperatives, and not-for-profit organizations and foster more diversity and women's representation on corporate boards and in management positions. Bill C-38 improves the state's capacity to combat human trafficking by inversing the onus of presumption for traffickers. Following a consultation process on the rights of disabled Canadians, the government introduced Bill C-81 called the Accessible Canada Act to ensure the equality of all persons, especially persons with disabilities. From the conflict between Quebec and Canada over the gun control registry (Bill C-52) to ending the postal strike before Christmas (Bill C-89), to problems with private pension plans (Bill C-27) or changes to public pension plans (Bill C-26), the Trudeau government showed how it exercises its independent mandate to govern.

In 24% of the legislative initiatives linked to the policy cycle (or 9% of all bills), various court decisions pushed issues onto the Trudeau government's agenda either because the courts ruled that clauses were unconstitutional or in violation or potential violation of the Charter of Rights and Freedoms or because court decisions revealed loopholes in laws that created injustices. For example, the government introduced Bill C-7 in response to the Supreme Court decision concerning the right of the RCMP to unionize, Bill C-10 following court decisions about Air Canada's fleet maintenance, and Bill C-14 following the *Carter v. Canada* (Attorney General) decision regarding medically assisted death. Finally, 9% of the bills in the category of public policy cycle initiatives (or 3% of all bills) involve the government adopting legislation to implement international treaties such as the WTO Trade Facilitation Agreement (Bill C-13) or the Canada-USA Agreement Beyond the Border Action Plan of 2011 (Bills C-21, C-23). Clearly, the public policy cycle, the budget cycle, and the election cycle regulate the flows of government legislative activity and reveal how the government fulfills its dual mandates to govern responsibly and to deliver on promises according to its vision of a change agenda.

## 2.4  PROMISES, LEGISLATIVE ACTIVITY, AND POLICY DOMAINS

Table 2-3 compares the Trudeau government's election promises to its legislative activity by policy domains. Government and democracy is the top policy domain in both cases. Although the next four top policy domains are the same, they vary in rank and weight for promises and bills. The law and order domain rises to second place on the legislative agenda mainly because of public policy cycle dynamics that required various modifications to the Criminal Code and other criminal justice laws following court decisions invalidating articles for constitutional reasons or charter rights. While the environment and the economy occupy third and fourth ranks for election promises, the economy rises to third place and the environment falls to sixth place.

The articulation of the government's mandate to deliver promises and its general overarching mandate to govern according to its vision and values is revealed further by comparing the bills that are linked to fulfilling specific promises and those that are not related to promises. Overall, 43% (40) of all government bills were linked to election promises showing the influence of the election cycle on the legislative agenda. Another 57% (53) of bills did not correspond to election promises, which reveals the impact of the policy cycle on government activity. By March 2019, only 53% (21) of the bills linked to promises compared to 68% (36) of the bills without promise linkages received royal assent. The legislative performance of previous Canadian governments measured by the percentage of government bills receiving royal assent varies widely from 92% for the Mulroney majority government to a low of 0% for the Harper minority government in 2008 (Conley 2011).

TABLE 2-3 – Comparison between the Political Program and the Legislative Program*

| RANK | 353 ELECTION PROMISES (POLITICAL PROGRAM) | | 93 GOVERNMENT BILLS (LEGISLATIVE PROGRAM) | |
|---|---|---|---|---|
| | PUBLIC POLICY DOMAIN | % (NUMBER) | PUBLIC POLICY DOMAIN | % (NUMBER) |
| 1 | Government and Democracy | 21%   (74) | Government and Democracy | 34% (33) |
| 2 | Health and Social Services | 15%   (53) | Law and Order | 15% (14) |
| 3 | Environment | 13%   (47) | Economy and Employability | 14% (13) |
| 4 | Economy and Employability | 11%   (38) | International Affairs and Defence | 12% (11) |
| 5 | International Affairs and Defence | 10%   (34) | Health and Social Services | 9%   (8) |
| 6 | Law and Order | 10%   (34) | Environment | 8%   (7) |
| 7 | Education and Research | 7%   (25) | Minorities | 5%   (5) |
| 8 | Minorities | 7%   (24) | Education and Research | 1%   (1) |
| 9 | Families | 3%   (12) | Families | 1%   (1) |
| 10 | Arts and Culture | 2%   (6) | Identity and Nationalism | 1%   (1) |
| 11 | Identity and Nationalism | 1%   (3) | Arts and Culture | 0%   (0) |
| 12 | Regions and Agriculture | 1%   (3) | Regions and Agriculture | 0%   (0) |
| | **Total** | **100% (353)** | **Total** | **100% (93)** |

* Rounded figures

Figure 2.2 shows the cumulative distribution of bills introduced by the presence and absence of linkages between bills and election promises from 2015–2016 through to 2018–2019. Figure 2.3 shows the number of government bills introduced each period by the presence or absence of linkages to promises. Figure 2.4 shows that the promise-keeping and legislative activities of the Trudeau government per period tend to follow the path suggested by the "deliverology" model (see Figure 2-1) with front-loading of activity in the first two years. These data suggest that the Trudeau government pursued both an imperative and an independent mandate, attending to promises made during the election cycle and to needs for legislative changes arising from the policy cycle. By contrast, the Couillard government in Quebec introduced 150 government bills during its mandate from 2014 to 2018, of which 111 (74%) were not linked to promises, suggesting that the Couillard government pursued an independent mandate via its legislative activity (Jacob et al. 2018).

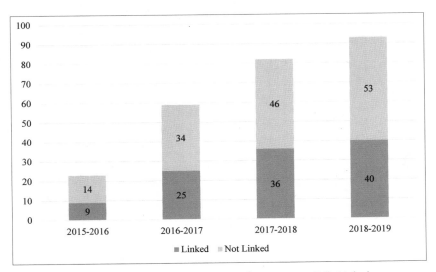

FIGURE 2-2 – Cumulative Evolution of Government Bills Linked or Not Linked to Election Promises

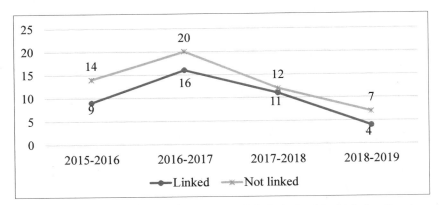

FIGURE 2-3 – Annual Evolution of Government Bills Linked or Not Linked to Promises

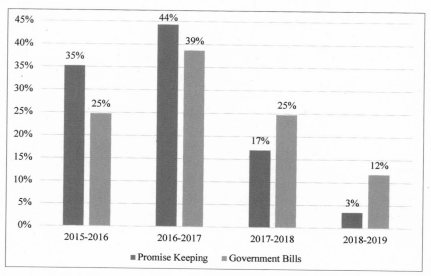

FIGURE 2-4 – Promise Keeping and Legislative Activities of the Trudeau
Government by Period (Percentage of Totals)*
* Promises kept or in the works (n = 318); Government bills introduced (n = 93)

These findings reflect those of our collaborators in other chapters. Overall, the Trudeau government fulfilled completely or partially 90% (318) of its 353 election promises, of which 64% (204) required legislative activity to fulfill. The election cycle nonetheless generated 43% of the bills on the legislative agenda. The Trudeau government proposed other bills outside its election promises in response to other agenda-setting dynamics arising from the longer public policy cycle. These data support the idea that the government has a dual mandate to implement its platform and to govern according to its vision on issues about which it made no promises. The government bills without election-pledge linkages tended to align with the Trudeau-Liberal vision of diversity, inclusion, and feminism. Accordingly, many government bills and their legislative summaries, either by their content, by their subject, or both, reflected the same human rights and justice perspective that guided promises.

## 2.5  VARIATIONS IN THE TIME REQUIRED TO ADOPT A GOVERNMENT BILL

The time required to move a government bill through the entire legislative process provides an indication of the degree of consensus among parliamentarians regarding government bills. The fewer the number of days between the introduction of a bill and its royal sanction, the more likely it is that the bill is supported by parliamentarians, and conversely, the greater the number of days, the more likely it is that the bill is controversial and subject to partisan conflict (Jacob et al. 2018). Figure 2-5 shows the average number of days for a bill introduced in each period to complete the legislative process depending on election-promise linkages. It took an average of 278 days in Parliament to move a government bill linked to an election promise through the legislative process and an average of 184 days to complete the legislative process for government bills unrelated to election promises.

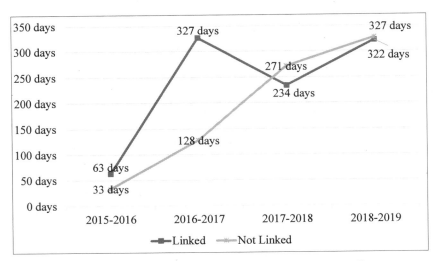

FIGURE 2-5 – Average Number of Days for a Government Bill to Complete the Legislative Process

Parliament adopted appropriation bills to allow the public administration to operate within 3 to 9 days, as these are straightforward, routine events each year. By contrast, complex subjects require technical expertise and broader consultations through parliamentary standing committees and may be a source of controversy and partisan politics. Budget bills took between 45 and 86 days to adopt. The time to adopt other bills varied from 64 days for C-14 on medically assisted dying that was not linked to any promises, to 133 days for C-79 on the implementation of the Progressive Trans-Pacific Partnership Agreement that was linked to a promise about trade diversification. It required 227 days for C-76 with less sensitive amendments to the Canada Elections Act, but 386 days for C-50 that brought amendments to the same Act regarding party financing, both of which were linked to promises. Issues of a more complex nature and ones linked to the Liberal vision of a diverse and inclusive Canada seemed to require more days. For example, Bill C-16 recognizing gender identity under the Canadian Human Rights Act took 398 days. Bills on the labour code and public sector labour relations took up to 508 days.

## CONCLUSION: A DUAL MANDATE

This examination of the influence of election, budgetary, and policy cycles on the legislative menu reveals how the Trudeau government proceeded to deliver on election promises and to act as a trustee with an independent mandate to govern. The Trudeau government fulfilled 90% of its promises in whole or in part as expected by the imperative mandate model of democracy. While the election cycle determined 41% of the legislative agenda for the 42nd Parliament, the policy and budget cycles accounted for 59% of all government bills. Through these bills, the Trudeau government shows how it fulfills its independent mandate to govern. Given the evidence in this chapter of how the Trudeau government navigated over the three cycles that regulate the rhythm of government, democratic mandates are necessarily dual mandates: one to implement election promises, which reflect the party's vision and values, and the other to govern on all other matters accordingly.

Come election night in October 2019, if voters decide mainly to hold the Trudeau government accountable for its promise-keeping record, they will be judging using imperative mandate criteria. Tools such as the Polimetre provide useful data about election promises and their fulfillment. If voters decide mainly to hold the Trudeau government accountable for its decision-making and governance record, they will assess based on independent mandate criteria. Books, such as this one, offer a retrospective of both the promise-keeping and decision-making records. If anything, this chapter shows two reasons why it is important for citizens to know the election platforms of parties. First, each party's election platform becomes the policy agenda it will prioritize if it forms the government. Second, it provides a sampling of how the party's vision translates into policy prefe-rences. That vision will guide the government as it exercises its independent mandate as a trustee of the public good to make policy decisions on matters about which its election platform remains silent.

## REFERENCES

Birch, Lisa, and Steve Jacob. 2019. Forthcoming. "'Deliverology' and evaluation: A tale of two worlds," *Canadian Journal of Program Evaluation*.

Canada School of Public Service MySchoolMonEcole. (2016a). *Results and Delivery—Lessons From Around the World*. [Video file]. Retrieved from https://www.youtube.com/watch?v=jUJlDAy6KbY

Conley, Richard S. 2011. "Legislative Activity in the Canadian House of Commons: Does Majority or Minority Government Matter?," *American Review of Canadian Studies*, 41 (4): 422–437, DOI: 10.1080/02722011.2011. 623237

Fagan, E. J. 2018. "Marching Orders? U.S. Party Platforms and Legislative Agenda Setting 1948–2014," *Political Research Quarterly*, 71 (4): 949–959. https://doi.org/10.1177/1065912918772681

Flynn, Greg. 2011. "Rethinking policy capacity in Canada: The role of parties and election platforms in government policy-making," *Canadian Public Administration*, 54 (2): 235–253. https://doi.org/10.1111/j.1754-7121.2011.00172.x

Jacob, Steve. 2006. "Élaboration, suivi et évaluation des engagements électoraux du Parti libéral du Québec". In *Le parti libéral: enquête sur les réalisations du gouvernement Charest*, François Pétry, Éric Bélanger et Louis Imbeau (eds.): 103-120. Québec: Presses de l'Université Laval.

Jacob, Steve, Lisa Birch, François Pétry and Antoine Baby-Bouchard. 2018. "Le gouvernement Couillard en tant que 'mandataire indépendant'." In *Bilan du gouvernement de Philippe Couillard: 158 Promesses et un mandat contrasté*, François Pétry and Lisa Birch (eds.): 77-90. Québec: Presses de l'Université Laval.

Mansbridge, Jane. 2003. "Rethinking Representation," *American Political Science Review*, 97 (4): 515–528.

Panova, Elena. 2017. "Partially Revealing Campaign Promises," *Journal of Public Economic Theory*, 19 (2): 312–330. https://doi.org/10.1111/jpet.12189

Sulkin, Tracey. 2009. "Campaign appeals and legislative action," *Journal of Politics*, 71 (3): 1093–1108. https://doi.org/10.1017/S0022381609090902

Trudeau, Justin. 2015. "Justin Trudeau, for the record: 'We beat fear with hope' Read a transcript of Justin Trudeau's victory speech after leading the Liberals to a majority," *MacLeans*, October 20, 2015. https://www.macleans.ca/politics/ottawa/justin-trudeau-for-the-record-we-beat-fear-with-hope/

# Chapter 3
# Federalism: An Institutional Constraint on the Fulfillment of Election Promises?[1]

FRANÇOIS ROCHER

| | |
|---|---|
| «Ma petite entreprise | "My little enterprise |
| Connaît pas la crise | Unaware of the crisis |
| Épanouie elle exhibe | Flourishing it exhibits |
| Des trésors satinés | Satiny treasures |
| Dorés à souhait» | Felicitously gilded" |

Alain Bashung

There are few areas where the federal government can propose policies on its own without considering the provinces, the territories, and the existing division of powers. The election platform of the Liberal Party of Canada (LPC) reflects this reality well. In most areas where the LPC government wished to intervene, the success of its proposed policies partly depended on the provincial/territorial governments' cooperation and sometimes resulted in the signing of agreements (bilateral or multilateral). Federal-provincial "complicity" appears to be a necessary condition to fulfill a number of election promises, whether the electorate is fully aware of this or not.

1. I would like to thank Jade Boivin and Yvan Giroux for helping me with data collection.

First, it should be noted that the LPC has not made any promises that directly (or even indirectly) affect the way Canadian federalism works. However, the federal dimension often comes into play in the context of specific promises, either because what the federal government is proposing has an impact on provincial/territorial activities or because their cooperation is necessary for the federal government to fulfill its promise. This chapter therefore asks two relatively simple questions: (1) What federal dimensions were associated with the promises made? and (2) What model of federalism has this government favoured?

## 3.1  FEDERALISM: A FEW REFERENCE POINTS

Since the creation of the welfare state, the notion that each level of government is sovereign in its jurisdiction areas, namely the dualistic vision of federalism, has almost fallen into obsolescence. The interdependence between the federal government and the provinces/territories[2] has become the norm. This reality has resulted in at least three terms qualifying this interaction, namely *cooperative*, *collaborative*, or *competitive* federalism. These terms refer to distinct political realities and dynamics.

Table 3-1 maps the differences and similarities between these approaches. Cooperative or collaborative federalism is the result of the constitutional boundaries easing between the two levels of government (Brouillet 2017, 141–142). Overlaps and joint actions are increasing. In terms of policy formulation, the first form emphasizes interdependence, even if the federal government is responsible for most of the initiatives. This has manifested itself through creating common bodies, delegating of administrative tasks, signing intergovernmental agreements (bilateral or multilateral, symmetrical or asymmetrical), or cooperation agreements to coordinate the exercise of concurrent or shared jurisdictions (Poirier 2018). Collaborative federalism emphasizes the federal partners' equality in the co-development of objectives (Cameron and Simeon 2002, 49). Therefore, there are no subordinate relationships from one order of government to the other. In the cooperative model, leadership is usually exercised by the federal government, which has repeatedly used its spending power to get the provinces to intervene in their jurisdiction areas according to the

---

2.    It should be noted that provinces have their own powers under the Canadian Constitution whereas Canada's three territories (Nunavit, the Yukon and the Northwest Territories) only have devolved powers, which means the powers that the federal government has delegated to them by law all while remaining the central authority. Unlike territories, provinces have power and authority that is determined by the Constitution, not the federal government.

federal objectives. In fact, this approach is essentially administrative (Banting 1987; Simeon, Robinson, and Wallner 2014, 75–76). Collaborative federalism can also lead to bilateral or multilateral agreements or arrangements (symmetrical or asymmetrical) and is not opposed to measures that meet the specific needs of some provinces as long as both levels of government consider themselves equal partners.

TABLE 3-1 – Models of Federal-Provincial Relations

| CHARACTERISTICS | MODEL OF FEDERALISM | | |
|---|---|---|---|
| | COOPERATIVE | COLLABORATIVE | COMPETITIVE |
| Jurisdictions and Responsibilities | Overlapping | Overlapping | Exclusive and shared |
| Policy Formulation | Interdependence with federal predominance | Co-determination | Autonomy of each order of government |
| Interventions | Conjoint actions | Equal partners | Limited to each order of government |
| Institutional Frameworks | Common bodies; administrative delegation; cooperation agreements; federal spending powers | Common bodies; administrative delegation; cooperation agreements | Competition between federal and provincial/ territorial bodies |
| Leadership | Federal government | Shared | Contested |

Cooperation and collaboration are not always possible. There may be times when the interests of federal partners are not aligned, where some of them are using their bargaining power, which may be a refusal to participate, in order to put conditions to their adherence, or simply to use their veto, to derail negotiation processes. The consensus decision rule grants uncooperative governments disproportionate power and stimulates bargaining behaviour in support of an agreement based on the lowest common denominator (Painter 1991, 274). Competitive federalism is characterized by escalating inter-regional and intergovernmental conflicts and greater pressure in favour of decentralization (Simeon et al. 2014, 76). Complementary to this is competitive federalism where behaviours and interactions are more those of strategic players competing with each other and ultimately finding compromises (Simmons and Graefe 2013, 33). Competitive federalism is close to the dualistic model because the provinces affirm their constitutional jurisdictions and challenge the federal government's authority to impose policies against their will.

## 3.2   LIBERAL PROMISES: COLLABORATIVE FEDERALISM?

The Liberal platform contains 37 promises that call for provincial and territorial involvement in one way or another. In the French version of the document, the term *collaboration* appears 35 times, whereas in the English version, the different versions of the term (collaborative, collaborative, collaboration) are mentioned only four times. The expression "work with" is favoured, being used 33 times. On the surface, it would appear that the Liberal government has endorsed the collaborative approach. It is important to note that provincial/territorial involvement is presented generally in a complementary manner as a condition for fulfilling promises. In other words, the platform does not present a coherent and unified vision of the federal government's role regarding the provinces and territories. Their take on federalism, being implicit, is nowhere to be found.

As shown in Table 3-2, the number of promises and their fulfillment varies by intervention areas. A first reading shows that only 8% of promises have remained unaddressed, 49% are in the works or partially fulfilled, and 43% have been fulfilled. However, these promises are not all of the same nature. Some financially enhance existing programs, others involve consultation with the provinces and territories in areas of public policy, some aim to better align federal and other levels of government policies, and many encroach on areas of provincial jurisdiction. Finally, despite the emphasis on the need for collaboration, several promises, whether fulfilled or in the process of being fulfilled, have created tension and conflict with some provincial governments, while others have generated little debate. Similarly, many of them have not received any media attention, while others, more controversial, have been discussed extensively in the public arena.

TABLE 3-2 – Promise Fulfillment by Policy Domain

| DOMAINS WITH F/P/T PROMISES * | KEPT | PARTIALLY KEPT | NOT YET RATED | TOTAL |
|---|---|---|---|---|
| Economy and Employability | 3 | 2 | 0 | 5 |
| Education and Research | 1 | 2 | 0 | 3 |
| Environment | 4 | 6 | 0 | 10 |
| Families | 1 | 1 | 0 | 2 |
| Government and Democracy | 2 | 1 | 2 | 5 |
| Law and Order | 2 | 1 | 0 | 3 |
| Indigenous Peoples | 0 | 2 | 0 | 2 |
| Health and Social Services | 3 | 3 | 1 | 7 |
| **Total** | **16** **(43%)** | **18** **(49%)** | **3** **(8%)** | **37** **(100%)** |

\* These are domains that contained promises that referred to federal/provincial/territorial relations.

It is possible to assess the actions of Trudeau's government by sectors of activity, as proposed by the Polimetre. However, this approach makes it harder to see the bigger picture and, more importantly, does not reflect how federal-provincial-territorial relations have unfolded throughout the LPC's mandate, which is what we are proposing to do.

## 3.3   BROKEN/NOT YET RATED PROMISES

First of all, there are three promises not yet rated. They deal with areas of exclusive provincial jurisdiction. The first promise concerned the application of federal regulations allowing more flexible working conditions for workers under federal jurisdiction to all workers from provinces and territories (promise 7.73). The second concerned the modification of the labour codes to adjust them to the new federal parental benefits (promise 7.74). They proposed amendments to provincial labour codes over which the federal government has no jurisdiction. The third was in the area of health care and concerned the development of a system allowing regulated companies to hire caregivers on behalf of families (promise 12.08). These promises illustrate a phenomenon in which a party makes promises in areas over which it has little or no control, either through imprudence, thoughtlessness, or pure electoral calculation (Pétry, Duval, and Birch 2018).

This leaves 34 promises considered fulfilled or in the works. We are therefore proposing another way of proceeding by focusing on the confrontational or non-confrontational nature of intergovernmental relations by sector, echoes of the initiatives in the media, the jurisdiction area of promises, and the type of actions favoured by the government with respect to intergovernmental relations. Table 3-3 shows where intergovernmental relations have been conflicting or not. This table calls for three general observations.

TABLE 3-3 – Number of Promises Fulfilled or Partially Fulfilled According to the Nature of the Relation, Federal-Provincial Jurisdictions, and the Nature of the Action

| PUBLIC POLICY DOMAIN* | INEXISTENT RELATION | | CONSENSUAL RELATION | | CONFLICTUAL RELATION | | JURISDICTION | | | TYPE OF ACTION | | |
|---|---|---|---|---|---|---|---|---|---|---|---|---|
| | IM | NIM | IM | NIM | IM | NIM | F | P | FP | U | M | B |
| Economy and Employability | | | 2 | 3 | | | | 3 | 2 | | 3 | 2 |
| Education and Research | | 1 | | 2 | | | | | 3 | 1 | 1 | 1 |
| Environment | | 1 | 2 | 2 | 4 | 1 | 1 | | 9 | 2 | 6 | 2 |
| Families | | 1 | 1 | | | | 2 | | | 2 | | |
| Government and Democracy | 1 | 1 | | 1 | | | 2 | | 1 | 2 | 1 | |
| Law and Order | 2 | 1 | | | | | | | 3 | 3 | | |
| Indigenous Peoples | 2 | | | | | | | 1 | 1 | 2 | | |
| Health and Social Services | | 3 | 1 | 1 | 1 | | 1 | 3 | 2 | 3 | 2 | 1 |
| **Total** | **5** | **8** | **6** | **9** | **5** | **1** | **6** | **7** | **21** | **15** | **13** | **6** |

*Only domains with promises that mention federal-provincial-territorial relations.

Legend:
IM: Issue mediatization          NIM: No or little issue mediatization          FP: Shared jurisdiction
F: Federal jurisdiction          P: Provincial jurisdiction          M: Multilateral Action
U: Unilateral Action          B: Bilateral Action

## 3.4   A FEDERALISM NOT INVOLVING THE PROVINCES

A relatively high number of promises (13/34 or 38%), although fulfilled, resulted in a collaboration with the provinces and territories that can be described at best as tenous. In other words, the government has put in place measures that only affected the federal portion of promises. For example, the LPC committed to establish a federal-provincial task force to study the development of a cannabis sales and distribution network (9.03) (see Chapter 10). This group, composed of nine members appointed exclusively by the federal government, was established in June and tabled its report in December 2016. Although provincial representatives were met, it is not the "federal-provincial task force" announced during the election campaign. However, the report raises many legislative and regulatory issues that the provinces and territories will have to face in order to comply with the new federal framework (Task Force on Cannabis Legalization and Regulation 2016; Beauchesne 2018).

We can also point to two other election promises affecting Indigenous Peoples this time (see Chapter 13 for all promises affecting Indigenous peoples). The LPC committed to work with the provinces and territories to implement the 94 recommendations of the Truth and Reconciliation Commission (TRC) and the obligations arising from the signing of the United Nations Declaration on the Rights of Indigenous Peoples (10.09). To this day, there is still no coordinated federal-provincial plan in place on this matter. The Liberals also promised to establish a process to resolve Métis self-government claims in collaboration with the provinces (10.20). In April 2017, the Canada-Métis Nation Accord came into force. Provinces are not signatories (Prime Minister of Canada 2017). However, many of its provisions require the establishment of bilateral mechanisms or agreements in areas such as education and health services that are under provincial jurisdiction. Bilateral meetings between the Canadian government and the Métis Nation presidents have taken place, but provincial government representatives do not appear to have been invited (Indigenous and Northern Affairs Canada 2018). More generally, when the media reported on any of these 13 promises, the intergovernmental dimension was not mentioned. Most of the time, these initiatives have received little attention.

## 3.5  COMPETITIVE FEDERALISM

The implementation of a relatively small number of promises (6 or 17%) has led to conflicts between the federal government and the provinces and territories. It is in the environmental area that conflicts have been most prominent and highly publicized (see Chapter 14). It is an area of shared jurisdiction, which is increasing the likelihood of tensions on key issues. The federal government must navigate between the need to protect the environment and the need to support the important natural resource extraction and commercialization sector (minerals, gas, oil, etc.). Interests between producing provinces are often opposed to those who have to assume some of the risks associated with the transportation of these pollutants, not to mention the citizens' concern about environmental issues. For example, the federal government has set Canada-wide greenhouse gas reduction targets (promise 5.18). In June 2018, it passed legislation to that effect and, by order in council, determined that the provinces and territories had to comply with the carbon pricing system. While the framework is flexible for the provinces and territories embracing the objectives, it is binding for those who would refuse to cooperate, in which case the "federal government will introduce an explicit price-based carbon pricing system that will apply in jurisdictions that do not meet Benchmark" (Canada Gazette 2018). In this area of environmental protection, "collaboration" is not optional. However, few provinces have put such a system in place. Until Jason Kenney's election in Alberta, Quebec, British Columbia, and Alberta had established their own pricing mechanism. Since the Conservative government was elected in Ontario, the province has opposed the federal government's price on carbon, as have the governments of Saskatchewan and New Brunswick, which lost their constitutional challenge before the Saskatchewan Superior Court on May 3, 2019. The Manitoban government has also decided to challenge the federal strategy.

In addition, the LPC wanted to review the environmental assessment process in areas under federal jurisdiction, in consultation with the provinces' and territories' administrations, to avoid duplication (promise 5.07). The problem is that this is still an area of shared jurisdiction. The division of roles and responsibilities between the two levels of government are unclear and often determined by the courts (Becklumb 2013). The Quebec government objected to the federal government's claim that only federal rules apply in the case of the Trans Mountain pipeline (Fournier 2018). The same question arose in the case of the Kinder Morgan pipeline when the Attorney General of British Columbia asked the court to rule on the validity of provincial environmental protection regulations (Hunter, McCarthy, and Lewis 2018). These conflicts have been widely publicized.

In short, while the Liberal government has kept some promises, many of them have created and fueled conflicts with provinces that do not share the objectives, or the means put forward by the federal authority. Collaboration is much easier to achieve when it comes to funding provincial and territorial initiatives as part of the transition to clean energy (such as the retirement of coal-fired power plants or the integration of renewable energy into the electricity grid). It is much less so when it comes to imposing a framework that involves pricing emissions according to thresholds unilaterally determined by the federal government. These initiatives open the door to competitive federalism in which the provinces invoke the principle of autonomy in their areas of jurisdiction and challenge the federal government's authority to impose measures without their approval.

A conflict also arose during the negotiation of the new Health Accord with the provinces and territories (promise 12.04) (see Chapter 11). A meeting between the Minister of Finance and the provincial and territorial ministers of Health in December 2016 resulted in the rejection of the federal proposal to offer a 3.5% transfer increase over five years (a 0.5% increase compared to the agreement made under the Conservative government), and a targeted investment of $5 billion over 10 years for mental health care and $6 billion for home care. The provinces' common front, which were calling for a 5.2% increase, dissolved after New Brunswick showed a willingness to negotiate an agreement with the federal government. Ottawa subsequently signed bilateral agreements with the provinces, and a number of them expressed dissatisfaction with the amounts that will be transferred in the future. These negotiations were echoed widely in the national press.

## 3.6 COOPERATIVE FEDERALISM

Finally, 15 promises (44%) resulted in intergovernmental relations that we might call consensual. This is particularly true when it comes to the financial enhancements of labour market development, training, and apprenticeship programs. They resulted in federal-provincial agreements that did not raise any tensions and did not really attract media attention (see Chapter 6). The same is true when it comes to funding federal initiatives extended to the provinces and territories. For example, the LPC promised to develop a new National Early Learning and Child Care Framework, in collaboration with the provinces, territories, and Indigenous communities (promise12.10). Following a meeting with the aforementioned stakeholders, separate announcements were made regarding subsidies to childcare systems across the country (see Chapter 9). As part of a multilateral agreement reached in June 2017, the federal government committed $7.5 billion over 11 years to the provinces in order to create 40 000 new subsidized spaces across Canada. Quebec did not take part in this agreement, but under the right to opt out with financial compensation, it got 23% of the amount announced by the federal government (Radio-Canada 2017). Bilateral agreements must be reached with the provinces to determine how funding will be provided.

The 2015 platform also promised to provide provinces, territories, and municipalities with predictable federal funding to implement their transit plans. In addition, it committed to providing loan and capital guarantees to provinces and municipalities through the Canada Infrastructure Bank (CIB). The federal government was acting as a funder. Hundreds of subsidies have been given to municipalities to develop their public transit systems. They have been the subject of federal-provincial agreements (Infrastructure Canada 2018). The Prime Minister also noted that some projects were struggling to get off the ground due to the lack of cooperation from some provinces, further delaying projects and fueling discontent among some large municipalities' mayors (Blatchford 2019). The same approach characterizes the new CIB. It is still in its beginnings and is considering a dozen projects for financial support (Press 2019). It has been criticized for its slowness and lack of clear direction (Macklem and Lynch 2019).

These generally unpublicized initiatives are part of the traditional approach to cooperative federalism where the federal government adopts "national" policies and invites the provinces to join, with fiscal transfers to follow. Therefore, it is the federal use of its spending power that makes it possible to keep a promise in an area of exclusive or shared provincial jurisdiction through multilateral or bilateral agreements. The provinces are not opposed to it because they can enhance their own programs or, in some cases, it allows them to reduce their investments in the affected sector, as was the case for federal infrastructure funding (Office of the Parliamentary Budget Officer 2019).

## CONCLUSION

From the outset, the Liberal government's record may seem impressive. Only three of the 37 promises were unaddressed, and none were publicly repudiated. This can be misleading, however, because while some commitments may have been partially met, they have sometimes been met despite the lack of an upstream cooperation process with the provinces and territories. For example, the Canada-Métis Nation Accord (promise 10.20) or the action on post-traumatic stress (promise 12.30) indicate collaboration to come and were not developed in partnership with the provinces and territories. Other Liberal commitments could only be well received by the provinces, since they were the ones who had first developed initiatives, such as the joint purchase of prescription drugs (promise 12.29). In addition, some promises avoided getting to the heart of some issues that were debated extensively and challenged by some provinces. The commitment to legalize the use of marijuana, while having significant implications for the provinces regarding public health and safety, did not address the issue of consultation with the provinces before proceeding. It should also be noted that some of the promises that ultimately hardly involved the federal government were very vague, as was the case with the public awareness campaigns against harassment (promise 12.30) or the education savings plans promotion (promise 4.19).

However, when it comes to intergovernmental relations, it is not enough to only do what was announced; it is also important to fulfill a promise without reviving or creating tensions, if not conflicts, between the two orders of government. It is much easier to achieve this when it comes to improving existing programs. This was the case in the area of economics and employability (see Chapter 5), where Liberal promises involved increased funding for worker training, or public transit infrastructure projects. Other financial commitments, however, are more difficult to meet without conflict with the provinces. For example, the LPC had no choice but to negotiate a new Health Accord since it had not been renewed under the previous government. Of course, the government managed to do it, but in total discord and discontent. The use of the federal spending power to force provinces to invest where the central government wishes has long been criticized by provincial and territorial players. Moreover, the desire to adopt a carbon pricing policy could only lead to confrontation, as could the desire to review the environmental assessment process. Provincial governments that do not share the same approach, ideology, or vision of the current Liberal government may occasionally be less receptive to federal policy initiatives.

In the end, although the Liberal platform made much of the collaboration notion, Justin Trudeau's government did not follow the model of so-called collaborative federalism, which respects the jurisdiction vested in each order of government. It should be based on the principle of co-determination and implies that they consider themselves equal partners, but it has not been the case. Instead, the fulfillment of Liberal promises, when endorsed by the provinces and territories, resulted in the use of cooperative or confrontational models that gave predominance to the central government. This has resulted in administrative or financial arrangements, but also in unilateral actions when deemed necessary by the Liberal government. The preferred model often relied on unilateral initiatives that provinces and territories had to endorse. This approach takes us away from collaborative federalism and reminds us of the golden age of cooperative federalism, in its positive aspects, or competitive federalism in areas where provinces and territories seek to preserve their autonomy.

REFERENCES

Banting, Keith. 1987. *The Welfare State and Canadian Federalism. 2nd ed,* Montréal and Kingston: McGill-Queen's University Press.

Beauchesne, Line. 2018. "Légaliser le cannabis au Canada: les défis à venir," *Drogues, santé et société,* 16 (1): 31–69.

Becklumb, Penny. 2013. *Federal and Provincial Jurisdiction to Regulate Environmental Issues.* Ottawa: Library of Parliament.

Blatchford, Andy. 2019. "Some provinces not co-operating to get infrastructure projects off the ground: Trudeau," *The Globe and Mail,* January 28, 2019. https://www.theglobeandmail.com/canada/article-some-provinces-not-co-operating-to-get-infrastructure-projects-off-the/

Brouillet, Eugénie. 2017. "The Supreme Court of Canada: The Concept of Cooperative Federalism and Its Effect on the Balance of Power". In *Court in Federal Countries. Federalists or Unitarists?,* Nicholas Aroney and John Kincaid (eds.): 135–164. Toronto: University of Toronto Press.

Cameron, David, and Richard Simeon. 2002. "Intergovernmental Relations in Canada: The Emergence of Collaborative Federalism", *Publius,* 32 (2): 49–71.

Canada Gazette. 2018. "Order Amending Part 2 of Schedule 1 to the Greenhouse Gas Pollution Pricing Act: SOR/2018-212", *Canada Gazette,* Part II, 152 (22) (October). http://gazette.gc.ca/rp-pr/p2/2018/2018-10-31/html/sor-dors212-eng.html.

Fournier, Jean-Marc. 2018. "Évaluation d'impacts environnementaux. Le fédéral doit respecter les lois provinciales," *LaPresse+*, 14 avril, 2018. http://plus.lapresse.ca/screens/71cd2fb0-5bbd-4a2d-bee9-84e331a18781__7C___0.html.

Hunter, Justine, Shawn McCarthy and Jeff Lewis. 2018. "B.C. takes pipeline fight to court, asking for power to restrict oil shipments," *The Globe and Mail*, April 26, 2018. https://www.theglobeandmail.com/canada/british-columbia/article-bc-seeks-jurisdiction-over-oil-shipments-with-court-reference/.

Indigenous and Northern Affairs Canada. 2018. *Canada and the Métis Nation move forward on Canada-Métis Nation Accord.* https://www.canada.ca/en/indigenous-northern-affairs/news/2018/03/canada-and-the-metis-nation-move-forward-on-canada-metis-nation-accord.html

Infrastructure Canada. 2018. "Public Transit Infrastructure." Ottawa: Infrastructure Canada. https://www.infrastructure.gc.ca/plan/pti-itc-eng.html.

Macklem, Tiff and Kevin Lynch. 2019. "What will it take to restore Canada's potential growth?," *The Globe and Mail*, January 31, 2019. https://www.theglobeandmail.com/business/commentary/article-what-will-it-take-to-restore-canadas-potential-growth/.

Office of the Parliamentary Budget Officer. 2019. *Infrastructure Update: Investments in Provinces and Municipalities.* Ottawa: Office of the Parliamentary Budget Officer.

Painter, Martin. 1991. "Intergovernmental Relations in Canada: An Institutional Analysis," *Canadian Journal of Political Science*, 24 (2): 269–288.

Pétry, François, Dominic Duval and Lisa Birch. 2018. "Do regional government fulfill fewer election promises than national governments? The case of Quebec in comparative perspective," *Party Politics*, First published July 9, 2018. https://doi.org/10.1177/1354068818787353

Poirier, Johanne. 2018. "Le fédéralisme coopératif au Canada: Quand les registres juridique et politique jouent au chat et à la souris," *Fédéralisme Régionalisme*, 18. https://popups.uliege.be/1374-3864/index.php?id=1772#bodyftn8

Prime Minister of Canada. 2017. "Canada-Métis Nation Accord." https://pm.gc.ca/fra/accord-canada-nation-metisse.

Press, Jordan. 2019. "Infrastructure bank narrows gaze to more than a dozen projects, CEO says," *The Star*, January 26, 2019. https://www.thestar.com/business/2019/01/26/infrastructure-bank-narrows-gaze-to-more-than-a-dozen-projects-ceo-says.html.

Radio-Canada. 2017. "Ottawa s'entend avec les provinces pour créer 40 000 places en garderie," June, 12, 2017. https://ici.radio-canada.ca/nouvelle/1039215/ottawa-gouvernement-federal-provincial-service-garderie-40000-places.

Simeon, Richard, Ian Robinson and Jennifer Wallner. 2014. "The Dynamics of Canadian Federalism." In *Canadian Politics*, 6th, James Bickerton and Alain-G. Gagnon (eds.): 65-91. Toronto: University of Toronto Press.

Simmons, Julie M., and Peter Graefe. 2013. "Assessing the Collaboration That Was 'Collaborative Federalism' 1996–2006," *Canadian Political Science Review*, 7 (1): 25–36.

Trudeau Polimetre. 2019. https://www.polimetre.org/fr/canada/42-trudeau-plc.

# Chapter 4
# The Liberal Fiscal Plan: Left-Wing Promises, Right-Wing Government?

GENEVIÈVE TELLIER AND CHEICK ALASSANE TRAORÉ

The 2015 federal election campaign was full of surprises. Among those was the resounding victory of the Liberal Party, which few observers could have predicted a few months earlier. It is true that the campaign style of the Liberals, and especially their leader Justin Trudeau, put them at an advantage over their opponents. However, one should not think that the Liberal victory was only the result of a battle of images and style. Justin Trudeau's election platform also put forward a number of markedly progressive ideas, breaking somewhat with the Liberal tradition of supporting centrist policies.

Many of these progressive ideas relate directly to the Liberal financial plan. A few months before the federal election, Stephen Harper's Conservatives had adopted a balanced budget and a bill prohibiting the government from running budget deficits. The New Democratic Party promised to balance budgets for the duration of its mandate if elected. The Liberal platform took the opposite direction to the Conservatives and the New Democrats. If voters elected the Liberals to power, there would be deficits, taxes would increase for the better-off in society, and the state would be more interventionist in terms of economic and social policies. In short, the Liberal platform presented a progressive discourse that the party had neglected for a long time. Enough voters supported this discourse and the associated election pledges to grant the Liberals a majority mandate to govern for four years.

What was the message conveyed by the Liberals' election commitments and to what extent was this message subsequently implemented? As the 2019 elections draw near, it seems appropriate to try to answer these questions. Our analysis begins with a review of the budget-related Liberal promises during the 2015 election campaign, focusing on the ideas conveyed in its financial plan and comparing them with those of the other parties. Next, we look at the fulfillment of these promises, including whether the economic environment has forced the Liberal government to review its commitments or whether it has stayed the course throughout its mandate. We conclude our analysis by taking stock of the Liberal government's budgetary and financial achievements.

## 4.1  THE LIBERAL FINANCIAL PLAN

Unveiled on September 26, 2015, less than a month away from the federal general election, the Liberal Party's fiscal plan synthesized all the costs and revenues generated by its platform pledges. Table 4-1 outlines the financial plan, as it was unveiled at the end of the Liberal Party platform (Liberal Party of Canada 2015).[1] The election pledges in the Liberal platform were numerous and diverse. However, it is clear that the Liberal Party's priority was to fund initiatives for individuals. Nearly 70% of new spending and promised tax cuts were targeting specific groups in the population, mainly families with children, seniors, students, workers, the unemployed, Indigenous peoples, veterans, immigrants, and refugees. Many other election pledges were related to economic initiatives such as workforce training, support for job creation, infrastructure development, the green economy, and support for the cultural and agricultural industries. Among all these pledges, the centrepiece of the Liberal platform was undeniably the introduction of a new family policy, the Canada Child Benefit (CCB), to enhance direct assistance to families. The cost of this program was estimated at nearly $90 billion for the next four years, which represented 60% of the new spending promised by the Liberal Party (see Chapter 9 by Daniel Béland and Michael J. Prince for more details on this and other social spending programs).

---

1.    We have simplified somewhat the categories in the financial plan to lighten the presentation while remaining as faithful as possible to the original document.

TABLE 4-1 – Financial Plan of the Liberal Party of Canada (millions of dollars)

| BUDGET ITEMS | 2016–2017 | 2017–2018 | 2018–2019 | 2019–2020 |
|---|---|---|---|---|
| **New Expenditure** | | | | |
| Tax Cuts and Benefits | 25,550 | 26,136 | 26,747 | 27,293 |
| *Including the Canada Child Benefit* | *21,725* | *22,160* | *22,600* | *23,000* |
| Infrastructure | 5,025 | 5,025 | 3,450 | 3,450 |
| Employment Insurance | 524 | 2,100 | 2,140 | 2,185 |
| Jobs and Training | 2,155 | 2,254 | 2,267 | 1,689 |
| Health | 415 | 665 | 900 | 1,000 |
| Environment and the Economy | 415 | 1,445 | 1,400 | 400 |
| Arts and Culture | 185 | 380 | 380 | 380 |
| Indigenous Peoples | 275 | 575 | 455 | 355 |
| Veterans | 325 | 309 | 311 | 313 |
| Strengthening Communities | 155 | 155 | 158 | 158 |
| Immigration | 133 | 108 | 58 | 58 |
| **Total New Expenditure** | **35,157** | **39,152** | **38,266** | **37,281** |
| **New Revenue[2]** | | | | |
| Replacing UCCB, CCTB, and NCBS **Expenditures** | 17,960 | 18,245 | 18,550 | 18,825 |
| Tax Expenditure and Harper Spending Review | 500 | 1,000 | 2,000 | 3,000 |
| Tax on Wealthiest One Percent | 2,800 | 2,856 | 2,913 | 2,971 |
| Reduce EI Premiums from $1.88 to $1.65 | 523 | 2,100 | 2,140 | 2,185 |
| Cancel Family Income Splitting (Not Pension Income Splitting) | 1,995 | 2,050 | 2,110 | 2,165 |
| Cancel Education/Textbook Credits to Boost Grants | 725 | 825 | 890 | 925 |
| Cancel TFSA Limit Increase from $5,500 to $10,000 | 160 | 235 | 295 | 360 |
| Continue to Phase Out Fossil Fuel Subsidies | 0 | 125 | 250 | 250 |
| **Total New Revenue** | **24,663** | **27,436** | **29,148** | **30,681** |
| **Net Value of Commitments** | **10,494** | **11,716** | **9,118** | **6,600** |
| Budget Balance without Commitments | 600 | 2,200 | 3,400 | 7,600 |
| **Budget Balance with Commitments** | **(9,894)** | **(9,516)** | **(5,718)** | **1,000** |
| Projected GDP Growth Rate (Real GDP) | 2.7 | 2.4 | 2.2 | 2 |
| Projected Debt-to-GDP Ratio | 0.30 | 0.29 | 0.28 | 0.27 |

1. includes reduced fiscal expenses (such as tax credits);
2. includes increased fiscal expenses
Source: Liberal Party of Canada platform, 2015, pp. 73–88

The Liberal financial plan also outlined the tax measures planned to fund its new social programs. A large proportion of the additional income required was to come from the abolition of existing programs, such as the universal child care program (UCCB), the income splitting program (except pension income), the reduction in allowable contributions to tax-free savings accounts (TFSA), and other tax deductions. The Liberal government implemented tax increases for 1% of the wealthiest Canadians, while taxes for the middle class were to be reduced. Finally, the Liberal Party intended to reduce program costs by revising them and to increase revenues by fighting tax evasion.

However, this set of measures would not be enough to fund all the promised new initiatives. The Liberal Party also planned to use short-term borrowing: "We will run modest deficits for three years so that we can invest in growth for the middle class and credibly offer a plan to balance the budget in 2019." (Liberal Party of Canada 2015, 73). It should be noted that the financial plan did not take into account some potential revenues such as those that could be obtained through the legalization of cannabis or the carbon tax. It may be that the Liberal Party did not want to plan formally for funds to be obtained from promises that had yet to be fulfilled with the cooperation of other decision-makers (especially provincial governments).

The 2015 Liberal financial plan is noteworthy for at least two reasons. On the one hand, many of the initiatives announced marked a significant shift in direction for the Liberal Party. For the first time since the early nineties, the Liberals abandoned their commitment to balancing the budget when the country was not in economic recession. It was the first time that the Liberals proposed a redistribution of the tax burden between the most affluent individuals and the middle class. In the past, the Liberal Party promised and adopted measures to lower taxes across the board. This time, a rise in the taxes paid by those who are better off was supposed to lower the tax rates for the middle class. It was the first time that the Liberals targeted the middle class, and not the private companies, as the main driver of economic growth. The following statement illustrates the new vision of the Liberal Party in this regard:

> A strong economy starts with a strong middle class. Our plan offers real help to Canada's middle class and all those working hard to join it. When our middle class has more money in their pockets to save, invest, and grow the economy, we all benefit (Liberal Party of Canada 2015, 4).

The Liberal platform stood out clearly from the platforms of its main political opponents. Table 4-2 provides a summary comparison of the major commitments of the Liberal Party with those contained in the fiscal appendices at the end of the 2015 platforms of the New Democratic Party and of the Conservative Party of Canada. The comparison shows that the Liberal Party was the only one to propose an increase in the federal government's debt. The willingness by the Liberals to increase government spending and go into debt contrasts, not surprisingly, with the Conservative commitment to respect stricter budgetary orthodoxy. The comparison with the New Democrats reserves a surprise. Contrary to expectations, the new spending announced in the Liberal financial plan is four times higher than that found in the New Democratic platform's fiscal appendix (nearly $150 billion in four years compared to $34 billion). A more detailed comparison of the Liberal and New Democratic platforms shows that the two parties proposed many initiatives that were quite similar. For example, both were committed to abolishing several fiscal measures adopted by the Conservative government (e.g., contributions to TFSAs, Employment Insurance (EI) premiums, income splitting, and fossil fuel subsidies). For other initiatives, the Liberal Party was even more resolutely interventionist than the New Democratic Party. The New Democrats did not commit to reviewing the personal tax system, they did not promise to spend as much on family support as the Liberals, and they were planning to dedicate fewer resources to fund transit and social infrastructures than the Liberals. In short, the Liberal Party seemed to be more left-wing than the New Democratic Party in many ways. Let us examine now what the Liberals did deliver on their fiscal and budget promises once in power.

TABLE 4-2 – Value of Commitments of the Three Main Political Parties, 2016–2017 to 2019–2020 (in millions of dollars)

| BUDGET ITEMS | BUILDING THE COUNTRY OF OUR DREAMS | A NEW PLAN FOR A STRONG MIDDLE CLASS | PROTECT OUR ECONOMY |
|---|---|---|---|
| | NEW DEMOCRATIC PARTY | LIBERAL PARTY OF CANADA | CONSERVATIVE PARTY OF CANADA |
| Budget Balance without Commitments* | 13,800.0 | 13,800.0 | 18,700.0 |
| New Expenditure | (33,820.8) | (149,856.0) | (7,599.2) |
| New Revenue | 29,966.6 | 111,928.0 | 2,350.0 |
| Total net with the New Commitments | (3,854.2) | (37,928.0) | (5,249.2) |
| Reserves for Contingencies | 0.0 | 0.0 | (7,000.0) |
| Budget Balance with Commitments | 9,945.8 | (24,128.0) | 6,450.8 |

* The NDP and the LPC used the estimates presented by the Parliamentary Budget Officer in July 2015 to project the budget balance without their commitments, whereas the CPC used the figures presented in its last budget from April 2015.
Sources: Costing plans in each party's 2015 platform

## 4.2  THE LIBERAL GOVERNMENT BUDGETS

Once elected, the Liberal government took great care to inform the public that it intended to fulfill its election promises. Mandate letters from the Prime Minister provided cabinet ministers with clear guidelines on the importance of fulfilling election pledges, and soon after the election, the Privy Council Office started to make a careful count of how the government was progressing towards fufilling its election promises. In addition to keeping a running tally of the committments kept, it also seems relevant to know when the government fulfilled these promises and to whom or for what purposes they were made. Table 4-3 presents this information with regard to the promises relating to the implementation of the financial plan. The specific promises in Table 4-3 are drawn from the Trudeau Polimetre.

TABLE 4-3 – Fulfillment of Liberal Promises Related to Fiscal and Budgetary Matters

| GROUP OR ITEM AFFECTED BY A FISCAL OR BUDGET TARGET | KEPT | | | | | KEPT IN PART | IN THE WORKS | BROKEN | TOTAL |
|---|---|---|---|---|---|---|---|---|---|
| | 2016 | 2017 | 2018 | 2019 | TOTAL | | | | |
| Individuals | 8 | 0 | 2 | 0 | 10 | 2 | 4 | 0 | 16 |
| Businesses | 5 | 2 | 5 | 0 | 12 | 1 | 2 | 0 | 15 |
| Infrastructure | 1 | 1 | 1 | 0 | 3 | 0 | 1 | 0 | 4 |
| Budget Balance | 0 | 0 | 0 | 0 | 0 | 0 | 0 | 4 | 4 |
| Budget Transparency | 0 | 1 | 1 | 0 | 2 | 0 | 0 | 0 | 2 |
| Total | 14 | 4 | 9 | 0 | 27 | 3 | 7 | 4 | 41 |

As shown in Table 4-3, half of the promises kept by the Liberal government were fulfilled during the first year in office. In fact, from the day after the election, the Liberal government seemed in a hurry to act. In December 2015, the Parliament was summonded and the first bill that was introduced by the government aimed at changing certain tax provisions to reduce inequalities between individuals. A few weeks after the election, the Parliamentary Budget Officer, followed by the Department of Finance, both confirmed that economic growth was weaker than anticipated and this was going to have a negative impact on the budget balance. The federal government was now forecasting a deficit of $3.0 billion for the current year rather than a surplus of $2.4 billion as projected in the April 2015 budget submission by the previous Conservative government (Department of Finance 2015). This shortfall of $5.4 billion in the financial balance meant that the Liberal government was no longer able to meet all its financial commitments. The Liberal government chose to address the new fiscal situation by deliberately breaking its promises to balance the budget. This would allow it to continue to focus on reducing tax inequality and enhancing public programs to help the middle class.

The first fiscal measure introduced by the government fulfilled the promise to redistribute the personal tax burden. Without even waiting until its first budget, the Liberal government introduced Bill C-2, an Act to amend the Income Tax Act. As promised, the bill modified the structure of the personal income tax brackets, lowering the middle-class tax rate and raising the highest-income taxpayers, while abolishing income splitting for tax purposes, and reducing the limit permitted for contributions to a TFSA. These measures came into effect on January 1, 2016.

The government's first budget, presented a few weeks later, fulfilled another key promise by the Liberals, namely the introduction of the Canadian Child Benefit (CCB). If families were the big winners of this first budget, many other groups in the population would also benefit from the government's new initiatives: students, workers, seniors, veterans, Indigenous peoples—in short, all the groups in the population that had been targeted for attention in the Liberal campaign platform. The economic sector was not left out, but the aid that was granted to it was more modest and largely focused on infrastructure programs. The government announced an increase in infrastructure spending of $120 billion over the next ten years, double the amount promised in the election campaign. However, the expenditures announced in the 2016 budget for the first three years were lower than what had been promised in the election platform. Essentially, the Liberal government delayed the fulfillment of some of these promises in the short term while pledging to fulfill them in the longer term. The new expenditures announced in the 2016–2017 budget were distributed as follows: 58% directly targeted individuals, 34% focused on infrastructures, and the remaining 8% were in the form of direct assistance to various economic sectors (environment, arts, innovation, research, etc.). These percentages are quite similar to the percentages in the Liberal platform's financial plan.[2]

Throughout its mandate, the Liberal government has not deviated from its overall plan to assist the middle class; however, the form of this assistance has varied over time. While the first budget initiatives aimed to deliver benefits directly to individuals or to reduce their tax burden (except for the better-off) the two subsequent budgets have focused on measures to stimulate economic growth, which was in turn intended to benefit the middle class. These economic measures especially targeted innovation, including the creation of industrial "super-clusters," the supply of venture capital, the creation of Innovation Canada in the 2017-2018 Budget (Department of Finance 2017). and scientific research, with funding for innovation, university research, industrial research, and government-business partnerships in the 2018-2019 Budget (Department of Finance 2018). The amount of money spent on these new measures was also much smaller. The Liberal government planned to increase total spending by

---

2.    This calculation is based on the data presented in Table A24 of the 2016-2017 Budget (Department of Finance 2016).

9.8% in 2016-2017, but only by 5.1% in 2017–2018 and by 2.5% in 2018–2019.[3] The message behind these economic measures is clear:

> Smart and ambitious investments in people, communities and high-growth sectors create opportunities. Opportunities lead to job creation. More jobs give rise to a more confident and growing middle class. And a more confident and growing middle class is the only way to strong and sustained economic growth (Ministry of Finance 2017, 6; see Chapter 5 by Marcelin Joanis and Stéphanie Lapierre for more details on the economic initiatives of the Liberal government).

With the last budget presented before the General Elections of 2019, the Liberal government tried to reconcile support for the middle class and economic development. This budget has an electoral flavour and announces the creation of programmes directly targeting individuals, while keeping an economic development objective. This budget proposes measures to support individuals seeking professional development training (Creation of the Canadian Training Benefit to stimulate "ongoing learning and retraining"),[4] buying their first home, purchasing an electric vehicle, and accessing high-speed Internet networks. The elderly, students, war veterans and indigenous communities are not overlooked in this budget. In brief, the budget is reaching the same groups of voters who were targeted by the Liberals during the 2015 election campaign. This last budget of the Liberal government is relatively generous: expenditures increase by 5.0%, even if the anticipated increase in revenues is lower (4.8%). Thus, there will be a deficit for the fourth consecutive year.

More generally, the Liberal government's mandate is characterized, from its beginning, by a willingness to implement programs intended to fulfill its key promises, which primarily target the middle class. The last years of the Liberal mandate have been devoted to consolidating these programs and, with its last budget, to initiate new proposals that could help its relection. However, some new developments have emerged along the way, although they did not fundamentally change the direction of the Liberal government. Indigenous communities have received more funding than promised (including an additional $4.8 billion over five years beginning in 2018-2019). The Liberal government has also shown a commitment to eliminating disparities between men and women. A series of initiatives and objectives were announced in the 2018-2019 budget to

---

3.   This calculation is based on annual budget documents.
4.   Finance Canada. Budget 2019-2020, The Canada Training Benefit. https://www.budget. gc.ca/2019/docs/themes/good-jobs-de-bons-emplois-en.html

promote, among other things, the increased presence of women in the labour market. Although these new measures were not in fulfillment of formal election pledges, they are not surprising either, as the Indigenous and gender issues are themes that are central to the Liberal platform (see Chapter 13 by Thierry Rodon and Martin Papillon and Chapter 12 by Karen Bird). A third, unplanned initiative was a bit more surprising: the federal government's purchase of the Kinder Morgan Trans Mountain pipeline in the spring of 2018 (see Pierre-Olivier Pineault's chapter). This investment disappointed environmental groups for which there is no social acceptability for this project. However, the purchase of the Kinder Morgan pipeline demonstrated the government's desire to reassure the business community:

> Getting the Trans Mountain Expansion Project built will preserve thousands of good, well-paying jobs — the kind of jobs that will strengthen and grow the middle class [...] It will reassure investors that Canada is a country that respects the rule of law and is carrying out major projects. It's important to remember, though, that Canada is also a place where we understand that the environment and the economy go hand in hand (Morneau 2018, para. 4-7).

This willingness to reassure the business community may explain why the Liberal government failed to implement all its fiscal reform aimed at limiting certain provisions that allow private companies to benefit from advantageous tax measures. Indeed, the Minister of Finance has had to face strong opposition from the business community (both large corporations and small-business owners) to this reform.[5]

Last, there were unanticipated revenues that were not included in the Liberal Party's financial plan. The government plans to use them largely to fund public programs rather than to reduce anticipated deficits. Thus, the revenue generated by the legalization of cannabis is to be redistributed to the provinces. Carbon taxes levied in provinces that do not have their own action plan to combat greenhouse gas emissions are to be redistributed to individuals in these provinces. Finally, tariffs on steel and aluminum imported from the United States are to be used to compensate Canadian producers affected by American protectionist measures.

On the other hand, economic growth was stronger than expected in 2017-2018, as GDP grew by 3.0% rather than the anticipated 1.9% which

---

5.   At the time of writing, the Liberal government has announced its intention to amend the provisions that allow some well-off taxpayers to benefit from a tax deduction through the stock option. The bill implementing this initiative has not yet been tabled.

has helped the government reduce its borrowing. Delays in financing infrastructure will also reduce the total amount of short-term expenditures. Thus, the observed deficits are lower than the anticipated deficits ($17.8 billion rather than the anticipated $29.4 billion for the 2016-2017 fiscal year; $19.0 billion instead of $28.5 billion for 2017-2018; and $14.9 billion instead of $18.1 billion for 2018-2019).[6] However, the government has not yet reached its target for balanced budgets. According to the latest published estimates, the federal government's debt would amount to 30.9% of GDP, while the Liberal Party promised to reduce it to 27% of GDP. Throughout its mandate, the Liberal government's approach has remained consistent with its primary objective of helping the middle class, through substantial investments of public funds.

## CONCLUSION

There is an old saying in politics that the Liberal Party of Canada acts as a left-wing political party during election campaigns, yet governs as a right-wing party once in power. That is to say, it seduces the Canadian electorate by promising to implement so-called progressive initiatives, yet does not dare to go against the business community once elected. The Liberal mandate of Justin Trudeau contradicts this vision, but only in part. According to many observers, the Liberal Party ran its 2015 election campaign on a clearly interventionist platform (David 2015; Hébert 2015). This is supported by our own analysis of the Liberal financial plan (and by our comparison with the financial plans of the two other major federal parties) both in terms of the scale of the proposed spending and their objectives. The Liberal platform advocated a larger and more sustained involvement of the state in society than the platforms of its political opponents. Once elected, the Liberal Party did not attempt to modify its roadmap. It has pursued the same objectives, even if the economic circumstances were not as favourable as anticipated.

However, state interventionism by the Trudeau government was not limited to an extension of the social safety net for the middle class; it also targeted the business sector. The Liberal Party still sees businesses as an engine of the economy and, for that reason, justifies state support for them. Liberal support for business became manifest only once promises to help the middle class were fulfilled or on their way to being fulfilled. The

---

6.    The data come from the Public Accounts of Canada (Receiver General for Canada 2017, 2018) and the 2019-2020 Budget (Minister of Finance, 2019).

Liberal government has shown a sustained interest in funding activities related to innovation and scientific research, but this was more apparent in the second half of the Liberal mandate. Liberal support for the economy was also evident in other initiatives, such as the decisions to purchase the Trans Mountain pipeline to "reassure investors," and to put into place incentives to promote the presence of women in the labour market. In this regard, it should be noted that the Trudeau government's feminist measures are essentially economic measures.

Have the Liberals ruled as a right-wing party? To a certain extent, the Liberal Party feels a desire to create conditions conducive to economic development and full employment as well as innovative and dynamic industries, a position generally held by right-wing parties. However, unlike right-wing parties that try to support economic development with policies that mainly benefit the owners of private companies, the Liberal government of Justin Trudeau has supported economic development with policies that benefit the middle class. Its more interventionist orientations marked a clear break with the previous Conservative government. The next few years will tell us whether the Liberal government's strategy of betting on the middle class to stimulate the economy will produce the desired results.

## References

Conservative Party of Canada. 2015. *Protect our Economy. Our Conservative Plan to Protect the Economy.*

David, Michel. 2015. "La fin du purgatoire?," *Le Devoir*, October 10, 2015.

Hébert, Chantal. 2015. "Les scénarios du 19 octobre," *L'Actualité* 40 (15) November 1st 2015:36–37.

Department of Finance. 2015. *Update of Economic and Fiscal Projections, 2015.* Ottawa: Department of Finance. https://www.budget.gc.ca/efp-peb/2015/pub/efp-peb-15-en.pdf

Department of Finance. 2016. *Growing the Middle Class.* Ottawa: Department of Finance. https://www.budget.gc.ca/2016/docs/plan/budget2016-en.pdf

Department of Finance. 2017. *Budget 2017—Building a Strong Middle Class,* Remarks by the Honourable Bill Morneau. Ottawa: Department of Finances.

Department of Finance. 2018a. *2018 Fall Economic Statement: Investing in Middle Class Jobs.* Ottawa: Department of Finance. https://www.fin.gc.ca/n18/18-107-eng.asp

Department of Finance. 2018b. *Equality and Growth for a Strong Middle Class.* Ottawa: Department of Finance. https://www.budget.gc.ca/2018/docs/plan/budget-2018-en.pdf.

Department of Finance. 2019. *Investing in the middle class. Budget 2019*, Ottawa, Department of Finance. https://www.budget.gc.ca/2019/docs/plan/budget-2019-en.pdf.

Morneau, Bill. 2018. *Agreement Reached to Create and Protect Jobs, Build Trans Mountain Expansion Project*. Ottawa, Department of Finance, 2018. https://www.canada.ca/en/department-finance/news/2018/05/agreement-reached-to-create-and-protect-jobs-build-trans-mountain-expansion-project.html

New Democratic Party. 2015. *Building the Country of our Dreams. Tom Mulcair's plan to bring change to Ottawa.*

Liberal Party of Canada. 2015. *Real Change: A New Plan for a Strong Middle Class.*

Receiver General for Canada. 2017. *Public Accounts of Canada, 2017. Volume 1: Summary Report and Consolidated Fiancial Statetments*. Ottawa: Public Services and Procurement Canada.

Receiver General for Canada. 2018. *Public Accounts of Canada. Volume 1: Summary Report and Consolidated Fiancial Statements*. Ottawa: Public Services and Procurement Canada.

# Chapter 5
# Economic Policies: Did the Liberals Strengthen the Middle Class?

Marcelin Joanis and Stéphanie Lapierre

## 5.1 THE OBSESSION WITH THE MIDDLE CLASS

"A New Plan for a Strong Middle Class" was the title of the Liberal Party of Canada's electoral platform presented by its leader, Justin Trudeau, during the 2015 election campaign. As it stated, "A strong economy starts with a strong middle class […] When our middle class has more money in their pockets to save, invest, and grow the economy, we all benefit." (Liberal Party of Canada 2015, 4). A strong economy also includes sustainable development and the green economy (see Chapter 14 by Pierre-Olivier Pineau). This economic vision contrasts clearly with the Conservative Party's vision of "protecting the economy" through control of spending to eliminate "waste" and measures to support the private sector (Conservative Party of Canada 2015). In addition to being ubiquitous during the campaign, the middle-class theme was repeated as a mantra throughout the Liberal mandate, the phrase appearing in most government speeches and announcements.

But, exactly, what is the middle class? In simple terms, the middle class corresponds to the middle section of the population, which includes more or fewer people depending on the boundaries that will be chosen to delimit the interval. Although there are some precise definitions of the concept in the literature, the fact remains that experts do not agree on a common definition (Delorme et al. 2014). One economic definition affixes the "middle class" label to individuals whose income is between

75% and 150% of the median income.[1] Other (sociological) definitions of the middle class place more emphasis on belonging to the intermediate occupations or call for a self-evaluation of the respondent's social position. In sum, the middle class is a rather blurred concept and it is reductive to hammer that every measure adopted by a government has the potential to influence the middle class.

In the case of promises affecting the entire economy and promoting job creation, it is conceivable that these measures will have a positive effect on the middle class, whatever its definition. However, when it comes to more specific promises, it becomes essential to clarify what is meant by the "middle class" to assess whether a promise has actually achieved its purpose. In this regard, it is interesting to note that several of the Trudeau government's flagship social policy measures (e.g., the Guaranteed Income Supplement, the Canada Child Benefit, Canada's National Housing Strategy, Employment Insurance, the Canada Pension Plan, and the establishment of an official poverty line) are in fact targeting groups that are not part of the middle class (see Chapter 9 by Daniel Béland and Michael J. Prince). Instead, these measures target "those who work hard to be part of the middle class" (Department of Finance Canada 2018a). Commitments to Indigenous peoples, notably the promises to fulfill the Kelowna Accord of 2004 and the 94 recommendations of the Truth and Reconciliation Commission of Canada of 2015, will also require significant expenditures that do not target the middle class (see Chapter 13 by Thierry Rodon and Martin Papillon).

## 5.2   A DYNAMIC LABOUR MARKET AS A BACKDROP

The main economic policy objective of the Trudeau government was to "generate more jobs and opportunities for the middle class and those who work hard to be part of it" (Department of Finance Canada 2019). While it is true that not everyone can be part of the middle class, an economic policy objective thus formulated avoids the trap of a quantified job-creation promise, which is much more risky because the economic and fiscal policies of a government are just one of many factors that influence the economy in general and job creation in particular. Just think of the impact on Canada of the economic performance of our trading partners,

---

1.   Based on this definition, the 2016 Census data indicate that 32.8% of Canadian households had after-transfer but before taxes incomes in the middle class in 2015, a decrease of 1.0 percentage point since 2005.

the protectionist behaviour of the United States, changes in international demand for commodities, or the exchange rate.

In this respect, it must be acknowledged that there was no lack of job creation in recent years. Labour market data show that in January 2019, the Canadian economy had 887,300 more jobs than in November 2015. Ontario, followed by Quebec and British Columbia, created the most jobs during this period. In contrast, Newfoundland and Labrador and Saskatchewan experienced a decline in employment. An analysis of the labour market over the last 18 years (Figure 5-1) shows that if the trend continues, Justin Trudeau's mandate will be the one in which job creation has been the highest since the early 2000s.

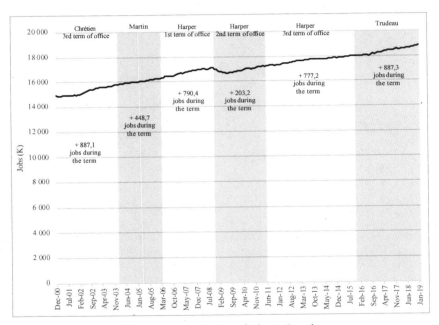

FIGURE 5-1 – Evolution of Jobs in Canada
Source: Statistics Canada, Table 14-10-0287-01

In the run-up to the 2019 election, the national unemployment rate is at a historic low (Figure 5-2) and economic growth remains positive since the last major recession (Figure 5-3). The main economic indicators show a positive trend since the Canadian economy emerged from the Great Recession of 2008–2009. The data in Figure 5-3 also show that the Canadian economy was in recession in early 2015, the election year that brought the Trudeau government to power. Although the 2015 recession was much smaller than the 2008–2009 recession, that is when the Canadian economy had its worst performance since 2009. In addition, three provinces and one territory (Alberta, Saskatchewan, Newfoundland and Labrador, Nunavut) were in recession in 2015. At the time of writing, economic forecasts for 2019 point to positive growth, despite a slowdown, with growth in investment, exports, and employment, despite the economic uncertainty stemming in particular from the protectionist threat from the United States (Bank of Canada 2019). The current strength in the Canadian economy cannot be attributed solely to the Liberal government's own economic program — far from it. However, Justin Trudeau's government has avoided the political pitfall that an economy in recession inevitably constitutes.

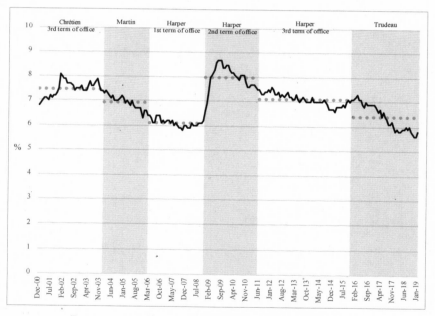

FIGURE 5-2 – Evolution of the Unemployment Rate in Canada
Source: Statistics Canada, Table 14-10-0287-01
Note: The dotted lines correspond to the average rate during the mandate.

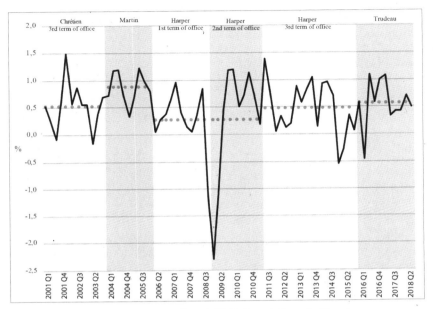

FIGURE 5-3 – Quarterly real GDP Growth Rates in Canada
Source: Statistics Canada, Table 36-10-0104-01
Note: The dotted lines correspond to the average rate during the mandate.

## 5.3 AN ECONOMIC PROGRAM PARTLY FULFILLED

What was the economic program of Justin Trudeau's Liberals? The Trudeau Polimetre lists 55 Liberal promises related to the economy (Trudeau Polimetre 2019). At first glance, the Trudeau government has fulfilled entirely 60% of them, and an additional 25% are kept in part or in the works. About one quarter of the 55 economic promises are associated with low-cost measures, involving new spending between $25 and $500 million compared to an annual budget of more than $300 billion. Other promises are associated with changes in existing programs and tax measures or the cancellation of policies that were put into place by the Harper government, particularly with respect to employment insurance. For the most part, these promises have been fulfilled at least in part, although they are not central to the Liberal government's economic policy. To assess the economic performance of the Trudeau government, the rest of this chapter will look at promises related to three major levers of economic policy: (1) public finance management; (2) infrastructure; and (3) support for innovation. First, however, we will discuss some government achievements in international and interprovincial trade that were not announced in the Liberal platform.

### 5.3.1    International and Interprovincial Trade

Many pledges in the Liberal platform promise to increase trade and diversify export markets in a "progressive and inclusive" way. With international trade accounting for nearly a third of the Canadian economy, negotiating and implementing agreements that facilitate the free trade of goods and services is undoubtedly a key component of Canadian economic policy (for more on Liberal promises on international trade, see Chapter 15 by Julien Lauzon Chiasson and Stéphane Paquin). However, while the Liberals promised to increase trade with established and emerging markets, particularly in China and India, the election of Donald Trump as president of the United States suddenly forced the Canadian government to fall back on defending its commercial interests under an existing trade agreement (North American Free Trade Agreement or NAFTA) and an already signed agreement (the Comprehensive and Progressive Agreement for Trans-Pacific Partnership or CPTPP), both of which involved the United States. In the end, Justin Trudeau's ambitious international trade program has been reduced mostly to the renegotiation of NAFTA. After several months of difficult discussions, Canada, the United States, and Mexico have agreed to sign the Canada-United States-Mexico Agreement (CUSMA), which will replace NAFTA.

Neither the CUSMA nor the TPP had been the subject of election pledges in 2015. However, it is perhaps on the domestic front that the biggest commercial surprise came, namely the Canadian Free Trade Agreement (CFTA), which became effective July 1, 2017. The press release issued on this occasion stated that thanks to this new agreement, "Canadians will be able to buy and sell goods and services more freely within their own country, which will create more job opportunities for the middle class" (Innovation, Science and Economic Development Canada 2017, para 1). The following year, in his mandate letter to the Minister of Intergovernmental Affairs, Justin Trudeau emphasized the priority of "collaborat[ing] with the provinces and territories to eliminate barriers to trade between each other and to work toward a stronger economy and a more integrated Canadian economy" (Trudeau 2018, para. 13).

### 5.3.2    Public Finance: Boosting the Economy with Broken Promises

Table 5-1 shows that the Trudeau government broke its main public finance promises to achieve a balanced budget in 2019, a modest deficit in the first two fiscal years alone, a debt-to-GDP ratio of 27% in 2019, and a declining debt-to-GDP ratio each year. The scrapping of these promises was a deliberate choice because, as we saw earlier, it was not directly forced upon the Liberal government by a struggling economy. In fact, the Trudeau government's budget deficits sit side by side with an economy running at full speed and a labour market posting record health, albeit with inevitable differences between the provinces and territories. Public account data show that Canada has had continual budget deficits since the Great Recession. The decision not to return to a balanced budget, even if it has been criticized by few economists, is still surprising because it is a break with the economic policies advocated by the Liberals since the Chrétien-Martin era and a change from the Harper government's balanced budget (see Chapter 4 by Geneviève Tellier and Cheick Traoré). There even seems to have been a change in philosophy during the Trudeau term given the nature of the budget promises contained in the 2015 platform.

TABLE 5-1 – Economic Promises and Verdicts I:
Public Finance Management

| # | PROMISE | VERDICT |
|---|---------|---------|
| **3.01** | **After the next two fiscal years, the deficit will decline and our investment plan will return Canada to a balanced budget in 2019.** | **Broken** |
| 3.02 | We will run modest short-term deficits of less than $10 billion in each of the next two fiscal years to fund historic investments in infrastructure and our middle class. | Broken |
| 3.03 | In 2019/20, we will reduce the federal debt-to-GDP ratio to 27 percent. | Broken |
| 3.04 | Reduce Canada's federal debt-to-GDP ratio each year. | Broken |

\* Sources: Trudeau Polimetre and Liberal Party of Canada platform
\*\* The most important pledges are in **bold**.

In the fall 2018 economic statement, Finance Minister Bill Morneau put the federal deficit at $19.6 billion for the 2019-2020 fiscal year. He said, "Across the country, a strong and growing middle class is driving economic growth and creating new jobs and new opportunities for people to succeed" (Department of Finance Canada 2018b). Invoking the need for a strong middle class, the Trudeau government continues to stimulate the economy at the top of the economic cycle. Historically, at this stage of the economic cycle, we would have rather favoured a balanced budget (even surplus in the Chrétien-Martin era) and public debt control.

### 5.3.3 Infrastructure at the Heart of Economic Policy

The multiplication of investments in infrastructure is another manifestation of the Trudeau government's resolutely expansionary fiscal policy. According to Infrastructure Canada (2017, para. 1):

> Investing in Canada's infrastructure strengthens communities and helps to grow the middle class, setting the stage for sustained economic growth in the future. Through the Investing in Canada plan, the Government of Canada is making historic, long-term investments in infrastructure.

In this area, the Trudeau government has indeed been a good student (see Table 5-2), having implemented most of its promises and following the guidelines of the International Monetary Fund (among others) to focus on infrastructure investments to support economic growth. In summary, as we wrote (translated from Eklou et al. 2017):

> public investment in infrastructure is an important determinant of economic growth, as it allows, for example, the construction of infrastructure connecting the different economic agents to economic possibilities. However, it is essential that public investment be efficient in order to be able to generate the maximum benefits without increasing the burden of public debt.

Efficient investments require organization, planning, and transparency. With this in mind, the Liberal government created the Canadian Infrastructure Bank in June 2017: "The Bank, as an innovative financing tool, will partner with public and private sector partners to transform the way Canada's infrastructure projects are planned, financed and delivered" (Infrastructure Canada 2017). The creation of the Canadian Infrastructure Bank was in response to a promise that was both an action and an outcome pledge according to the expression used in Chapter 1 by François Pétry and Lisa Birch; however, it could take up to a decade before we can see and begin to assess its real impact (policy outcome) on economic development.

TABLE 5-2 – Economic Promises II and Verdicts: Infrastructure

| # | PROMISE | VERDICT |
|---|---------|---------|
| 3.19 | We will establish the Canadian Infrastructure Bank to provide low-cost financing for new infrastructure projects. | Kept |
| **3.20** | **Over the next decade, we will quadruple federal investment in public transit, investing almost $20 billion more in transit infrastructure.** | **Kept in part** |
| 2.04 | We will make significant new investments in cultural infra-structure as part of our investment in social infrastructure. | Kept |
| 5.32 | We will make the New Building Canada Fund is more focused. By providing significant, separate investments in public transit, social infrastructure, and green infrastructure. | Kept |
| 5.27 | To support renewable energy projects, the new Canada Infrastructure Bank will issue Green Bonds to fund projects like electric vehicle charging stations and networks, transmission lines for renewable energy, building retrofits, and clean power storage. | Kept in part or in the works |

\* Sources: Trudeau Polimetre and Liberal Party of Canada platform
\*\* The most important pledges are in **bold**.

### 5.3.4    Innovation: Priority for Small- and Medium-Sized Enterprises and Green Technologies

Finally, in the area of support for innovation (see Table 5.3), the Trudeau government also fulfilled most of its 2015 campaign pledges. Two priorities clearly emerge from the innovation policies promised in 2015: small- and medium-sized enterprises (SMEs) and green technologies. The innovative manufacturing sector, emblematic of the so-called "Industry 4.0," is also directly targeted. Once again, these pledges are being fulfilled through policy output in the form of budget allocation, internal government policies, or support programs for SMEs. It is too early to analyze in depth the impact of these measures that will be realized well after the end of this four-year term.

TABLE 5-3 – Economic Promises III and Verdicts: Innovation

| # | PROMISE | VERDICT |
|---|---------|---------|
| 3.08 | **We will invest $200 million each year in a new Innovation Agenda to significantly expand support for incubators and accelerators, as well as the emerging national network for business innovation and cluster support.** | Kept in part or in the works |
| *Small- and Medium-Sized Businesses* | | |
| 3.09 | We will invest an additional $100 million each year in the Industrial Research Assistance Program, which has a proven track record of helping small- and medium-sized businesses to innovate and become world leaders. | Kept |
| 3.11 | Reduce the small business tax rate to 9 percent from 11 percent. | Kept |
| 3.15 | We would ensure that employees with up to $100,000 in annual stock option gains will be unaffected by any new cap. | Kept |
| *Green Technologies* | | |
| 5.14 | We will invest $100 million more each year in clean technology producers, so that they can tackle Canada's most pressing environmental challenges, and create more opportunities for Canadian workers. | Kept |
| 5.15 | We will also invest $200 million more each year to support innovation and the use of clean technologies in our natural resource sectors, including the forestry, fisheries, mining, energy, and agricultural sectors. | Kept |
| 5.08 | We will deliver more support to emerging clean tech manufacturing companies, making it easier for them to conduct research and bring new products to market. | Kept |
| 5.09 | We will look for ways for government to be an "early adopter" of emerging green technologies. | Kept |
| 5.12 | We will enhance existing tax measures to generate more clean technology investments. | Kept |
| 3.06 | **As the country's single largest employer, customer, and landlord, we will lead by example and increase government use of clean technologies.** | Kept in part or in the works |
| 5.13 | We will work with the provinces and territories to make Canada the world's most competitive tax jurisdiction for investments in the research, development, and manufacturing of clean technology. | Kept in part or in the works |

\* Sources: Trudeau Polimetre and Liberal Party of Canada platform
\*\* The most important pledges are in **bold**.

## CONCLUSION: WHAT PROGRESS
## FOR THE MIDDLE CLASS SINCE 2015?

In this chapter, we have made a critical assessment of the fulfillment of the economic promises of Justin Trudeau's government. It should be noted that none of the promises that we have identified as the most salient are entirely fulfilled according to the Trudeau Polimetre. While it is easy to observe the Trudeau government's policy actions (outputs) in terms of trade, infrastructure, and innovation, it is much more difficult to determine their impact (outcome) in the short, medium, and long term.

Throughout the mandate, the leitmotif of the government's economic policy has been to support the middle class. After almost four years, it seems legitimate to ask this question: How is the middle class doing? Better, according to the government (Department of Finance Canada, 2018a). However, as we mentioned at the outset, the middle class is a vague economic concept whose definition does not reach a consensus. In attempting to track the economic situation of the middle class during Justin Trudeau's tenure, we quickly encountered a data problem. The current income data that are available at the time of writing are not recent enough to provide a convincing diagnosis of the progress of the middle class since 2015.[2] However, a partial portrait can be established from salary data, which are available as of January 2019 at the time of writing. Table 5.4 shows the growth rate of real earnings over the last five government mandates.[3]

---

2.  For example, disposable income data, when available, will take into account the redistributive effect of the Canadian tax system and better reflect the effect on the middle class of the tax cuts announced in December 2015.
3.  Constant 2002 dollars with a six-month moving average.

TABLE 5-4 – Growth Rates of Real Average Weekly Earnings
by Profession over Different Government Mandates

| CATEGORIES OF PROFESSIONAL SALARIES | GROWTH RATES OF REAL AVERAGE WEEKLY SALARIES (MOVING AVERAGE LAGGED 6 MONTHS) BY PROFESSIONAL REVENUE CATEGORY (% CHANGE) | | | | |
|---|---|---|---|---|---|
| | MARTIN | HARPER I | HARPER II | HARPER III | TRUDEAU |
| | JAN. 2004– FEB. 2006 | 1ST MANDATE, MAR. 2006– OCT. 2008 | 2ND MANDATE, NOV. 2008– MAY 2011 | 3RD MANDATE, JUNE 2011– OCT. 2015 | NOV. 2015– JAN. 2019 |
| Salaries below the Middle Class | 0.1 | 4.4 | 0.4 | 5.2 | 0.2 |
| Middle-Class Salaries | 2.1 | 1.8 | 3.9 | 3.7 | -0.2 |
| Salaries above the Middle Class | 0.5 | 2.2 | 1.2 | 3.0 | 0.7 |
| **Total, All Professions** | **1.9** | **2.8** | **2.1** | **4.6** | **1.1** |

Source: Calculated by the authors from Statistics Canada data (Tables 14-10-0306-01 and 18-10-0004-01)

Note: The real average weekly salary (in constant dollars) by category corresponds to the weighted average by profession.

We have classified occupations into three categories based on both economic and sociological definitions of the middle class (Delorme et al. 2014):

1.  Wages below the middle class: The average weekly earnings of these occupations are less than 75% of the average weekly earnings for the total of all occupations.

2.  Middle class: The average weekly earnings of these occupations are between 75% and 150% of the average weekly earnings for the total of all occupations.

3.  Salary above the middle class: The average weekly earnings of these occupations are greater than 150% of the average weekly earnings for the total of all occupations.[4]

Even though the Canadian economy is growing, the unemployment rate is the lowest in 18 years, and the number of people with jobs is increasing, our calculations show a 0.2% reduction in average real weekly earnings for middle-class occupations since the beginning of the Trudeau

---

4.    Occupations are divided into categories based on average weekly earnings in January 2019. Readers interested in learning more about the method of ranking occupations are invited to contact the authors.

government's mandate. For all occupations, there is a growth of 1.1% due to growth at the bottom of the wage distribution (+ 0.2%) and at the top of it (+0.7).

These results show that the Liberal Party is right in targeting the middle-class, but it has not yet succeeded in curbing the economic forces that place this segment of the population in a difficult position in the current economic context. The Trudeau government has fulfilled entirely or in part most of its economic promises. Clearly, however, the actions (outputs) of a government do not necessarily guarantee that the desired effects (outcomes) will manifest themselves before the end of its four-year term. The ultimate verdict will nonetheless belong to middle-class citizens when they put on their voting shoes!

## References

Bank of Canada. 2019. *Monetary Policy Report. January 2019.* https://www. bankofcanada.ca/wp-content/uploads/2019/01/mpr-2019-01-09.pdf

Conservative Party of Canada. 2015. *Protect our Economy. Our Conservative Plan to Protect the Economy.* https://www.poltext.org/sites/poltext.org/files/plate-formes/conservative-platform-2015.pdf

Delorme, François, Suzie St-Cerny and Luc Godbout. 2014. *La classe moyenne au Québec s'érode-t-elle vraiment? Contour et évolution. Working Paper* 2014/04. Chaire de recherche en fiscalité et en finances publiques, Université de Sherbrooke.

Eklou, Kodjovi M., Étienne Farvaque and Marcelin Joanis. 2017. "Des investisse-ments publics efficients pour une dette publique soutenable." In *Le Québec économique 6*, Marcelin Joanis (ed.). Québec: Presses de l'Université Laval.

Department of Finance Canada. 2018a. *Real Progress for Canada's Middle Class.* Ottawa: Department of Finance. https://www.fin.gc.ca/n18/data/18-077_1-eng.asp

Department of Finance Canada. 2018b. *2018 Fall Economic Statement: Investing in Middle Class.* Ottawa: Department of Finance. https://www.fin.gc.ca/n18/18-107-eng.asp

Department of Finance Canada. 2019. *Minister Morneau Welcomes New Telecom Investment.* Ottawa: Department of Finance. https://www.fin.gc.ca/n19/19-013-eng.asp

Global Affairs Canada. 2018a. Canada signs new trade agreement with the United States and Mexico. *News release.* Ottawa: Global Affairs Canada. https://www. canada.ca/en/global-affairs/news/2018/11/canada-signs-new-trade-agreement-with-united-states-and-mexico.html

Infrastructure Canada. 2017. *Statement of Priorities and Accountabilities—Canada Infrastructure Bank*. Ottawa: Infrastructure Canada. https://www.infrastructure.gc.ca/CIB-BIC/letter-lettre-eng.html

Innovation, Science and Economic Development. 2017. *Historic trade accord strengthens Canada's economic union*. https://www.canada.ca/en/innovation-science-economic-development/news/2017/04/historic_trade_accordstreng-thenscanadaseconomicunion.htm.

Trudeau Polimetre. 2018. https://www.poltext.org/en/trudeau-polimeter

Trudeau, Justin. 2018. *Minister of Intergovernmental and Northern Affairs and Internal Trade Mandate Letter*. August 28, 2018 https://pm.gc.ca/eng/minister-intergovernmental-and-northern-affairs-and-internal-trade-mandate-letter-august-28-2018

# Chapter 6
# Political Communication and the Trudeau Liberal Government

Alex Marland and Vincent Raynauld

This chapter explores to what extent the Liberal government led by Justin Trudeau pursued its campaign commitments to change some of the rules and practices of public sector advertising and communication in Canada. Our examination, which zeroes in on four interrelated commitments, is underpinned by a conviction that political actors engage in permanent campaigning by exploiting government resources and political communication to their own advantage. We identify the circumstances of the Conservative government led by Stephen Harper that prompted the Liberals to make the four policy pledges. Finally, we summarize the progress made by the Trudeau government on each promise and reflect on broader trends toward digital and social media-based communication.

## 6.1 POLITICAL COMMUNICATION BY THE HARPER CONSERVATIVES AND PROMISES BY THE TRUDEAU LIBERALS

Since taking office on November 4, 2015, Prime Minister Justin Trudeau and his government deployed substantial efforts to reshape the structure and tone of the public political discourse in Canada. During the Harper years, the Prime Minister's Office (PMO) tightly controlled flows of political communication from the government to the public, aligning all points of contact under a common—and highly strategic—messaging rubric. The Conservatives' permanent campaign mentality of availing of public resources to establish and reinforce a partisan agenda hardened during a precarious hold on power in successive minority governments. The ensuing Conservative majority government put the party on a firm footing to assert its core messages and to advance the trend of centralized political communications. Often this involved challenging norms and changing rules in order to improve the party's electoral prospects while agitating, and in some cases undermining, its opponents.

Among the many controversies surrounding the Harper Conservatives' communications activities was the partisan tone of government advertising. Thanks to public tendering processes, historical practices of government contracts being dished out to party-friendly advertising agencies are no longer a significant concern. However, the temptation by a governing party to use public funds to persuade citizens about the merits of its policy goals and accomplishments has not been resolved (e.g., Rose 2000). The breadth of the Conservative government's use of advertising as a tool of permanent campaigning was especially evident in its mammoth Economic Action Plan publicity campaign (see Marland 2016, 335–349; Thomas 2013, 74). Government advertisements, photo-op props, and digital information hubs tended to echo party messaging and display hues of blue commonly associated with that party's colours. As a political pressure tactic, the Conservative government sometimes purchased ads to promote policies not yet approved by Parliament. The government spent tens of millions of dollars annually on government advertising that survey research suggested was delivering poor value for money (Globe and Mail 2013). Toward the end of the Conservatives' time in office, a Liberal MP fashioned a private Member's bill to appoint an independent advertising commissioner in the hope this would ensure that government ads are non-partisan (Harris 2015). This bill, which was inspired by an oversight model used by the Ontario provincial government, informed the Liberals' subsequent campaign pledge.

The Conservatives saw a communications advantage in their fundraising prowess. They ran negative advertising campaigns whenever the Liberals anointed a new leader. Their government passed the Fair Elections Act, which, among many things, included a provision that parties may spend an extra $650,000 per day that a campaign extends beyond 37 days. The ensuing 11-week election campaign in 2015, the longest campaign since the 19th century, was a strategic move intended to deplete the opposition parties' resources (Gollom 2015).

The Conservatives were agitated over Stephen Harper's participation in the traditional televised leaders' debates. Ever since Brian Mulroney's infamous "knockout punch" of Prime Minister John Turner in a July 25, 1984, leaders' debate, a consortium of mainstream media settled into a tradition of organizing English- and French-language televised policy debates among party leaders. The tradition is so deeply rooted that the leaders' debate has become a "crucial" campaign event that marks the point at which many electors begin paying attention (Blais and Boyer 1996, 144). Each iteration involved political wrangling about the format of the debate and participation eligibility. In other words, a debate about debates.

In 2015, the Conservatives strategized ways to avoid providing their opponents with a national forum to disparage the Prime Minister, his government, and their accomplishments. For several months before the campaign, there was gamesmanship about which debates the Conservatives would recognize. Effectively, they held a veto because of the legitimacy associated with a prime minister's participation. The main party leaders ended up participating in five debates. The traditional French consortium debate was supplemented by a second French debate organized by French-language broadcast television network TVA. The traditional English consortium debate was replaced with three English debates: a general debate organized by national news magazine *Maclean's*, a debate on the economy presented by national newspaper *The Globe and Mail* and Google Canada, as well as a debate on foreign policy sponsored by Munk Debates and Facebook Canada. With the possible exception of the *Maclean's* event, the English media did not seem to treat the debates as focusing events commanding public attention.

In their campaign platform, the Trudeau Liberals pledged to address and resolve many of the aforementioned political tactics (Table 6.1). While these issues can irritate partisans and Ottawa insiders, they have little bearing on Canadian's everyday lives. What matters is the overall crux of promoting good governance and leveling the playing field for political parties in an era of 24/7 politicking.

TABLE 6-1 – Promises and Verdicts for Political Communication

| # | PROMISE | VERDICT |
|---|---------|---------|
| 7.32 | Significantly reduc [e] the advertising budget of the government of Canada and end the use of government advertising for partisan activities. | Kept |
| 7.33 | **We will appoint an Advertising Commissioner to help the Auditor General oversee government advertising. The Commissioner will review proposed messages to ensure that they are non-partisan and represent a legitimate public service announcement.** | Kept in part |
| 7.41 | We will review the limits on how much political parties can spend during elections, and ensure that spending between elections is subject to limits as well. | Kept in part |
| 7.52 | We will establish an independent commission to organize leaders' debates and bring an end to partisan gamesmanship. | Kept |

\* Sources: Trudeau Polimetre and Liberal Party of Canada platform
\*\* The most important pledges are in **bold**.

## 6.2 PROMISES TO REDUCE PARTISAN GOVERNMENT ADVERTISING

Two entwined Liberal promises proposed to address the perception of partisan government advertising. The first advertising commitment (promise 7.32) is to significantly reduce spending on government advertising and for any such ads to be non-partisan. Since 2004, in the wake of the Liberal sponsorship scandal involving partisan misappropriation of funds intended for government advertising (see Kozolanka 2006), the Canadian government produces annual reports on its advertising and public opinion research activities. Spending data show that the Trudeau government did indeed scale down advertising spending (Table 6-2). In fact, the Liberals are spending less on advertising than any previous government since the Canadian government started publishing annual reports. The 2016–2017 federal budget announced reduced annual spending on professional services, travel, and government advertising to the tune of $221 million of which the advertising reduction comprised approximately $32 million. During this period, the Liberal government tripled the amount spent on public opinion research.

TABLE 6-2 – Government of Canada Spending on Advertising
and Public Opinion Research, Fiscal Years 2003–2018

| PARTY (PRIME MINISTER), FISCAL YEAR | ADVERTISING | PUBLIC OPINION RESEARCH |
|---|---|---|
| Liberal (Chrétien), 2003 | $111 million | $23.7 million |
| Liberal (Martin), 2004 | $69.8 million | $25.4 million |
| Liberal (Martin), 2005* | $49.5 million | $29.1 million |
| Conservative (Harper), 2006* | $41.3 million | $26.8 million |
| Conservative (Harper), 2007 | $86.9 million | $31.4 million |
| Conservative (Harper), 2008 | $84.1 million | $24.8 million |
| Conservative (Harper), 2009* | $79.5 million | $8.1 million |
| Conservative (Harper), 2010 | $136.3 million | $8.3 million |
| Conservative (Harper), 2011 | $83.3 million | $7.9 million |
| Conservative (Harper), 2012* | $78.5 million | $6.5 million |
| Conservative (Harper), 2013 | $69.0 million | $4.3 million |
| Conservative (Harper), 2014 | $75.2 million | $4.9 million |
| Conservative (Harper), 2015 | $68.7 million | $1.9 million |
| Liberal (Trudeau), 2016* | $42.2 million | $3.8 million |
| Liberal (Trudeau), 2017 | $36.1 million | $12.5 million |
| Liberal (Trudeau), 2018 | $39.2 million | $11.3 million |

Source: Government of Canada advertising annual reports and public opinion research annual reports
Note: Rounded figures. Data are for the end of a fiscal year. Total amounts may not be definitive due to different reporting practices.
*Activity was postponed during an election campaign in the preceding fiscal year.

Political communication always requires context. The numbers in Table 6.2 reflect that advertising declines in fiscal years featuring a federal election because government advertising must be paused during the official campaign period. Additionally, there is less advertising in the first year in office for a new government, as it initiates a new round of strategic planning and creative development. A noticeable uptick in government advertising beginning in fiscal year 2009–2010 was justified by the H1N1 health pandemic and the need to instill public confidence in the economy after the global financial crisis. The Trudeau Liberals faced no such crisis warranting supplementary advertising. Moreover, they did not introduce rules preventing additional spending on advertising or media relations, which tend to be common when a government gets long in the tooth.

A mitigating factor is the Trudeau government's interest in media relations. Liberals tend to be more comfortable than Conservatives with communicating information through earned (free) media, such as by holding news conferences and making ministers available to journalists. The Liberal government's departmental communication plans pay considerable attention to ways that messages can be promoted at little to no cost via media relations and social media channels (Marland 2017). While the Trudeau PMO was initially more relaxed about controlling messaging, many centralized coordination activities are entrenched in government, and gradually ministers and government backbenchers resumed their predecessors' pattern of repeating and reinforcing core talking points.

Further changes in communications activities reflect the Liberals' digital-first philosophy and broader societal trends. The government's advertising expenses declined in part because of the cost savings realized by purchasing more affordable targeted messaging via foreign-owned Facebook, Google, Yahoo, Twitter, YouTube, Snapchat, and Bing (Thompson 2016; Wright 2019). The 2016–2017 fiscal year marked the first time that the government of Canada spent more on digital advertising than any other medium, including television. Specifically, digital media accounted for 54.7% of all advertising expenditures, with social media representing 23.3% of the costs (Wright 2018) — a proportion that increased to 43% of digital spending just a year later (Wright 2019). This evolution in advertising spending follows media consumption trends among the Canadian public. Indeed, a growing number of Canadians — especially those aged between 15 to 34 years — are turning to the Internet to follow news and current events (Statistics Canada 2016). Relatedly, the Canadian news industry is suffering from declining advertising revenues, prompting the Liberal government to commit funding to the media sector. The 2019 federal budget created a multimillion dollar news media fund featuring several measures for journalistic organizations that meet specific conditions. Eligible media can register as donees to receive money from donors and issue tax credits, much like charities; they can receive up to $13,750 dollars in tax credits per researcher, reporter, or editor working a minimum of 26 hours per week; and tax credits are available to Canadians who buy eligible digital subscriptions (Pinkerton 2019).

The hypertargeting of audiences delivers value for money at a cost of excluding some Canadians. Several authors (e.g., Howlett, Craft et al. 2010; Kozolanka 2015) have documented how government communication in Canada can be tailored for and delivered to narrow slices of the public likely to be receptive to specific political and policy messages. In other words, different citizens can be intentionally exposed to different government messaging based on their preferences, interests, and goals. This practice can have positive effects. Targeted government appeals have been used on several occasions to address issues plaguing specific communities, such as reducing levels of smoking among youth smokers or increasing voter turnout among segments of the public less likely to go to the polls on Election Day (Howlett, Craft et al. 2010). However, hypertargeted government communication can be utilized by the party in power to support its permanent campaign agenda, manage and build support among the electorate, as well as agitate its political opponents. Furthermore, a digital-first approach excludes people who are not significant consumers of digital media, and advertising is created that may evade public scrutiny. From a broader perspective, it can contribute to the slow and progressive breakdown of the broadly shared understanding of political and policy landscape among the Canadian public.

There is little question that the Trudeau team, including the Prime Minister himself, have embraced social media in ways that their Conservative predecessors were unable or unwilling to do. Trudeau and many of his PMO staff are digital natives who understand the expectations of the online audience and regularly post to their social media sites content that is often personal and informal in nature (e.g., Lalancette and Raynauld, forthcoming; see also McGregor 2018). The Prime Minister's official photographer doubles as a videographer and is a veritable content production machine who constantly uploads fresh updates about his boss and his activities across a variety of digital platforms. More importantly, Trudeau is leveraging social media's distinct properties to present a more humanized and relatable version of himself that is rooted in key elements of his personal brand, including his "youth, athleticism, open-mindedness, interpersonal skills, and support of feminist causes" (Lalancette and Raynauld, forthcoming, 13; see also Marland 2016). Ultimately, this fosters a more meaningful identity-based and intimate connection with some segments of the public. By comparison, Prime Minister Harper was panned for adopting a more traditional and formal approach. His photographer gained exclusive behind-the-scenes access to create a daily digital photo of the prime minister at work and material for the unidirectional *24 Seven* video newsmagazine on the prime minister's website (Lalancette and Tourigny-Koné 2017). Norms of communication and public engagement have evolved so much that it is difficult to imagine how the Harper-led Conservative government would cope in today's fast-paced, personalized, and increasingly informal political communication environment.

The second advertising commitment (promise 7.33) was to create an Advertising Commissioner position to flag partisanship in draft advertisements. The Auditor General would be responsible for oversight in consultation with the Commissioner. A problem with this promise that the Liberals surely realized is that Ontario softened its model when that province's auditor general was too exacting (Taber 2015).

In May 2016, the federal Liberals announced that the government's communications policy was being revised to include a definition of non-partisan communications. The policy now states that government programs not yet approved by Parliament may not be advertised. The policy also stipulates that government advertising may not occur in the 90 days prior to a scheduled federal election. However, the Advertising Commissioner position did not materialize. Instead, the government announced that it would pay $65,000 annually (later increased to $87,500) to the advertising industry's oversight body to review, on an interim basis, all government advertising and it would invite the Auditor General to assess the effectiveness of this interim measure.

Advertising Standards Canada (ASC) maintains a code of conduct that it encourages Canadian advertisers to follow, including governments, government departments, and Crown corporations (Ad Standards 2019). The code has long exempted political and election advertising on the basis of free speech. In lieu of referring draft ads to an Advertising Commissioner, the Liberal government decided to require that all advertising campaigns exceeding $500,000 be reviewed by the ASC for partisanship, and to leave it up to departments to volunteer to do so for smaller amounts. The government sets the parameters of the non-partisan review criteria as follows:

(1) objective, factual, and explanatory;

(2) free from political party slogans, images, identifiers, bias, designation or affiliation;

(3) the primary colour associated with the governing party is not used in a dominant way, unless an item is commonly depicted in that colour; and

(4) advertising is devoid of any name, voice or image of a minister, member of Parliament or senator (Treasury Board of Canada Secretariat 2018).

The multistage review process is as follows. Government department personnel complete a form that collects basic information, including the name of the campaign, its budget, its proposed dates, and a list of types of media requiring review. The form and creative content are submitted to Public Service and Procurement Canada (PSPC). Next, the PSPC provides the materials to the ASC for an initial arms-length assessment. The form provides the ASC with six policy guidelines to consider. The guidelines encompass the above list and the stipulation that "initiatives that require parliamentary approval, or trade agreements that require ratification, are not advertised until such approval has been received" (Treasury Board of Canada Secretariat 2018). The preliminary review is relayed back to the applicable department via the PSPC and informs decisions about how to proceed before a major spend commitment. The final materials are provided to the ASC for a supplementary assessment as partisan or non-partisan before the advertising campaign begins.

Results are posted online. The initial batch of assessed ads submitted by nearly a dozen departments were deemed to meet all criteria in both rounds of review (Treasury Board of Canada Secretariat 2019). Our general impression is that advertising by the Trudeau government is indeed non-partisan as per the stated criteria. However, the criteria do not go far enough to differentiate advertising that seeks to inform and persuade citizens about a policy or to nudge behaviour compared with the neutrality of a public service announcement. A challenge is that a risk-adverse process generates advertising that offers poor value for money because it is not noticeable, memorable, or likely to change behaviours. It is possible that the government's social media communication has more punch. However, this is difficult to assess because of its more clandestine nature and the volume of digital content.

The campaign pledge is therefore fulfilled only in part. The Trudeau government replaced the promised creation of an Advertising Commissioner by an interim measure by mandating an independent, industry body. The adjustment strikes us as sensible because it engages industry professionals and is cost efficient. Further transparency is required about which members of the ASC conduct reviews and surely a political scientist should be included as occurs in Ontario. As well, the Office of the Auditor General has not yet released the outcome of the requested audit of the appropriateness of the ASC review process. The government indicated its intentions to use the audit to inform draft legislation.

The setup was outdated before it was even in place because of emerging concerns about government use of digital communication and social media analytics. There is no scrutiny of how governments use public resources to earn publicity via media relations and social media channels. Standards of good governance and ethics are needed as the government allocates tens of millions of dollars to generate traffic for Facebook and Instagram posts, quizzes, ads, and videos (Wright 2018). Privacy advocates call for rules about how the government mines citizens' information from social media posts and subsequent use. There are also concerns about the ways in which and to what degree social media companies protect personal details (Thompson 2017). As well, there is no scrutiny of the Liberal government's engagement in the deceptive practice of authoring advertisements masking as news editorials (Korski 2018), nor is there oversight of the government's practice of hiring citizens with an online following to produce blogs and videos about government initiatives (Thibedeau 2019). The promises to limit government advertising illustrate that more work is required to depoliticize further government communication as a whole in the digital era.

## 6.3   PROMISES TO LIMIT POLITICAL PARTY SPENDING

A third Liberal campaign promise was to limit the amount that political parties can spend during the interelection and official campaign periods (promise 7.41). The pledge is a delicate one because it straddles the Charter of Rights and Freedoms constitutional protection of "freedom of thought, belief, opinion and expression, including freedom of the press and other media of communication" (section 2b) and the Supreme Court of Canada's decisions upholding reasonable spending limits, which promote equality of that freedom.

An omnibus bill passed in December 2018 introduced new rules for the next federal election campaign. The Elections Modernization Act (Bill C-76) amended the Canada Elections Act and other acts. Among the amendments was setting a limit of $1.4 million on advertising spending by political parties and interest groups during the three months prior to a scheduled federal election. Advertising by those entities during that period must identify them as the sponsor. The official campaign period is now a minimum of 37 days and a maximum of 50 days. The rule introduced by the Conservatives that permitted an additional $650,000 spending per day after 37 days has been repealed.

Other related changes in Bill C-76 include broadening the ability of Elections Canada to engage in public information activities; a requirement that political parties' websites include a policy about the protection of citizens' personal information; and prohibiting advocacy groups from accepting foreign money for partisan campaigns. Digital media companies are now required to maintain a registry of digital advertisements by political parties and groups. Henry Milner discusses the electoral reform aspects of Bill-76 in another chapter of this edited volume.

## 6.4 PROMISES TO END PARTISAN GAMES OVER LEADERS' DEBATES

The fourth related commitment is to establish an independent commission in charge of organizing the leaders' election debates and bringing an end to partisan gamesmanship (promise 7.52). Televised leaders' debates constitute pivotal moments during any election. They can be seen as a one-stop shop for voters seeking a better understanding of key campaign issues. Specifically, they enable voters to compare and contrast party leaders' policy offerings. They also give party leaders an unparalleled opportunity to connect with French- and English-speaking members of the Canadian public and share their views on political and policy matters (Blais and Perrella 2008).

Through this commitment, the Liberals wished to prevent a repeat of the strategic political plays by the Conservatives during the organization of the 2015 leaders' debates. This gaming of the leaders' debates resulted in a different approach, which garnered a smaller audience than debates during the previous campaign (see Bastien 2015), partly due to the fact that there was a lesser televised presence. The Liberals sought to address key issues in order to reposition leaders' debates as a widely accessible, high-visibility, and high-impact moment of the electoral process.

In November 2017, the Standing Committee on Procedure and House Affairs launched consultations on the creation of an independent commissioner with a mandate to organize leaders' debates during future federal election campaigns in Canada. The Committee heard from 33 witnesses, including journalists, academics,[1] civil servants, and representatives of the public and private media industry over the course of nine

---

1. Both authors of this book chapter appeared before the Standing Committee on Procedure and House Affairs to testify on the creation of an independent commissioner in charge of organizing the leaders' debates during federal elections in Canada.

meetings. The Standing Committee also considered written submissions by political parties as well as other interested stakeholders during the period of consultations. It explored different facets of the role and responsibilities of such a commissioner. These areas include the mechanics of the leaders' debate organization, the function of leaders' debates in the electoral and democratic process, and the changing nature of the mass media environment in Canada, especially with the growing traction of social media among the Canadian public (see House of Commons 2018).

Following the submission of a report by the Standing Committee on Procedure and House Affairs in March 2018, the government announced the nomination of former governor general David Johnston as Canada's first independent commissioner on October 30, 2018. Johnston will be in charge of the organization of two leaders' debates during the 2019 federal campaign. The commissioner's mandate includes responsibility for setting up a seven-member advisory board, reaching out to and engaging with Canadians in order to generate public awareness, and presumably, anticipation for the leaders' debates during elections. A post-campaign report will be required. From a broader perspective, the commissioner's role will be to inject reliability, stability, and predictability in the way in which debates are organized, thus addressing issues that plagued the organization of debates (Government of Canada 2019). While this campaign pledge can be viewed as fulfilled, it will be possible to assess the impact of the independent commissioner and advisory group on the organization of leaders' debates in the next federal election.

## CONCLUSION

In addition to the campaign pledges discussed in this chapter, the Liberals mentioned in different sections of their campaign platform document titled "Real Change: A New Plan for a Strong Middle Class" that they needed to deploy more efforts to engage first-time voters as well as younger segments of the public. Through these campaign pledges and other initiatives, such as turning to social media for public political outreach and engagement, it can be argued that the Liberals have been taking steps to alter—and to some degree modernize—some aspects of public sector advertising and communication in Canada. However, partisan and strategic considerations remain, especially in the illusive domain of digital communications. Some of these changes will arguably assist the Liberals' electoral prospects in future elections.

## REFERENCES

Ad Standards. 2019. "The Canadian Code of Advertising Standards." http://www. adstandards.com/en/standards/cancodeofadstandards.aspx

Bastien, Frédérick. 2015. "Leaders' Debates in a Post-Broadcast Democracy." In *Canadian Election Analysis: Communication, Strategy, and Democracy*, Marland, Alex and Thierry Giasson (eds): 68–69. Vancouver: UBC Press.

Blais, André and Andrea M. Perrella. 2008. "Systemic effects of televised candidates' debates." *The International Journal of Press/Politics*, 13 (4): 451–464.

Blais, André and M. Martin Boyer. 1996. "Assessing the impact of televised debates: The case of the 1988 Canadian election," *British Journal of Political Science*, 26 (2): 143–164.

Gollom, Mark. 2015. "Federal election 2015: How a long campaign will benefit the cash-rich Tories," *CBC News*, July 30, 2015. https://www.cbc.ca/news/politics/federal-election-2015-how-a-long-campaign-will-benefit-the-cash-rich-tories-1.3173208

Government of Canada. 2018. "The leaders' debates commission." Ottawa: Governement of Canada. https://www.canada.ca/en/democratic-institutions/news/2018/10/the-leaders-debates-commission.html

Harris, Sophia. 2015. "Taxpayer-supported ad on-message with Conservative themes," *CBC News*, May 18, 2015. https://www.cbc.ca/news/business/taxpayer-supported-ad-on-message-with-conservative-themes-1.3076424.

House of Commons. 2018. "The creation of an independent commissioner responsible for leaders' debates: Report of the Standing Committee on Procedure and House Affairs." Ottawa: House of Commons. https://www.ourcommons.ca/Content/Committee/421/PROC/Reports/RP9703561/procrp55/procrp55-e.pdf

Howlett, Michael, Jonathan Craft, and Lindsay Zibrik. 2010. "Government communication and democratic governance: Electoral and policy-related information campaigns in Canada," *Policy and Society*, 29 (1): 13–22.

Korski, Tom. 2018. "Feds' fake news cost $577K," *Blackrock Reporter* [blog], April 12, 2018. https://www.blacklocks.ca/feds-fake-news-cost-577k/

Kozolanka, Kirsten. 2006. "The sponsorship scandal as communication: The rise of politicized and strategic communications in the federal government," *Canadian Journal of Communication*, 31 (2):343–366.

Kozolanka, Kirsten. 2015. "Communicating strategically in government." In *The Routledge Handbook of Strategic Communication*, D. Holtzhausen and A. Zerfass (eds.): 396–408. New York, Routledge.

Lalancette, Mireille and Vincent Raynauld. Forthcoming. "The power of political image: Justin Trudeau, Instagram, and celebrity politics," *American Behavioral Scientist*. Online first, https://doi.org/10.1177/0002764217744838

Lalancette, Mireille and Sofia Tourigny-Koné. 2017. "24 Seven videostyle: Blurring the lines and building strong leadership." In *Permanent Campaigning in Canada*, A. Marland, T. Giasson and A. Lennox Esselment (eds.): 259–277. Vancouver: UBC Press.

Marland, Alex. 2016. *Brand Command: Canadian Politics and Democracy in the Age of Message Control*. Vancouver: UBC Press.

Marland, Alex. 2017. "Strategic management of media relations: Communications centralization and spin in the Government of Canada," *Canadian Public Policy*, 43 (1): 36–49.

McGregor, Shannon C. 2018. "Personalization, social media, and voting: Effects of candidate self-personalization on vote intention," *New Media & Society*, 20 (3): 1139–1160.

Pinkerton, Charlie. 2019. "Budget 2019: Budget reveals details of government's news media fund," *iPolitics*, March 19, 2019. https://ipolitics.ca/2019/03/19/budget-2019-budget-reveals-details-of-governments-news-media-fund/.

Rose, Jonathan W. 2000. *Making "Pictures in Our Heads": Government Advertising in Canada*. Westport, CT: Praeger.

Statistics Canada. 2016. "Spotlight on Canadians: Results from the general social survey—The use of media to follow news and current affair." https://www150.statcan.gc.ca/n1/pub/89-652-x/89-652-x2016001-eng.htm

Taber, Jane. 2015. "Ontario auditor-general laments planned ad-law changes," *The Globe and Mail*, April 29, 2015. https://www.theglobeandmail.com/news/politics/ontario-auditor-general-laments-planned-ad-law-changes/article24178795/

The Globe and Mail. 2013. "Action-plan ads are ineffective," July 22, 2013. https://www.theglobeandmail.com/opinion/editorials/action-plan-ads-are-ineffective/article13351559/.

Thibedeau, Hannah. 2019. "The influencers: How Ottawa uses popular online hosts to get its messages out," *CBC News*, January 4, 2019. https://www.cbc.ca/news/politics/online-influencers-youtube-trudeau-1.4965417

Thomas, Paul G. 2013. "Communications and prime ministerial power." In *Governing: Essays in Honour of Donald J. Savoie*, J. Bickerton and B.G. Peters (eds.): 53–84. Montreal and Kingston: McGill-Queen's University Press.

Thompson, Elizabeth. 2016. "Trudeau government spending millions on digital ads," *iPolitics*, July 6, 2016. https://ipolitics.ca/2016/07/06/trudeau-government-spending-millions-on-digital-ads/

Thompson, Elizabeth. 2017. "Privacy experts call for rules on government monitoring social media," *CBC News*, January 25, 2017. https://www.cbc.ca/news/politics/privacy-facebook-cra-surveillance-1.3950796

Treasury Board Secretariat. 2018. "Advertising oversight mechanism." https://www.canada.ca/en/treasury-board-secretariat/services/government-communications/advertising-oversight-mechanism.html

Treasury Board of Canada Secretariat. 2019. "Review results and decisions." https://www.canada.ca/en/treasury-board-secretariat/services/government-communications/advertising-oversight-mechanism/review-results-decisions.html

Trudeau Polimetre. 2019. https://www.polimetre.org/fr/canada/42-trudeau-plc.

Wright, Teresa. 2018. "Canadian government spending tens of millions on Facebook ads, boosted posts," *Financial Post*, May 22, 2018. https://business.financialpost.com/technology/canadian-government-spending-tens-of-millions-on-facebook-ads-boosted-posts

Wright, Teresa. 2019. "Social media sites like Facebook take in lion's share of federal ad dollars," *The Star*, February 11, 2019. https://www.thestar.com/politics/federal/2019/02/11/social-media-sites-like-facebook-take-in-lions-share-of-federal-ad-dollars.html

# Chapter 7
## What Electoral Reforms?

HENRY MILNER

S everal promises in the Liberal platform during the 2015 election concerned improving the way we elect members of Parliament. Most of them relate to accessibility to the ballot box and the role of the Chief Electoral Officer and the Commissioner of Canada Elections. But a few, and by far the most visible and controversial, are related to the commitment to making the 2015 federal election the last one to be held under the first-past-the-post electoral system. When unexpectedly declared winner of the elections with a majority government in October of that year, the new prime minister, Justin Trudeau, reiterated this commitment upon taking power.

In all, out of fifteen promises contained in the Open and Fair Elections section of the Liberal platform (Liberal Party of Canada 2015), eight are rated "fulfilled", three are "partially fulfilled", one is "in the works" and four have been broken (see Table 7.1). This chapter examines whether and how the Liberal promises related to accessibility to the ballot box found their way into government legislation. Then, it turns to a more detailed analysis of the process under which electoral system reform proceeded and, in the end, came to an abrupt halt.

TABLE 7-1 – Promises and Verdicts for Open and Fair Elections

| # | PROMISE | VERDICT |
|---|---------|---------|
| 7.28 | Any incident of electoral fraud must be prosecuted. To that end, we will restore the independence of the Commissioner of Canada Elections, so that they are accountable to Parliament and not the government of the day. | Kept |
| 7.29 | **We are committed to ensuring that 2015 will be the last federal election conducted under the first-past-the-post voting system.** | **Broken** |
| 7.30 | **We will convene an all-party Parliamentary committee to review a wide variety of reforms, such as ranked ballots, proportional representation, mandatory voting, and online voting. This committee will deliver its recommendations to Parliament.** | **Kept** |
| 7.31 | **Within 18 months of forming government, we will introduce legislation to enact electoral reform.** | **Broken** |
| 7.32 | Significantly reduce the advertising budget of the government of Canada and end the use of government advertising for partisan activities. | Kept |
| 7.33 | We will appoint an Advertising Commissioner to help the Auditor General oversee government advertising. The Commissioner will review proposed messages to ensure that they are non-partisan and represent a legitimate public service announcement. | Kept in part |
| 7.34 | We will give Elections Canada the resources it needs to investigate voter fraud and vote suppression, illegal financing, and other threats to free and fair elections. | Kept in part |
| 7.35 | We will increase penalties so that there are real deterrents for deliberately breaking our election laws. | Broken |
| 7.36 | Every young person should be registered to vote when they turn 18. We will work with interested provinces and territories, and Elections Canada, to register young Canadians as a part of their high school or CEGEP curriculum. | Kept in part |
| 7.37 | To encourage more voter participation, we will support Elections Canada in proactively registering Canadians from groups that historically have lower turnout, such as students. | Kept |
| 7.38 | To ensure that no young person loses the opportunity to vote, we will mandate Elections Canada to stay in contact with them if they change addresses after graduation. | Kept |
| 7.39 | We will help encourage more Canadians to vote, by removing restrictions on the ways in which the Chief Electoral Officer and Elections Canada can communicate with voters. | Kept |

| # | PROMISE | VERDICT |
|---|---------|---------|
| 7.40 | We will repeal the anti-democratic elements in Stephen Harper's Fair Elections Act, which make it harder for Canadians to vote and easier for election lawbreakers to evade punishment. We will restore the voter identification card as an acceptable form of identification. | Kept |
| 7.41 | We will review the limits on how much political parties can spend during elections, and ensure that spending between elections is subject to limits as well. | Kept |
| 7.52 | We will establish an independent commission to organize leaders' debates and bring an end to partisan gamesmanship. | Kept |

\* Sources: Trudeau Polimetre and Liberal Party of Canada platform
\*\* The most important pledges are in **bold**.

## 7.1 IMPROVING ACCESSIBILITY TO THE BALLOT BOX: THE ROLES OF THE CHIEF ELECTORAL OFFICER AND THE COMMISSIONER OF CANADA ELECTIONS

On April 30, 2018, Karina Gould, Minister of Democratic Institutions, responsible for democratic reforms, introduced the Elections Modernization Act (Bill C-76). It replaced an earlier version, C-33, introduced by her predecessor, Maryam Monsef, in November 2016, but not taken further. It followed the completion of online consultations and cross-country round tables with Canadians on C-76 in February 2018. Among other changes, the legislation proposed improvements to the integrity of the electoral system by repealing provisions in the Fair Elections Act enacted by the Harper government that made it harder for Canadians to vote.

The legislation included the measures that were previously contained in Bill C-33, notably the changes that reinstate the voter information card as authorized identification (ID), restore vouching for those without proper ID, and expand voting rights to more than one million Canadians living abroad. In particular, it removed two limitations on voting by non-resident voters: (1) the requirement that they have been residing outside Canada for less than five consecutive years; and (2) the requirement that they intend to return to Canada to resume residence in the future.

Bill C-76 also expands the Chief Electoral Officer's ability to educate Canadians to improve civic literacy and knowledge. These provisions include helping future young voters participate in the electoral process by pre-registering youth aged 14–17 so they can more easily vote when they turn 18 and removing limitations on public education and information activities that can be conducted by the Chief Electoral Officer under the Fair Elections Act (S.C. 2014, c. 12). Additional provisions make it easier for new Canadians to vote for the first time.

The bill amends the Act in order to establish spending limits for third parties and for the political parties during a defined period before the beginning of the official election period of a general election held on a day fixed under that Act. It also establishes measures to increase transparency regarding the participation of third parties in the electoral process. Finally, Bill C-76 enhances the independence of the Commissioner of Canada Elections (CCE) by repealing the obligation for the CCE to report to the Minister of Justice introduced earlier by the Harper government and by granting the CCE new powers to investigate and lay charges in the case of alleged violations of election laws. Essentially, Bill C-76 fulfilled many Liberal commitments (see promises 7.28 and 7.36 to 7.41 in Table 7-1).

On October 22, 2018, the Standing Committee on Procedure and House Affairs reported on Bill C-76 with amendments. These amendments were proposed by the Chief Electoral Officer and by a number of other organizations, including representatives of disabled persons and Democracy Watch (2018), which had submitted a petition to "stop secret, fake online election ads and invasions of privacy by political parties" with over 17 000 signatures.

Bill C-76 passed the Senate on December 10, 2018, and received royal assent on December 13, 2018. This paved the way for this new law to apply in the 2019 general election. Given the various measures in this bill and the clarification of offences related to false information and foreign meddling in domestic elections, the Chief Electoral Officer and the Commissioner of Canada Elections have the authority to ensure open and fair elections.

## 7.2 ELECTORAL SYSTEM REFORM AT THE FEDERAL LEVEL: THE POLITICAL ART OF TREADING IN PLACE

This brings us to the three promises about electoral system reform. They have been highlighted in bold characters in Table 7-1 to underline the fact that they are the most salient promises in the electoral reform domain based both on the volume of parliamentary activity and media coverage they generated, on the durableness of the issue, and on potential budgetary implications. Discussion of electoral system reform is not new in Canada, especially at the provincial level, particularly in British Columbia where a proposal to bring in a form of proportional representation was rejected for the third time in December 2018, and in Quebec where the recently elected government is committed to electoral reform within a year. While there has been much activity at the provincial level regarding electoral system reform, there have been discussions at various moments at the federal level, none of which reached the point that real reform was on the table — until this past decade.

In 1979, the Pépin-Robarts Commission recommended moving toward a mixed electoral system. In 2001, the Law Commission of Canada initiated a study of Canada's electoral system, and by 2004, after public consultation, recommended a mixed member proportional electoral system (MMP) in a 209-page report titled "Voting Counts: Electoral Reform for Canada." It was, however, only seven years later that a real discussion of electoral reform took place for the House of Commons following a motion by the NDP on March 3, 2011. The motion proposed that a Special Committee be set up to engage with Canadians and make recommendations on how best to achieve a House of Commons that more accurately reflects the votes of Canadians by combining direct election by electoral district and proportional representation to the distribution of popular votes by political party. The Special Committee was to report its recommendations in no more than one year.

As the 2015 election approached, the Green Party took up the idea through a resolution in August 2014 that called for the immediate appointment of an all-party commission with expert assistance. It was to review previous studies, consult the public, devise a system of elected proportional representation in the House of Commons within the constraints imposed by Canada's geography and federal system, and report its recommendations to the House, including draft legislation, within 12 months. By February 2014, the Liberal Party had adopted its own priority resolution 31

> … that immediately after the next election, the Liberal Party of Canada institute an all-Party process, involving expert assistance and citizen participation, to report to Parliament within 12 months with analysis and recommendations for an electoral system including, without limitation, a preferential ballot and/or a form of proportional representation, to represent all Canadians more fairly and to allow Parliament to serve Canada better (Liberal Party of Canada, 2014).

It was learned subsequently that the new leader, Justin Trudeau, favoured a preferential ballot, but the caucus was divided.

The election was called in August. On October 19, 2015, the Liberal Party, which had been third in the polls when the writs were issued, unexpectedly won a majority in Parliament. Having committed itself to electoral reform when in opposition, its leader and incoming prime minister, Justin Trudeau, when pressed, confirmed his intentions to live up to the specific promises about electoral reform found in the Liberal platform. The Liberal platform contains three specific promises about electoral reform: (1) ensuring that 2015 will be the last federal election conducted under the first-past-the-post voting system; (2) convening an all-party Parliamentary committee, which would deliver its recommendations to Parliament; and (3) introducing legislation to enact electoral reform (see promises 7.29, 7.30, and 7.31 in Table 7.1).

It took many months for the all-party Special Committee on Electoral Reform (ERRE) to be established. The Trudeau government initially insisted that its composition reflect the proportion of seats each party held in the House of Commons, giving the Liberals a majority and thus a veto. However, it finally accepted to make the committee's partisan composition proportional to the popular vote, reluctantly establishing the precedent of proportionality. In June 2016, the House of Commons passed a motion creating this special committee, which included all five parties represented in the House of Commons, with a clear mandate to study alternatives to the first-past-the post voting system and other election reforms and assess them relative to the guiding principles, expressed as follows:

(1)  Effectiveness and legitimacy: that the proposed measure would increase public confidence among Canadians that their democratic will, as expressed by their votes, will be fairly translated and that the proposed measure reduces distortion and strengthens the link between voter intention and the election of representatives;

(2)  Engagement: that the proposed measure would encourage voting and participation in the democratic process, foster greater civility and collaboration in politics, enhance social cohesion and offer opportunities for inclusion of underrepresented groups in the political process;

(3)  Accessibility and inclusiveness: that the proposed measure would avoid undue complexity in the voting process, while respecting the other principles, and that it would support access by all eligible voters regardless of physical or social condition;

(4) Integrity: that the proposed measure can be implemented while safeguarding public trust in the election process, by ensuring reliable and verifiable results obtained through an effective and objective process that is secure and preserves vote secrecy for individual Canadians;

(5) Local representation: that the proposed measure would ensure accountability and recognize the value that Canadians attach to the community, to Members of Parliament understanding local conditions and advancing local needs at the national level, and to having access to Members of Parliament to facilitate resolution of their concerns and participation in the democratic process (Parliament of Canada, House of Commons 2018a).

Ultimately, the government did not act on this engagement. On the Liberal government's Mandate Letter Tracker website, which sets out its commitments and how well it has lived up to them, we find the following rather terse statement:

In addition to the consultation undertaken by the ERRE, the Minister consulted Members of Parliament of all parties, and oversaw an engagement process with 360,000 Canadians through mydemocracy.ca. Following extensive consultation with Canadians, it was determined that no clear preference for a new electoral system had emerged. The Government will not proceed with electoral reform (Government of Canada 2018).

The ERRE engaged in vast, inclusive, and engaged consultations through formal hearings, e-consultations, open-mic sessions, written input, and MP town hall reports. It produced three reports, all of which are available online (Parliament of Canada 2018b). According to an analysis made public in November 2016 by Fair Vote Canada, a pro-change lobby, the four months of expert and public consultations by the ERRE and the hundreds of public town halls organized by members of Parliament that took place on the issue produced an unmistakably clear consensus. Altogether, 89% of the 122 witnesses who came before the Committee with a position on specific voting systems recommended proportional representation (Special Committee on Electoral Reform 2018). Graves (2016) reported the results of an online EKOS poll found that 59% of Canadian respondents wanted the government to follow through on its electoral reform pledge, with only 21% opposed.

Fair Vote Canada was responding to the Prime Minister's statement in a newspaper interview to mark the one-year anniversary of his Liberal Party's election victory. Prime Minister Trudeau told *Le Devoir*, "If we are going to change the electoral system, people must be open to it," and indicated that he planned to look at how consultations have unfolded, then gauge the public's reactions (Vastel 2016). He added that substantial support would be required to significantly change the electoral system, giving a partisan spin to the issue by claiming that there was less need for electoral change now that the Conservatives were no longer in power, since the people had a government with which they are satisfied.

Prime Minister Trudeau was taken to task on this assertion (Coyne 2016). His remarks were followed up at a roundtable held on October 27, 2016, in Victoria, British Columbia, by the responsible Minister Maryam Monsef. She stated that she "won't be advocating for PR" as she had "not heard that sentiment" in her tour of the country. However, Fair Vote Canada (2016) showed data from the ERRE's consultations supporting the opposite. Moreover, Prime Minister Trudeau's preference for a ranked ballot pretty much disappeared from the Committee's consultations, despite efforts by the Liberal members of the Committee to broaden the discussion beyond proportional representation. Hence, the issue came down to maintaining the status quo or changing the electoral system, something it was becoming increasingly evident the government was unprepared to do.

Around this time, the media revealed that the government was planning to send postcards to every Canadian household (approximately 13 000 000) asking residents to respond to an Internet survey on the issue. In response to questioning in Parliament, Minister Monsef said the government was simply looking for new and innovative ways to consult as many Canadians as possible about "the values that matter most to them" in their voting system (Bryden 2016).

During this period, the New Democratic Party dropped its opposition to holding a national referendum on electoral reform. This move was aimed at finding a basis for a compromise recommendation that could win support from the Conservatives who, though not favouring proportional representation per se, had indicated they were open, in light of the many pro-proportional representation briefs presented to the Committee, to a referendum on the issue.

On December 1, 2016, as promised, the ERRE made public its 338-page majority report. The report stressed that its recommendations emerged from a comprehensive gauging of the views of both experts and interested citizens. Its first recommendation was that "the Government should, as it develops a new electoral system, use the Gallagher Index[1] in order to minimize the level of distortion between the popular will of the electorate and the resultant seat allocations in Parliament." The ERRE specified that the objective should be a .5 or less Gallagher score. The lower the Gallagher score, the more closely the distribution of seats reflects the distribution of popular vote.

A reformed election system that would generate Gallagher scores of .5 or less would make Canada's system among the most proportional in the world—even more proportional than Denmark's multiparty system (average Gallagher score of .72 over the last three elections computed by Gallagher 2019). It would also make it more difficult for a leading party to win a majority government without strong popular support. For example, the outcomes of the current election system yielded Gallagher Index scores of 12.02 in 2015 (Liberal majority with 55.44% of the seats based on 39.7% of the popular vote) and 12.42 in 2011 (Conservative majority with 54% of the seats based on 39.62% of the popular vote). Electoral reform proposals seek to redress this bias of the current election system.

The ERRE excluded all pure party-list systems to guarantee that some linkage would remain between citizens and their representatives. It recommended that once the government had designed the new election system, it should submit it to the people of Canada in a referendum in which the status quo would be one of the options.[2]

During Question Period in Parliament that afternoon, in answering questions from the New Democrat members, the Minister downplayed the report, stressing that the government was about to consult Canadians the following week. The Conservatives' only question was in hypothetical form: Will the government respect the report's insistence that a referendum on the issue be held before it made changes to the electoral system? In response, the Minister criticized the ERRE for failing to come up with a single system on which to consult Canadians, thus depriving Canadians of

---

1.  For more about this index, see Gallagher (1991). The index (based on the method of least squares) measures the difference between the percentage of votes each party gets and the percentage of seats each party gets in the resulting legislature. It involves taking the square root of half the sum of the squares of the difference between percent of vote and percent of seats for each party. The greater the differences between the percentage of the vote and the percentage of seats summed over all parties, the greater the index value and the more disproportional the election results.

2.  All attempts to implement a proportional representation system by referendum in Canadian provinces have failed (PEI, 2005, 2016, 2019; Ontario, 2007; British Columbia, 2005, 2009, 2018).

a concrete proposal on which to vote. She argued that the Gallagher rule was incomprehensible to voters. Instead, she in effect endorsed the minority report from the five Liberal ERRE members, which dissented from the referendum proposal and from the objective of changing the electoral system in time for the fall 2019 election. She suggested that the next step was to go back to Canadians and have a conversation not about the recommendations of the Committee, but about values.

The conversation about values was to begin the following week when postcards arrived inviting Canadians to go to MyDemocracy.ca and fill out an interactive, online survey between December 5, 2016 and January 15, 2017. Social and data scientists from Vox Pop Labs, the group behind the Vote Compass, designed the consultation tool to provide Canadians with real-time analysis of their views relative to those of other Canadians. The goal of this consultation tool was "to engage as many Canadians as possible in a conversation about how representative democracy ought to be practiced in Canada" (Vox Pop Labs 2017). The questions reflected trade-offs in democratic values associated with electoral reform.

In late January 2017, the MyDemocracy.ca survey report became public (Vox Pop Labs Inc. 2017). Table 7-2 presents the questions most relevant to outcomes of different electoral systems along with the percentage of the 243 057 unique user respondents out of 383 074 who agreed, disagreed, or remained neutral for whom there was sufficient sociodemo-graphic information for analysis. The results show that Canadians value some changes to governance and accountability in the current election system. When asked to choose between specific options, 70% of respondents preferred cooperation among several parties to govern with shared accountability to single-party government and accountability.

TABLE 7-2 – MyDemocracy.ca Survey Responses Linked to Electoral Reform

| POSITION RELATIVE TO THE CURRENT ELECTORAL SYSTEM | STATEMENTS RELATED TO ELECTORAL REFORM | SOMEWHAT AND STRONGLY AGREE | NEUTRAL | SOMEWHAT AND STRONGLY DISAGREE |
|---|---|---|---|---|
| Change | It is better for several parties to have to govern together than for one party to make all the decisions in government, even if it takes longer for government to get things done. | 62% | 9% | 29% |
| Change | Governments should have to negotiate their policy decisions with other parties in Parliament, even if it is less clear who is accountable for the resulting policy. | 62% | 15% | 24% |
| Change | A party that wins the most seats in an election should still have to compromise with other parties, even if it means reconsidering some of its policies. | 68% | 10% | 22% |
| Change | There should be greater diversity of views in Parliament. | 65% | 22% | 13% |
| Status quo | It should always be clear which party is accountable for decisions made by government, even if this means that decisions are only made by one party. | 53% | 16% | 31% |
| Status quo | A ballot should be easy to understand, even if it means voters have fewer options to express their preferences. | 49% | 16% | 35% |
| Change | There should be parties in Parliament that represent the views of all Canadians, even if some are radical or extreme. | 41% | 14% | 45% |

Source: Compiled and adapted from Vox Pop Labs, 2017

The Canadian experience confirms what Pilet and Bol (2011) found in their comparative research: parties used to exercising power over a long period of time are reluctant to change electoral systems. This certainly applies to the Liberal Party of Canada, which though it had been relatively weak in the years before 2016, dominated Canadian politics for much of its history, and continues to see itself as Canada's natural governing party.

The Liberals' commitment to this being "the last federal election conducted under the first-past-the-post voting system" (Liberal Party of Canada, 2015, p. 27) reflected the expectation of a minority government, under which it would be dependent on the support of the New Democratic Party that had long advocated proportional representation. When they found themselves with an unexpected majority, the Liberals' initial reaction was to delay. They undoubtedly faced internal dissension, especially from many newly elected caucus members who had not been present in the debate when the Liberals were weak. However, the fact that they had four years to carry out their promise meant that delay would not suffice. Hence, consultations ultimately led to reneging on their promise, using the absence of the needed consensus on an alternative system as a justification.

## CONCLUSION

One clear lesson emerging from the Canadian experience is that even with the most advantageous proposal, the odds are stacked against change. Politicians in or near power have a stake in the status quo. When the rare strong movements for change emerge, such as under the circumstances described here, they are likely to seek to delay decisions about pre-electoral commitments through consultative commissions and referenda. They know that, as time passes, public pressure to live up to their commitments is likely to recede.

There is a parallel situation in Quebec at the time of this writing late in 2018. Upon election with a solid, unexpected majority, Premier François Legault reiterated the Coalition Avenir Québec Party's commitment to reform the electoral system. There will undoubtedly be grumbling in the caucus as the implications of the commitment on their electoral base becomes clear. However, Premier Legault has less wiggle room than Prime Minister Trudeau since the commitment is not simply to change the system, but to install a specific proportional one, namely Mixed Member Proportional. He also does not want to be accused of following Mr. Trudeau's example. Those of us who have been observing this process for years will be following events very closely.

## REFERENCES

Bryden, Joan. 2016. "Liberals accused of trying to skew results of electoral reform consults," *The Globe and Mail*, November 17, 2016. https://www.theglobeandmail.com/news/politics/liberals-accused-of-trying-to-skew-results-of-electoral-reform-consultations/article32906375/.

Coyne, Andrew. 2016. "Andrew Coyne: Is Trudeau trying to pull a fast one," *The National Post*, October 16 2016. http://news.nationalpost.com/full-comment/andrew-coyne-is-trudeau-trying-to-pull-a-fast-one-on-electoral-reform.

Democracy Watch. 2018. "More than 17,000 call on House Committee to strengthen Bill C-76 to stop secret, fake online election ads and invasions of privacy by political parties," October 22, 2018. https://democracywatch.ca/more-than-17000-call-on-house-committee-to-strengthen-bill-c-76-to-stop-secret-fake-online-election-ads-and-invasions-of-privacy-by-political-parties/.

Fair Vote Canada. 2016. "Consultations Provide Strong Mandate for Proportional Representation," *Fair Vote Canada*, Press Release, November 3, 2016. https://www.fairvote.ca/2016/11/03/strong-mandate/.

Gallagher, Michael, 2019. Electoral Systems Web site. Trinity College, Dublin. https://www.tcd.ie/Political_Science/people/michael_gallagher/ElSystems/.

Gallagher, Michael. 1991. "Proportionality, Disproportionality and Electoral Systems," *Electoral Studies*, 10 (1): 33–51.

Government of Canada. 2018. *Mandate Letter Tracker: Delivering results for Canadians. Fair and open government.* https://www.canada.ca/en/privy-council/campaigns/mandate-tracker-results-canadians.html.

Graves, Frank. 2016. "The Public Outlook on Electoral Reform: What Do Canadians Want?," *Canadian Politics and Public Policy*, 4 (6): 10–14. http://policymagazine.ca/pdf/22/PolicyMagazineNovemberDecember-2016-Graves.pdf.

Law Reform Commission of Canada. 2004. *Voting Counts: Electoral Reform for Canada.* Ottawa, ON: Public Works and Governmeny Services. http://publications.gc.ca/collections/Collection/J31-61-2004E.pdf.

Liberal Party of Canada. 2014. "31. Priority Resolution: Restoring Trust in Canada's Democracy." In Policy *Resolutions*, 2014. https://www.liberal.ca/policy-resolutions/31-priority-resolution-restoring-trust-canadas-democracy.

Liberal Party of Canada. 2015. Real Change: *A New Plan for a Strong Middle Class.* https://www.liberal.ca/wp-content/uploads/2015/10/New-plan-for-a-strong-middle-class.pdf.

Parliament of Canada, House of Commons. 2018a. *Committees: ERRE. Mandate.* http://www.ourcommons.ca/Committees/en/ERRE/About.

Parliament of Canada, House of Commons. 2018b. *Committees: ERRE. Reports.* http://www.ourcommons.ca/Committees/en/ERRE/Work?show=reports&parl=42&session=1.

Pilet, Jean-Benoît and Damien Bol. 2011. "Party Preferences and Electoral Reform: How Time in Government Affects the Likelihood of Supporting Electoral Change," *West European Politics*, 34 (3): 568–586.

Special Committee on Electoral Reform. 2018. *Synthesis of Witnesses' Statements and Views*. https://bit.ly/2RxQfMl.

Vastel, Marie. 2016. "Trudeau ne garantit plus une réforme électorale majeure," *Le Devoir*, October 19, 2016. https://www.ledevoir.com/politique/canada/482514/la-reforme-electorale-n-est-plus-garantie.

Vox Pop Labs Inc. 2017. "MyDemocracy.ca. Online digital consultation and engagement platform." https://www.canada.ca/content/dam/pco-bcp/documents/pdfs/mydem/MyDemocracy.ca.PDF.

# Chapter 8
# Selection, Humanitarianism, and Performance: Trudeau's Immigration Promises

Mireille Paquet

Traditionally, in Canada and elsewhere, immigration has not featured heavily in national elections and even less in party manifestos. This has started to change with the global politicization of immigration and refugee issues. Immigration is now more often a central theme of electoral contests. Political parties become more polarized toward the issue and they increasingly include specific immigration pledges in their manifestos (Grande et al. 2018; Green-Pedersen and Otjes 2017). While immigration is less of a polarizing electoral issue in Canada than in the United States and in some European countries, recent Canadian elections have nonetheless offered hints of a growing salience of immigration in electoral politics.

During the 2015 campaign, this emerging trend was visible in the actions of the two leading federal parties. Stephen Harper and the Conservatives campaigned on their achievements, following three consecutive mandates in which they implemented a considerable set of robust immigration reforms (Paquet and Larios 2018). They continued to link immigration with a law-and-order agenda. They also introduced the idea of a government phone line to denounce "barbaric cultural practices" (Powers 2015) and remained unclear for most of the campaign on how Canada would respond to the growing humanitarian crisis surrounding the resettlement of refugees.

Justin Trudeau and the Liberals, for their part, worked to activate the traditional values of the party when it came to liberalism, internationalism, and humanitarianism (Bauder 2008; Andersen 2012), pledging to review several Conservative reforms and to welcome more than 25 000 Syrian refugees. While it is impossible to ascertain whether the Liberals won because of immigration pledges, the 2015 election set the stage for a growing polarization of federal parties on this issue in elections to come.

The 2015 Liberal Party platform included 17 promises on immigration-related issues. Out of these 17 pledges, 12 have been fulfilled, 3 are partially kept, and 2 are not yet rated at the moment of writing this chapter. So far, Trudeau's government has fulfilled 71% of its immigration-related promises. This chapter contextualizes those pledges, while offering an explanation of the relative pattern of fulfillment of the Trudeau government during its 2015–2019 mandate. Generally speaking, Trudeau's performance is the function of the institutional configuration of immigration policy-making in Canada. In cases where the pledge could be achieved through the specific channels of Canada's immigration program or through federal policy action alone, Trudeau's performance at pledge fulfillment is literally perfect. On the other hand, when promises had to be fulfilled through horizontal policymaking across different federal programs and depart-ments or had to do with provinces and territories, arms-length agencies, or other stakeholders, pledge fulfillment lagged. Trudeau's pattern of meeting a large part of its immigration promises, then, shows the strength of executive immigration policymaking in Canada.

## 8.1 TRUDEAU'S IMMIGRATION PLEDGES

The immigration-related promises included in the 2015 Liberal manifesto fall into three main subcategories. First, there are pledges having to do with immigration selection processes and procedures. These promises have to do with visas, with how immigration applications are processed, with the establishment of new immigration categories and streams, as well as with specific rules of the immigration system in Canada. The second category is comprised of pledges having to do with refugee resettlement and global humanitarianism that address the target and design of the national refugee program as well as with Canada's engagement to global immigration governance. They also include funding for international immigration-related initiatives having to do with displacement or humani-tarianism. The third category of immigration pledges addresses themes associated with system performance and integrity. This category includes reforms having to do with transparency, administrative efficiency, and the establishment of coordination mechanisms across programs or units.

Note that these three categories do not represent the complete universe of potential immigration pledges. Indeed, the 2015 Liberal platform is completely silent on two important components of Canada's immigration program: annual immigration intakes and the management of the national integration program for non-refugee immigrants, the federal settlement program, and its various components. Considering, the fact that the Trudeau government did implement several reforms in immigration, including a return to a multiyear planning of immigration levels (Immigration, Refugees and Citizenship Canada 2017), these absences show that in 2015, Canadian federal parties remain somewhat shy on engaging on immigration in the electoral arena. This is also confirmed by the growing importance of mandate letters during Trudeau's tenure. These documents and the online tracker created by the government point to several achievements of the government that were not foregrounded in the 2015 platform.

Table 8-1 summarizes the 2015 pledges for each category, with an indication as to whether they have been fulfilled, according to the Trudeau Polimetre data. The five most important pledges are highlighted in bold based on two criteria. The first criteria was whether they reinforced a central orientation of Canada's contemporary immigration programs, which is to ensure that immigration can contribute to the economy and the labour market. Three pledges are especially important in this area: the reform of the Canadian Experience Class, the restoration of the residency time for students applying to naturalize, and the lift of the assessment fee to hire international caregivers. The second criteria, in the context of a growing displacement crisis, was whether the promises contributed to Canada's response to the needs of refugees and asylum seekers living abroad and in Canada. In relation to this criterion, the promise to welcome 25 000 Syrian refugees and the pledge to restore the Interim Federal Health Program are the most important.

TABLE 8-1 – Three Categories of Immigration Pledges*

| # | PROMISE | VERDICT |
|---|---------|---------|
| **1. Immigration Selection Processes and Procedures Pledges** | | |
| 1.16 | We will immediately lift the Mexican visa requirement that unfairly restricts travel to Canada. | Kept |
| **4.09** | **We will also make changes to the Canadian Experience Class, to reduce the barriers to immigration imposed on international students.** | **Kept** |
| **3.19** | **We will make it easier for international students and other temporary residents to become Canadian citizens by restoring the residency time credit.** | **Kept** |
| 8.01 | To help those who are new to Canada, we will change the rules so that spouses immigrating to Canada receive immediate permanent residency—rather than a two-year waiting period. | Kept |
| 10.11 | We will provide more opportunities for applicants who have Canadian siblings by giving additional points under the Express Entry system. | Kept |
| 10.12 | We will restore the maximum age for dependents to 22 from 19, to allow more Canadians to bring their children to Canada. | Kept |
| 12.25 | We will immediately double the number of applications allowed for parents and grandparents, to 10,000 each year. | Kept |
| 12.26 | We will nearly double the budget for processing family class sponsorship. Wait times will come down—which currently average almost four years for parent and grandparent applications. | Kept |
| **6.06** | **Canadian families looking for caregivers to help family members with physical or mental disabilities must pay a $1,000 Labour Market Impact Assessment fee. We will eliminate that fee.** | **Kept** |
| **2. Refugee Resettlement and Global Humanitarianism Pledges** | | |
| 1.30 | We will provide a new contribution of $100 million this fiscal year to the United Nations High Commission for Refugees to support critical relief activities in the region. | Kept |
| **12.25** | **We will expand Canada's intake of refugees from Syria by 25,000 through immediate government sponsorship.** | **Kept** |
| 10.14 | We will invest $250 million, including $100 million this fiscal year, to increase refugee processing, as well as sponsorship and settlement services capacity in Canada. | Kept |
| 10.15 | We will establish an expert human rights panel to determine designated countries of origin, and provide a right to appeal refugee decisions for citizens from these countries. | Kept in part or in the works |

| # | PROMISE | VERDICT |
|---|---------|---------|
| 4.08 | We will appoint individuals with appropriate subject-matter expertise to Canada's Immigration and Refugee Board. | Kept in part or in the works |
| 12.27 | **We will fully restore the Interim Federal Health Program that provides limited and temporary health benefits to refugees and refugee claimants.** | **Kept** |
| **3. System Performance and Integrity Pledges** | | |
| 12.05 | Performance will be independently assessed and publicly reported. We will start with the services hardest hit by years of cuts by Stephen Harper: [ … ] immigration [ … ]. | Not yet rated |
| 12.08 | We will work with the provinces and territories to develop a system of regulated companies to hire caregivers on behalf of families. | Not yet rated |

\* Source: Trudeau Polimetre and Liberal Party of Canada platform
\*\* The most important pledges are in bold.

## 8.2   IMMIGRATION SELECTION PROCESSES AND PROCEDURES PLEDGES

When it comes to immigration selection and procedures, Trudeau's record is one of promises kept. His government implemented several policy changes that aimed at reversing the Harper governments' decisions. These include lifting the visa requirement for Mexican visitors, restoring the time credit given to international students and temporary foreign workers wishing to naturalize, and reinstating a maximum age of 22 years for individuals to be considered dependents of principal applicants (Immigration, Refugees and Citizenship Canada; CBC News 2016.). Not all of the Trudeau government's actions broke with Harper's legacy. Indeed, two kept promises were rendered possible through an adjustment of the Express Entry system, first established by the Conservatives in 2015 (Citizenship and Immigration Canada 2015; Paquet and Larios 2018; National Post 2016). These cover reforms to the Canadian Experience Class to grant extra points to applicants who studied in Canada and to applicants with siblings already living in Canada. Moreover, these promises, and the other ones summarized in Table 8.1, confirm that when it comes to immigration, the Liberal Party through its 2015 manifesto and the subsequent Liberal government did not align with global trends toward restriction when it comes to immigration levels. They instead reflect a continued trend of favouring the mobility of highly skilled and economic migrants (Dauvergne 2003, 2016).

## 8.3 REFUGEE RESETTLEMENT AND GLOBAL HUMANITARIANISM PLEDGES

Considering the resettlement and global humanitarian pledges of Trudeau, a mixed pattern emerges. During the election campaign, Trudeau appealed to the tradition of Canadian internationalism and humanitarianism in response to public outcries at the sight of the iconic image of three-year-old Aylan Kurdi's drowned body on the Turkish seashore, focusing global attention to the Syrian refugee crisis (Slovic et al. 2017). A unique Canadian twist to this focusing event arose when the media interviewed the child's aunt, Tima Kurdi, a new Canadian living in Vancouver. This set the stage for the new Liberal government to fulfill its humanitarian role for Syrian refugees. From that standpoint, when it comes to the international arena, the government did good on its promises to contribute to the United Nations High Commission for Refugees (Blanchfield 2015). The government further worked to reinforce some of the protection it offers to asylum seekers and refugees through the restoration of the interim health protection program (Harris and Zuberi 2015; Enns et al. 2017)[1] and a reinvestment in Canada's refugee settlement capacity (Morneau n.d.). The most visible realization on this matter, however, remains the success of the 2015–2016 Syrian Refugee Initiative, implemented as a response to the pledge to welcome 25 000 Syrian refugees by April 2016 (Immigration, Refugees and Citizenship Canada 2016). The total intake of Syrian refugees was much greater than 25 000 since in addition to government-sponsored refugees, Canadians could also welcome refugees through the Private Sponsorship Program (Immigration, Refugees and Citizenship Canada 2016). As the biggest government-coordinated intake of refugees since the resettlement of about 70 000 Indochinese refugees from 1970–1985 (Molloy et al. 2017), this operation will remain a central achievement of the 2015–2019 Liberal government.

These achievements allowed the government to pose as a proactive actor responding to the global displacement crisis. Yet, it is important to note that Canada's contribution to refugee resettlement was modest when compared to other countries in the global North and the global South

---

1. This program provides access to public medical coverage for individuals who are not eligible to provincial or territorial health insurance programs, such as refugee claimants.

(United Nations High Commissioner for Refugees 2018). In addition, the government has not delivered on its pledges to review and improve Canada's inland refugee determination process through new appointments at the Canadian Immigration and Refugee Board and via the creation of a human rights panel to assist in decision making. These failures can partially be attributed to the arrival of irregular asylum seekers at the Canada-United States border throughout Trudeau's tenure (United Nations High Commissioner for Refugees Canada 2018; Immigration and Refugee Board of Canada 2018). These mediatized arrivals have created important pressures on the national settlement services and on the inland refugee determination procedures (Schertzer and Paquet 2019). Notwithstanding these unexpected events, the unaccomplished promises signal that the Trudeau government has not changed fundamentally the course of the reforms implemented by Harper when it comes to refugee protection (Atak, Hudson, and Nakache 2017). This is in large part due to the institutional complexity associated with such reforms, as well as with the sensitivity of public opinion when it comes to the "deservingness" of refugees as opposed to other immigrant groups (Lawlor and Tolley 2017).

## 8.4   SYSTEM PERFORMANCE AND INTEGRITY PLEDGES

The themes of program integrity and effectiveness had been central to the Conservative's immigration agenda between 2006 and 2015. These concerns supported the fight against a backlog in the processing of applications to the federal skilled workers program, a legislation on immigration consultants, and several reforms aimed at limiting or punishing "bogus" immigration claims (Gaucher 2014; Paquet and Larios 2018). The 2015 Liberal platform also included two immigration pledges having to do with ensuring the integrity and performance of Canada's immigration program. As part of a broader call for transparency, the party promised to ensure independent and public performance assessment of several public services, including the immigration service. While this was achieved for Veterans Affairs, this review is still forthcoming in the immigration sector (Immigration, Refugees and Citizenship Canada 2018). Framed as part of a larger bundle of reforms to allow Canadian families to hire affordable caregivers, the government also pledged to "[…] work with the provinces and territories to develop a system of regulated companies to hire caregivers on behalf of families, [to] make it simpler for families to hire caregivers, and protect caregivers by allowing them to change employers in the case of bad relations or abuse" (Liberal Party of Canada 2015, 63). Had it been implemented, this promise would have represented a major improvement in the current mechanisms through which foreign caregivers and domestic workers enter into Canada and work, by responding to tough criticism formulated by immigration scholars, lawyers, activists, and domestic workers themselves (Hanley et al. 2017; Boyd 2017). In this category, then, Trudeau did not effect a major break with the approach of the previous government.

## 8.5   TRUDEAU'S PATTERN OF IMMIGRATION PLEDGE FULFILLMENT

Overall, Trudeau's record of pledge fulfillment in the immigration sector is strong, with 71% of its promises fulfilled. Once the commitments are disaggregated into subcategories of immigration policies, a clear pattern emerges: between 2015 and 2019, the Liberal government performed especially well in the area of immigrant selection processes and procedures. When it comes to promises about who can enter Canada and how, the Trudeau government fulfilled 100% of its promises. This perfect record does not take into account other policy changes implemented during the 42nd legislature, notably the development and release of a multiyear immigration level plan that will bring Canada's immigration level to a record number by 2021 (Immigration, Refugees and Citizenship Canada 2018).

It might be tempting to see this high level of pledge fulfillment as an indication that Trudeau's government changed the way Canada's immigration program operates. As explored earlier, some of the promises kept indeed had to do with reversing programmatic decisions of the Harper government. Overall, however, Trudeau maintained in place a large portion of immigration reforms established under Harper and even benefited from the flexibility afforded by some of the innovations brought in place by the previous government, notably the Express Entry system (Paquet 2019). These innovations allowed for even greater executive autonomous policy-making in the immigration sector. The central features of Canada's immigration system—preference for economic migrants as opposed to refugees or family reunification, high degree of state selection, focus on the economic contribution of immigration—have remained in place during Trudeau's tenure.

This pattern of pledge fulfillment, more broadly, points to the importance of understanding the institutional context in which federal immigration policymaking unfolds in Canada. For one thing, as with other policy sectors, the parliamentary system and the convention of party discipline reinforces already strong tendencies for power centralization (Savoie 1999). This is amplified by the fact that the main law governing immigration in Canada—the Immigration and Refugee Protection Act (IRPA)—is a framework legislation (Canada 2013). In practice, this means that through "IRPA, Parliament has delegated to the Governor in Council the authority to make immigration-related regulations" (Elgersma 2015). Under Harper, this authority was channeled further through the use of Ministerial Instructions, an IRPA codified mechanism, "[…] that allow the Minister to issue special Instructions to immigration officers to enable the Government of Canada to best attain its immigration goals" (Immigration, Refugees and Citizenship Canada 2019). Because Ministerial Instructions are not statutory instruments, they provide the government of the day with the freedom to effect rapid policy change without "the same requirements concerning consultation and publishing as regulations" (Elgersma 2015). This institutional context provides the executive—the immigration minister, the cabinet and the prime minister—with a sizeable autonomy to develop immigration policies and to effect changes to Canada's immigration program (Kelley and Trebilcock 2010). From that standpoint, as long as the immigration pledges remain within the realm of the topics covered by IRPA, it is possible to expect high levels of fulfillment.

This institutional explanation also helps make sense of the pattern of pledge fulfillment in the category of refugee resettlement and global humanitarianism as well as in the category of system performance and program integrity. On these issues, Trudeau's record is more inconsistent. It features the historical realization of the Syrian Refugee Initiative, but also failure when it comes to reinforcing the inland protection and processing of refugees. One way to interpret this record is to highlight the fact that several of the unfulfilled pledges required collaboration with stakeholders, including provinces, territories and other federal agencies, with employers, or cooperation with arms-length agencies such as the Immigration and Refugee Board of Canada. In those cases, pledge fulfillment is contingent on the capacity and willingness of the government of the day to negotiate and collaborate with others in the immigration sector (Paquet 2015).

## CONCLUSION

Using the PolimetreTrudeau, this chapter shows that the Trudeau government fulfilled 71% of its 17 immigration-related pledges. When it comes to immigration selection and the associated procedures, the Liberal government has a perfect record of acting on its promises. On issues related to refugee resettlement, global humanitarianism, as well as system performance and integrity, the performance of Trudeau's Liberals has been less stellar with several pledges still in the works. Notably, the government has not broken its immigration promises between 2015 and 2019.

In this chapter, this pattern of pledge fulfillment is explored through the institutional context of federal immigration policymaking. It shows high performance in pledge fulfillment in immigration is associated with promises that could be achieved through executive policymaking, federal policy alone, and through the powers delegated by Canada's Immigration and Refugee Protection Act (IRPA). In contrast, less-effective pledge fulfillment has been associated with horizontal policymaking across different federal programs and departments, with federal-provincial-territorial relations, and with the need to collaborate with international organizations, arms-length agencies, and other stakeholders.

The 2015 election, finally, unfolded in the context of a global displacement crisis (Esses et al. 2017). Four years later, the number of refugees worldwide remains high and governments, everywhere, even less willing than before to welcome them. Up until the last election, Canada was one of the rare countries that remained insulated from this reality because of its geography and its capacity to control its borders. Trudeau's time in government has marked the end of this insulation, with the appearance of a large number of irregular border crossings at the Canada-United States border. In the wake of the 2019 election, these arrivals and the management of Canada's immigration program appear to have become even more politicized than before. What remains to be seen, however, is how parties' views and discourses on immigration will be translated into electoral pledges and what it will mean for the future of Canada's immigration politics.

## References

Atak, Idil, Graham Hudson, and Delphine Nakache. 2017. "'Making Canada's Refugee System Faster and Fairer': Reviewing the Stated Goals and Unintended Consequences of the 2012 Reform," *SSRN Electronic Journal*. https://www.ssrn.com/abstract=2977986.

Andersen, Christopher G. 2012. *Canadian Liberalism and the Politics of Border Control, 1867–1967*. Vancouver: UBC Press.

Bauder, Harald. 2008. "Dialectics of Humanitarian Immigration and National Identity in Canadian Public Discourse," *Refuge: Canada's Journal on Refugees*, 2 (1): 84–93.

Blanchfield, Mike. 2015. "Canada Gives United Nations $100 Million for Syrian Refugee Relief," *The Star*, November 26, 2015. https://www.thestar.com/news/canada/2015/11/26/canada-gives-united-nations-

Boyd, Monica. 2017. "Closing the Open Door? Canada's Changing Policy for Migrant Caregivers." In *Gender, Migration, and the Work of Care*, Michel Sonya, and Peng Ito (eds.): 167–189. Cham: Palgrave Macmillan.

Canada. 2013. *Immigration and Refugee Protection Act* (S.C. 2001, c. 27). http://laws-lois.justice.gc.ca/eng/acts/I-2.5/FullText.html.

CBC News. 2016. "Canada Drops Mexican Visa Requirement, Mexico Lifts Beef Ban," June 28, 2016. https://www.cbc.ca/news/politics/trudeau-pena-nieto-bilateral-visas-beef-1.3655746.

Dauvergne, Catherine. 2003. "Evaluating Canada's New Immigration and Refugee Protection Act in Its Global Context," *Alberta Law Review*, 41 (3): 725-44.

Dauvergne, Catherine. 2016. *The New Politics of Immigration and the End of Settler Societies*. New York: Cambridge University Press.

Elgersma, Sandra. 2015. *Immigration Policy Primer*. Ottawa: Library of Parliament.

Enns, Richard, Philomina Okeke-Ihejirika, Anna Kirova, and Claire McMenemy. 2017. "Refugee Healthcare in Canada: Responses to the 2012 Changes to the Interim Federal Health Program," *International Journal of Migration and Border Studies*, 3 (1): 24–42.

Esses, Victoria M., Leah K. Hamilton, and Danielle Gaucher. 2017. "The global refugee crisis: Empirical evidence and policy implications for improving public attitudes and facilitating refugee resettlement," *Social Issues and Policy Review*, 11 (1): 78–123.

Gaucher, Megan. 2014. "Attack of the Marriage Fraudsters!: An Examination of the Harper Government's Antimarriage Fraud Campaign," *International Journal of Canadian Studies* 50 (2014): 187–206.

Government of Canada. 2016. "Regulations Amending the Immigration and Refugee Protection Regulations (Age of Dependent Children)," *Canada Gazette*. http://gazette.gc.ca/rp-pr/p1/2016/2016-10-29/html/reg2-eng.html.

Grande, Edgar, Tobias Schwarzbözl, and Matthias Fatke. 2018. "Politicizing Immigration in Western Europe," *Journal of European Public Policy*. https://doi.org/10.1080/13501763.2018.1531909.

Green-Pedersen, Christoffer, and Simon Otjes. 2017. "A Hot Topic? Immigration on the Agenda in Western Europe," *Party Politics*. https://doi.org/10.1177/1354068817728211

Hanley, Jill, Lindsay Larios, and Jah-Hon Koo. 2017. "Does Canada" Care" about Migrant Caregivers?: Implications under the Reformed Caregiver Program," *Canadian Ethnic Studies*, 49 (2): 121–39.

Harris, Helen P., and Daniyal Zuberi. 2015. "Harming Refugee and Canadian Health: The Negative Consequences of Recent Reforms to Canada's Interim Federal Health Program," *Journal of International Migration and Integration*, 16 (4): 1041–1055.

Immigration and Citizenship. 2015. "Express Entry—Comprehensive Ranking System (CRS) Criteria." Ottawa: Immigration and Citizenship. https://www.canada.ca/en/immigration-refugees-citizenship/services/immigrate-canada/express-entry/eligibility/criteria-comprehensive-ranking-system/grid.html

Immigration and Refugee Board of Canada. 2018. "Irregular Border Crosser Statistics." https://irb-cisr.gc.ca/en/statistics/Pages/Irregular-border-crosser-statistics.aspx#inline_content_rpd.

Immigration, Refugees and Citizenship Canada. 2016. *Rapid Impact Evaluation of the Syrian Refugee Initiative*. Ottawa: Immigration, Refugees and Citizenship Canada.

Immigration, Refugees and Citizenship Canada. 2017. "Notice—Supplementary Information 2018–2020 Immigration Levels Plan." Ottawa: Immigration, Refugees and Citizenship Canada. https://www.canada.ca/en/immigration-refugees-citizenship/news/notices/supplementary-immigration-levels-2018.html

Immigration, Refugees and Citizenship Canada. 2018. *2018 Annual Report to Parliament on Immigration*. Ottawa: Immigration, Refugee and Citizenship Canada.

Immigration Refugees and Citizenship Canada. 2019. "Ministerial Instructions." Ottawa: Immigration Refugees and Citizenship Canada. https://www.canada.ca/en/immigration-refugees-citizenship/corporate/mandate/policies-operational-instructions-agreements/ministerial-instructions.html.

Kelley, Ninette, and Michael Trebilcock. 2010. *The Making of the Mosaic. A History of Canadian Immigration Policy*. Second Edition. Toronto: University of Toronto Press.

Lawlor, Andrea, and Erin Tolley. 2017. "Deciding Who's Legitimate: News Media Framing of Immigrants and Refugees," *International Journal of Communication* 11 (25): 967-991.

Liberal Party of Canada. 2015. *Real Change: A New Plan for a Strong Middle Class*. https://www.liberal.ca/wp-content/uploads/2015/10/New-plan-for-a-strong-middle-class.pdf.

Molloy, Michael, Peter Duschinsky, Peter Jensen, and Robert Shalka. 2017. *Running on Empty Canada and the Indochinese Refugees, 1975–1980*. Mcgill-Queen's University Press. Montreal.

Morneau, William Francis. 2016. *Growing the Middle Class: 2016 Federal Budget*. Ottawa: Department of Finance.

National Post. 2016. "Liberals to Scrap Two-Year Delay before Spouses from Overseas Win Permanent Residency," March 1, 2016. https://nationalpost. com/news/canada/liberals-to-scrap-two-year-delay-before-spouses-from-overseas-win-permanent-residency.

Paquet, Mireille. 2015. *La fédéralisation de l'immigration au Canada*. Montréal: Presses de l'Université de Montréal.

Paquet, Mireille, and Lindsay Larios. 2018. "Venue Shopping and Legitimacy: Making Sense of Harper's Immigration Record," *Canadian Journal of Political Science*, 51 (4): 817-836.

Paquet, Mireille. 2019." Immigration and Borders in Canada: Looking Outward, Looking Inward, and Breaking Away from Legacies." In *Applied Political Theory and Canadian Politics*, David McGrane and Neil Hibbert (eds.): pages. Toronto: University of Toronto Press.

Powers, Lucas. 2015. "Tories Pledge New RCMP Tip Line to Report Forced Marriage and Other 'barbaric Practices'," *CBC*. 2015. https://www.cbc.ca/ news/politics/canada-election-2015-barbaric-cultural-practices-law-1.3254118.

Savoie, Donald J. 1999. *Governing from the centre: The concentration of power in Canadian politics*. Toronto: University of Toronto Press.

Schertzer, Robert, and Mireille Paquet. 2019. "A lot is riding on how we manage asylum seekers," *Policy Options,* February 21, 2019. https://policyoptions.irpp. org/magazines/february-2019/lot-riding-manage-asylum-seekers/.

Slovic, Paul, Daniel Västfjäll, Arvid Erlandsson, and Robin Gregory. 2017. "Iconic photographs and the ebb and flow of empathic response to humanitarian disasters," *PNAS* 114 (4):640–644. https://doi.org/10.1073/pnas.1613977114

United Nations High Commissioner for Refugees. 2018. *Global Trends: Forced Displacement in 2017*. Geneva: United Nations High Commissioner for Refugees.

United Nations High Commissioner for Refugees Canada. 2018. "Irregular Arrivals at the Border in 2017: Background Information." https://www.unhcr. ca/wp-content/uploads/2018/09/Irregular-Arrivals-at-the-Border_JAN-JULY-2018.pdf

Veteran Affairs. 2018. *Delivering on Service Excellence. A Review of Veterans Affairs Canada's Service Delivery Model*. Ottawa: Veterans Affairs Canada.

# Chapter 9
## Social Policies for a Stronger Middle Class: Toward Policy Transformation

DANIEL BÉLAND AND MICHAEL J. PRINCE

A s the first chapter of this edited volume demonstrates, the Trudeau government has made more election promises than any federal government since 1984. This accomplishment is easy to see in the area of social protection, which is the focus of this chapter. In 2015, social protection was at the heart of many Liberal promises. These promises were rooted in a human rights-based approach and a willingness to help the most vulnerable in society. Some of these promises were potentially transformative, hence the importance of examining their eventual fulfillment.

The chapter provides a qualitative portrait of the Liberal promises found in the sections of the Liberal platform of Canada 2015 on Affordable Housing (p. 7), Fighting Poverty (p. 10), Employment Insurance (p. 20), and More Support for Veterans' Families (p. 50). We analyze more specifically 15 of the 55 promises in these areas, 12 of which are rated as "fulfilled," two as "partially fulfilled," and one as "not yet rated or broken" (see Table 9.1). We focus on promises of significant budgetary importance. The chapter consists of three main sections in which we assess the pledge fulfillment performance of the government of Justin Trudeau (2015–2019) across three policy domains: (1) family policies; (2) housing policies; and (3) income maintenance and the fight against poverty.

TABLE 9-1 – The Most Important Promises in Social Policy and Their Verdicts*

| # | PROMISE | VERDICT |
|---|---------|---------|
| **Family Policies** | | |
| 6.04 | We will introduce a new Canada Child Benefit to give Canadian families more money to raise their kids. | Kept |
| 6.05 | Tax-free, tied to income and delivered monthly, this benefit (Canada Child Benefit) provides greater support to those who need help most: single-parent families and low-income families. | Kept |
| 12.10 | With provinces, territories, and Indigenous communities we will work on a new National Early Learning and Child Care Framework, to deliver affordable and high-quality child care in the first 100 days, funded by our investments in social infrastructure. | Kept |
| 12.53 | We will provide greater education, counselling, and training for families who are providing care and support to veterans living with physical and/or mental health issues as a result of their service. | Not yet rated*** |
| **Housing Policies** | | |
| 12.21 | We will give communities the money they need for Housing First initiatives that help homeless Canadians find stable housing. | Kept |
| 12.24 | We will renew federal leadership in housing, starting with a new, ten-year investment in social infrastructure. | Kept |
| 12.23 | We will prioritize investments in affordable housing and seniors' facilities. | Kept in part |
| 12.32 | We will give support to municipalities to maintain rent-geared-to-income subsidies in co-ops. | Kept |
| **Income Support and Anti-poverty Policies**** | | |
| 12.35 | We will restore the eligibility age for Old Age Security and the Guaranteed Income Supplement to 65. | Kept |
| 12.36 | Because many seniors live on fixed incomes, we will introduce a new Seniors Price Index to make sure that Old Age Security and the Guaranteed Income Supplement benefits keep up with seniors' actual rising costs. | Kept in part |
| 12.37 | We will help to lift hundreds of thousands of seniors out of poverty by increasing the Guaranteed Income Supplement for single low-income seniors by ten percent. | Kept |
| 12.38 | We will not end pension income splitting for seniors. | Kept |
| 3.24 | Starting in 2017, we will reduce the waiting period for benefits. When a worker loses their job and applies for Employment Insurance, they will only be without income for one week, not two. | Kept |

| # | PROMISE | VERDICT |
|---|---------|---------|
| 3.28 | We will reverse Stephen Harper's 2012 EI reforms that force unemployed workers to move away from their communities and take lower-paying jobs. | Kept |
| 12.13 | We will ensure that the Employment Insurance system is providing real income security to workers, including those with precarious work. | Not yet rated*** |

\* Source: Trudeau Polimetre and Liberal Party of Canada platform

\** The most important pledges are in **bold**.

\*** For promises not yet rated at the time the authors wrote this chapter, if the Liberal government does not announce any concrete actions regarding this pledge before the elections are called, they will be rated as broken.

\**** The Liberal Party of Canada made a general pledge to work with the provinces to improve Old Age Security. Following CPPG guidelines, the Polimetre team retained the specific pledges that operationalized the improvements to pensions, rather than a vague general committment.

## 9.1   FAMILY POLICIES

In 2015, the Liberal Party of Canada (LPC) election platform contained many promises regarding children and families covering a range of programs, groups, and issues. These promises included improved access to compassionate care and parental leaves under Employment Insurance, increased support for veterans' families, a new program for families of disabled or deceased public safety officers, the new Teacher and Early Childhood Educator School Supply Tax Credit, a new First Nations child and family services program, the cancellation of family income splitting, and the elimination of processing fees for hiring foreign family helpers.

Three big ideas dominated the 2015 Liberal promises on family policy: the creation of a new income security program called the Canada Child Benefit (CCB), the establishment of a new framework agreement with the provinces and the territories on Early Learning and Child Care, and improved services and benefits for veterans and their families. After winning the 2015 election, the Trudeau government's Minister of Finance, Morneau, announced the creation of the CCB in its first budget, calling it "the most important social policy innovation in a generation" (Morneau 2016, 4). With the introduction of the CCB and the abolition of the Universal Child Care Benefit (UCCB) introduced in 2006 by the Harper government (and the cancellation of the related National Child Benefit Supplement), the Trudeau government ended the universality that had characterized the federal system of family benefits since its inception (Mahon with Prince 2019).

The CCB offers much more generous benefits to eligible families than the previous combination of selective and universal programs under the UCCB, with an average annual increase of almost $2,300 per child over the 2016–2017 reference year. In addition, benefits were increased in July 2018 and are expected to increase again in July 2019. While UCCB benefits were taxable, CCB benefits are tax-exempt, subject to an income test and paid monthly. According to the federal government, because of this new program, about 300,000 fewer children were living in poverty in 2017 than in 2013, a reduction of 40%. In July 2018, two years earlier than initially promised, CCB benefits were indexed to inflation to offset the rising cost of living related to raising children.

The promise of a new intergovernmental framework agreement on preschool education and childcare was the other major Liberal commitment in the area of family policies. In June 2017, a Multilateral Framework on Early Learning and Child Care was adopted by all federal, provincial, and territorial ministers responsible for families and social services, with the exception of the Quebec government, which received full compensation as it already had put in place early childhood centres and kindergarten at age four in disadvantaged areas. The Multilateral Framework set out a ten-year vision with clear principles and objectives, as well as substantial federal investments. Federal priorities were to invest in regulated centres, programs, and services for children under age six. Starting in 2018–2019, the Trudeau government has committed $7.5 billion over ten years. Bilateral agreements between the federal, provincial, and territorial governments for an initial three-year period aim to create up to 40,000 new subsidized child care spaces across the country. The federal government is also committed to ensuring that their annual budget allocation to 2027–2028 is not lower than that of 2017–2018.

In summary, in the area of family policies, the introduction of the CCB can be seen as a transformative pledge to thoroughly reform social protection in Canada. The Trudeau Liberals describe the CCB as "a plan to help families more than any other social program since universal health care" introduced in the late 1960s and early 1970s (Morneau 2016, 4). The CCB was quickly implemented, before being enhanced later. Similarly, the Multilateral Framework Agreement on Early Childhood Education and Child Care is also a transformative commitment with a long-term vision that revolves around a set of multilateral and bilateral agreements.

Many other promises regarding child and family benefits, however, are more transactional in nature and target specific clients interested in specialized services. These include support for caregivers who work, and support for families of public safety officers and families of veterans (for veterans, see also promises 12.42 to 12.57 on the Trudeau Polimetre web page).

## 9.2  HOUSING POLICIES

In 2015, the LPC's housing policy promises were linked to other important themes such as the fight against poverty, increased purchasing power, quality of life in communities, and ultimately, economic growth through investment in infrastructure. The Liberal election platform of 2015 promised to invest in affordable housing and financially support local initiatives to subsidize rents. Other specific housing-related commitments were to improve the flexibility of the Registered Retirement Savings Plan (RRSP) Home Ownership Plan, to increase and index the Northern Residents deduction, to increase investment in the network of shelters and halfway houses, to build more safe and affordable housing in Indigenous communities (see Chapter 13 by Thierry Rodon and Martin Papillon), and to eliminate the Goods and Services Tax (GST) on new investments in housing (Liberal Party of Canada 2015). In order not to unduly lengthen this chapter, these commitments are not analyzed here; however, the details of these promises and their fulfillment status can be found on the Trudeau Polimetre website.

Following extensive public consultations, in November 2017 the Trudeau government announced a National Housing Strategy (Canada 2017). The ten-year strategy is linked to the creation of a $5 billion National Housing Fund to address critical housing needs. In April 2018, nine provinces and three territories approved a multilateral partnership framework with the federal government on housing. The goals of the National Housing Strategy are to address the housing challenges of 530,000 Canadian families, reduce the number of chronically homeless people by 30%, create 100,000 new housing units, build 14,000 new housing units, and repair 300,000 existing homes.

As a result of bilateral agreements with provinces and territories, federal investments must target a number of vulnerable populations: women and children fleeing domestic violence, seniors, Indigenous communities, veterans, persons with disabilities, low-income Canadians, and people living with mental health problems and drug use. With respect to homelessness, the Trudeau government launched a Homelessness Partnering Strategy and announced $2.1 billion in spending over eleven years. Defining housing as a human right (Canadian Press 2018), the Trudeau government is committed to "progressively implement the right of every Canadian to access adequate housing." Based on the principles of inclusion, accountability, participation, and non-discrimination, this strategy creates, among other things, a community initiative for tenants that will "provide funding to local organizations which assist people in housing needs so that they are better represented and able to participate in housing policy and housing project decision-making" (Canada 2017, 8).

The establishment of the National Housing Strategy is also associated with the creation of the Canada Housing Benefit (CHB). This is a new cost-shared housing allocation with the provinces and territories aimed at reducing the rising cost of rental housing for low-income households. The CHB should be available from April 2020 to cover part of the annual rent paid by a low-income household. This program targets people "currently living in social housing, those on the waiting list for social housing and those who live on the private market, but who are struggling to make ends meet" (Canada 2017, 16). According to the Trudeau government, the CHB will allocate an average of $2,500 per year to each recipient household and by 2028, it will support at least 300 000 households across the country (Canada, 2017). This reform is transformative and has important implications for households, provincial and territorial governments, Indigenous communities, municipalities, the private sector, and civil society organizations. The National Housing Strategy and the Canada Housing Benefit mark the strong return of the federal government in this area of public action.

## 9.3 INCOME MAINTENANCE AND THE FIGHT AGAINST POVERTY

In the area of income maintenance, three main issues need to be discussed: old age pensions and, to a lesser extent, employment insurance and the fight against poverty. Regarding old age pensions, the Liberals made several particularly important promises. The first promise in this area was the cancellation of a controversial measure passed under the Harper government: the increase in the age of eligibility for benefits of the Old Age Security (OAS) and Guaranteed Income Supplement (GIS). Because these two programs are funded from the federal budget, population aging is expected to result in a significant increase in federal spending in this area. It is this demographic and fiscal situation that justified the Conservatives' decision to gradually increase the eligibility age for these two programs from 65 to 67 between 2023 and 2029. Announced in 2012, this measure was decried immediately by the Liberal Party and the New Democratic Party (NDP).

In this context, the promise to restore OAS and GIS eligibility to age 65 was not a big surprise. Given that the measure adopted in 2012 was not to be implemented until 2023, reversing it did not pose any particular technical problem even if, in the long run, it would significantly increase federal spending on old age pensions. Prime Minister Trudeau announced his decision in March 2016. A few days later, the first Liberal budget officially canceled the planned increase in the eligibility age for OAS and GIS benefits (Harris 2016). This is a fulfilled promise as stated by the Trudeau Polimetre. The same applies to another Liberal promise, the 10% increase in GIS benefits for seniors living alone, which became a reality in July 2015.

In the area of old age pensions, the Liberals committed to working with the provinces and territories, workers, employers, and pension organizations to enhance the Canada Pension Plan (CPP). In particular, the Liberal platform promised to implement a new Consumer Price Index for seniors, to increase the Guaranteed Income Supplement for low-income seniors, and not to eliminate pension income splitting. These promises were part of an ongoing debate on the potential expansion of the Canada Pension Plan, a debate that intensified in the aftermath of the 2008 financial crisis and its negative impact on Registered Retirement Savings Plans (RRSPs) and Retirement Savings Plans (RSPs).

Long supported by the NDP and the labour movement, the expansion of the CPP had become a major political issue in the context of a minority Conservative government seeking additional electoral support. However, due in part to the opposition of small- and medium-sized businesses and some provinces such as Alberta, the idea of increasing CPP benefits was officially dropped by the Harper government at the end of 2010 (Béland 2013). The labour movement and the NDP, however, continued to promote the expansion of the CPP during the majority Conservative government (2011–2015), leading the Liberals to seek support from left-wing voters by promising the expansion of this program in its 2015 campaign platform.

Once in power, the Liberals held discussions with the provinces on this issue. These are essential because any reform of the CPP requires the support of at least seven provinces representing at least two-thirds of the Canadian population. Here, Rachel Notley's NDP surprise win in Alberta in the spring of 2015 made it possible for the Trudeau government to enact its pledge to increase CPP benefits. This would have been impossible with Rachel Notley's Progressive Conservative predecessor Jim Prentice. In this context, an agreement between Ottawa and the provinces was reached in the summer of 2016.

This agreement provides for an increase in the CPP replacement rate from 25% to 33.3%, while increasing the combined contribution rate from 9.9% to 11.9% between 2019 and 2023 and the earnings ceiling covered by the plan from $54,900 to $82,700 between 2016 and 2025 (Department of Finance Canada, 2016). Hesitant about the possibility of adopting an identical increase in the benefits of the Québec Pension Plan (QPP) because of its already higher contribution rate than the CPP, the Couillard government finally announced its decision to do so at the same time. The promise made by the Trudeau government had direct consequences for the QPP, a program created at the same time as the CPP in the mid-1960s and whose benefits have remained largely similar since then (Béland and Weaver 2019).

In the area of income maintenance, the Liberals also made promises about Employment Insurance (EI) in their 2015 campaign platform. The three main promises in this area were, respectively, to improve access to compassionate leave benefits for employees, to reduce the "waiting period for EI benefits" from two weeks to one week, and to reverse "Stephen Harper's EI reforms that force unemployed workers to move away from their communities and take lower-paying jobs." The 2016 federal budget delivered on these promises by improving compassionate care benefits, by reducing the one-week EI waiting period, and by eliminating "a 2012 directive that forced unemployed people to accept any job even far from home or at a much lower wage than they were before" (Fortier 2016). The budget also put an end to the requirement for new entrants (youth or immigrants) to "work at least 910 hours over a one-year period" for "entitlement to employment insurance" (Fortier 2016). Despite these promises, it is not at all clear that the Liberals have achieved their goal of "providing real income security for workers, including those with precarious jobs." This is a major issue, especially for young precarious and self-employed workers. According to the Trudeau Polimetre, this last promise is "not yet rated."

Finally, an issue directly related to income maintenance is the fight against poverty. This issue explicitly intersects with the promises already mentioned, including the construction of "affordable housing," the creation of the CCB, and the enhancement of GIS benefits for "low-income seniors living alone." More generally, the Liberals promised to establish and evaluate "anti-poverty goals" while "publicly reporting results." A significant step in this direction was the unveiling in August 2018 of a federal anti-poverty strategy based on public consultations held in six Canadian cities starting in September 2016 (CBC News 2018). This is the first federal strategy of its kind, while similar strategies have been in place for a long time in most provinces.

Like many of these provincial strategies, the federal initiative does not currently include any new programs. However, according to Alain Noël (2018), the new federal strategy is "a big step forward" because it transforms the fight against poverty as a priority for the federal government, which for the first time adopts an official definition of poverty that is likely to help measure progress in this area in the years to come. At the same time, only time will tell if the federal government will be able to achieve its more ambitious goal of "reducing poverty by 20% from 2015 levels by 2020 and by 50% by 2030" (CBC News 2018).

In summary, in terms of income maintenance and the fight against poverty, we can speak of transformative commitments and achievements in at least two areas: increasing CPP benefits and creating a first federal strategy to fight poverty. In the area of retirement pension policies, the cancellation of the increase in the age of eligibility for OAS and GIS also represents a significant change that should affect millions of Canadians over the next decades.

## CONCLUSION

As our analysis points out, some of the social policies adopted during Justin Trudeau's mandate are potentially transformative, reflecting the ambition shown by the social promises of the 2015 Liberal platform. From the creation of the CCB and the renewed federal engagement in housing policy through to the expansion of CCP and the launching of the First Federal poverty strategy, the Trudeau government delivered on much of its social policy promises while improving social protection. While austerity still dominates social protection debates in other rich countries, Canada is clearly moving toward a gradual improvement in social policies that is illustrated perfectly by the achievements of the Trudeau government that, while often transformative, are nothing revolutionary. They do, however, reflect a real interest in social protection from the federal government that seems to be higher than the one that existed during the Harper years.

## References

Béland, Daniel and R. Kent Weaver. 2019. "Federalism and the Politics of the Canada and Quebec Pension Plans", *Journal of International and Comparative Social Policy,* 35(1), 25-40.

Canada. 2017. *Canada National Housing Strategy. A place to call home.* Ottawa: Government of Canada. https://www.placetocallhome.ca/pdfs/Canada-National-Housing-Strategy.pdf

CBC News. 2018. "Liberals vow to lift 2 million Canadians out of poverty by 2030, with no new spending", August 21, 2018. https://www.cbc.ca/news/politics/poverty-strategy-low-income-1.4792808

Canadian Press. 2018. "Liberals' $40B national housing plan to treat shelter as a human right", March 26, 2018. https://www.cbc.ca/news/politics/canada-national-housing-strategy-right-minister-duclos-1.4594100

Department of Finance Canada. 2016. *Backgrounder on Enhancing the Canada Pension Plan (CPP).* Ottawa: Department of Finance. https://www.fin.gc.ca/n16/data/16-113_3-fra.asp

Fortier, Marco. 2016. "L'assurance-emploi plus généreuse pour les chômeurs", *Le Devoir,* 23 mars 2016. https://www.ledevoir.com/politique/canada/466230/l-assurance-emploi-plus-genereuse-pour-les-chomeurs

Harris, Kathleen. 2016. "Justin Trudeau says OAS eligibility age to return to 65 in 1st Liberal budget", *CBC News,* March 17, 2016. https://www.cbc.ca/news/politics/trudeau-economy-bloomberg-new-york-1.3495331

Liberal Party of Canada. 2015. Real Change: *A New Plan for a Strong Middle Class.* https://www.liberal.ca/wp-content/uploads/2015/10/New-plan-for-a-strong-middle-class.pdf.

Mahon, Rianne with Michael J. Prince. 2019. "From Family Allowances to the Struggle for Universal Childcare in Canada." In *Universality and Social Policy in Canada,* Daniel Béland, Gregory Marchildon and Michael J. Prince (eds.): 83–102. Toronto: University of Toronto Press.

Morneau, Hon. Bill. 2016. *Budget Speech,* March 22. Ottawa: Department of Finance Canada.

Noël, Alain. 2018. "Un pas en avant dans la lutte contre la pauvreté", *Options politiques,* August 29, 2018. http://policyoptions.irpp.org/fr/magazines/august-2018/un-pas-en-avant-dans-la-lutte-contre-la-pauvrete/

# Chapter 10
# The Legalization of Recreational Cannabis

Jared J. Wesley

O n the surface, assessing the Trudeau government's fulfillment of its pledge to "legalize, regulate, and restrict access to marijuana" appears clear-cut. As of October 17, 2018, Canadian adults can consume most cannabis products in much the same way they consume tobacco or alcohol. The case raises deeper questions about democratic accountability, however. Should governments be held to account for achieving the long-term outcomes of their proposed policy changes, or is it enough that they deliver a set of short-term outputs that may or may not align with those broader objectives? From the latter perspective, the Liberals delivered on their narrower commitment to consult Canadians and pass two pieces of legislation.[1] This is not to diminish the gravity or difficulty of the feat. In three short years, the Trudeau Liberals accomplished what many of their predecessors had promised and failed to deliver. In acting with such speed, however, the Liberals placed the medium- and longer-term success of legalization at risk. Supply issues, the lack of reliable roadside testing technology, and uneven implementation of the laws across the country have cast a shadow over the legalization process. The Trudeau government delivered on its promise to legalize non-medical cannabis, but questions linger as to whether the new policy will achieve the broader public health and public safety objectives the Liberals have set.

---

1.  At the time of writing, the federal government had not legalized pre-packaged edible cannabis products. Given that this step is within the sole purview of Parliament, it is highly likely they will meet this commitment by their self-imposed deadline of October 2019.

This chapter begins by tracing the origins of the Liberal Party of Canada's policy positions on cannabis, with particular attention to the rapid evolution of Justin Trudeau's own attitudes toward decriminalization and legalization. It then explains how the Liberals were able to maintain focus on their two main policy objectives by orchestrating the public consultation process to centre around public health and public safety. The chapter concludes by assessing the implications of the Trudeau government's accelerated approach to policymaking.

## 10.1 THE EVOLUTION OF THE LIBERAL POLICY

Justin Trudeau was not the first federal leader to promise cannabis reform. He was not even the first in his family. In 1969, his father, Pierre Trudeau, launched a public inquiry into the non-medical use of drugs. The Le Dain Commission's recommendation to repeal prohibition against simple possession and home cultivation did not make it into the Liberal government's legislative agenda, however. Their primary opponents, the Progressive Conservatives, campaigned on decriminalization in 1979, but Prime Minister Joe Clark's short-lived PC government fell before it could introduce any legislation. The issue remained dormant on Parliament Hill for the next two decades. Events south of the border may have had influence in this regard. The salience of the Reagan administration's vaunted "war on drugs" helped frame efforts at cannabis reform as being too soft on crime. It also had a chilling effect on made-in-Canada efforts, for fear of American reaction and potential border-security retaliation amid free trade negotiations in the 1980s and 1990s.

Indeed, Canadian governments appeared forced into acting on the cannabis file, beginning with the medical system. As with other post-material issues such as abortion, marriage, and euthanasia, early progress on cannabis legalization was achieved through the Canadian courts. The Ontario Court of Appeal's decision in the *Parker* (2000) case pushed Jean Chretien's Liberal government to establish Canada's system of medical cannabis. Two years later, a Senate Special Committee on Illegal Drugs reiterated the Le Dain Commission's call to legalize possession for recreational purposes. These pressures forced the Chretien government's hand, prompting it to introduce decriminalization legislation in 2002 (Bill C-38). Amid changes in party leadership, the bill died on the order paper. Overt signals from the conservative George W. Bush administration convinced Chretien's Liberal successor, Paul Martin, to abandon the issue in favour of shoring up the medical cannabis system. Conservative Prime

Minister Stephen Harper needed no such encouragement from the Bush administration, whose tough-on-crime approach mirrored his own. In fact, under the Harper government, Health Canada's attention shifted from tobacco control to drugs with an anti-drug campaign. It was into this atmosphere that Justin Trudeau entered federal politics.

Branded by opponents on the left and right as being more style than substance and too inexperienced to become prime minister, Trudeau's cautious approach to public policy was understandable. First elected to Parliament in 2008, he initially sided with Harper by voting in favour of the Conservative government's new legislation establishing mandatory minimum sentences for cannabis-related offenses (Bill C-15). As late as 2010, Trudeau was on record as supporting prohibition and tough sentencing—a mainstream position among elites from most political parties in Canada at the time (Raphael 2010).

The chill on Canadian cannabis reform began to thaw in 2012. U.S. President Barack Obama had relaxed federal enforcement of recreational cannabis use in states that had legalized it. This created a window of opportunity to debate legalization without fear of the United States closing its border to Canadians who partake in legal cannabis consumption north of the 49th parallel. The Liberal Party of Canada seized the mantle at its January 2012 bi-annual policy convention, passing a resolution to the effect "that a new Liberal government will legalize marijuana and ensure the regulation and taxation of its production, distribution, and use, while enacting strict penalties for illegal trafficking, illegal importation and exportation, and impaired driving" (Liberal Party of Canada 2012). Importantly, the commitment went beyond these public health and public safety objectives to stress goals related to social justice and collaborative intergovernmental processes. The policy resolution included plans to establish "prevention and education programs; extend amnesty to all Canadians previously convicted of simple and minimal marijuana possession, and ensure the elimination of all criminal records related thereto" (Liberal Party of Canada 2012). All of this was to be accomplished through collaboration "with the provinces and local governments of Canada on a coordinated regulatory approach" (Liberal Party of Canada 2012).

As a contestant in the Liberals' 2012–2013 leadership race, Justin Trudeau initially distanced himself from the party's policy resolution, even after it passed. Media attention forced him to soften his stance, however, and he began embracing decriminalization as a good "first step" in improving Canada's cannabis regime (Mcknight 2013). This said, the issue was absent from his leadership campaign speeches, including his victory address at the April 2013 Liberal Leadership Convention. It was not until four months later that Trudeau adopted a pro-legalization position. This came as part of a public admission of smoking cannabis at a 2010 dinner party, during his first term as an MP (Raj 2013). At the time, he reported being convinced by research suggesting that legalization and strict regulation was the best way to keep cannabis out of the hands of youth (Janus 2013). From a strategic standpoint, the promise distinguished the Liberal leader from his opponents on both ends of the spectrum. On the left, the New Democrats (NDP) were longstanding supporters of decriminalization. Since full legalization remained a step too far for NDP members and strategists, decriminalization remained official NDP policy when Tom Mulcair assumed the leadership in 2012.[2] Days before becoming leader, Mulcair created confusion and controversy in a television interview when he appeared to reverse the party's support for decriminalization, saying "I think that would be a mistake because the information that we have right now is that the marijuana that's on the market is extremely potent and can actually cause mental illness" (Bryden 2012). He later clarified his remarks, stating that he had confused the terms decriminalization (which he supported) and legalization (which he opposed). Yet, Mulcair's response only helped highlight Trudeau's more progressive position on the issue. Meanwhile, the Liberal approach forced the governing Conservatives to double down on their tough-on-crime, anti-drug position.

Trudeau's move was risky nonetheless. Open admissions of smoking cannabis while serving in elected office played into opponents' claims that Trudeau was too immature and impulsive to assume the responsibilities of prime minister. In the end, the gamble worked to his favour. Canadians' attitudes toward legalization had shifted considerably, and more quickly than New Democratic and Conservative strategists had anticipated (CBC News 2015).

---

2.  Decriminalization would have involved removing criminal penalties for possession of small amounts of cannabis; administrative penalties, like fines, would likely remain. Legalization would have removed all sanctions associated with this sort of possession, while also opening up a legal system of production, distribution, and sale.

## 10.2 PLEDGE FULFILLMENT

From a public policy standpoint, governments should aim to achieve grander objectives (outcomes) by establishing shorter-term, measurable deliverables (outputs). The former are longer-term, often aspirational or nebulous goals that defy concrete evaluation, while the latter are precise milestones capable of being assessed. The conflation of outcomes with outputs is a perennial misstep. Simply because a government hits narrower targets does not mean it will achieve its broader goals, particularly when the outputs fail to align with the outcomes they are intended to accomplish. Let us examine the five specific 2015 Liberal Party campaign promises as reproduced in Table 10-1 through this lens.

TABLE 10-1 – Specific Pledges for a Cannabis Policy Shift

| # | PROMISE | VERDICT |
|---|---------|---------|
| 9.15 | We will create a federal/provincial/territorial task force, and with input from experts in public health, substance abuse, and law enforcement, will design a new system of strict marijuana sales and distribution [...] | Kept in part |
| 9.16 | We will create new, stronger laws to punish more severely those who operate a motor vehicle while under its [marijuana's] influence. | Kept |
| 9.17 | We will create new, stronger laws to punish more severely those who provide it [marijuana] to minors. | Kept |
| 9.18 | We will create new, stronger laws to punish more severely those who sell it [marijuana] outside of the new regulatory framework. | Kept |
| 9.19 | We will remove marijuana consumption and incidental possession from the Criminal Code. | Kept |

* Sources: Trudeau Polimetre and Liberal Party of Canada platform

The Liberal Party was clear in terms of its desired outcomes from legalization. Messaging on the campaign trail and in government was tightly controlled and entirely in sync: the ultimate objectives of the policy were to enhance both *public health* by keeping cannabis out of the hands of youth and *public safety* by cutting off organized crime from the proceeds of cannabis sales. How did the Liberals maintain this laser-like, dual focus throughout the legislative process and intergovernmental negotiations?

In large part, the answer lies in their strategic use and management of the public consultation process. Following the Speech from the Throne in December 2015, when the government promised to "introduce legislation that will… legalize, regulate and restrict access to marijuana," one can trace its public health/public safety frame from the initial discussion paper (June 2016) to the federal Task Force report (November 2016). In turn, this document shaped the federal legislation and influenced the provincial/territorial response (both in November 2017).

Government communications professionals and seasoned stakeholders know well: the outcome of a consultation is determined largely by the structure of the discussion paper that guides it. In "Toward the Legalization, Regulation and Restriction of Access to Marijuana," the Trudeau government outlined a total of nine policy objectives. The top two objectives were to "protect young Canadians by keeping marijuana out of the hands of children and youth" and "keep profits out of the hands of criminals, particularly organized crime" (Task Force on Marijuana Legalization and Regulation 2016). Public health and public safety figured prominently among the remaining seven objectives. These involved reducing burdens on the criminal justice system for simple cannabis offenses, preventing Canadians from receiving criminal records for the same, stiffening penalties, enhancing public education, establishing strict quality and safety controls, maintaining access to medical cannabis, and setting up a rigorous evaluation framework.

The government designed the discussion paper to focus the work of the new federal Task Force on Cannabis Legalization and Regulation, whose creation was foreshadowed in the 2015 Liberal Party platform. Crucially, the Trudeau government chose to deviate from its election pledge by making the Task Force a *federal* body—not the "federal/provincial/territorial" model promised in the platform. This allowed Ottawa to set the terms of the public consultation and influence the final report with input—but not direction—from provincial/territorial governments. Negotiating the Task Force's mandate with thirteen other partners would have likely led to a proliferation of policy priorities, particularly given the wide range of perspectives on the topic. While the overwhelming mood toward legalization among provincial/territorial governments was one of ambivalence, differences in the degree of support for the public health, public safety, and other components of the process could have delayed the Task Force's work and produced a less-focused final report (Wesley 2018). The choice to keep the Task Force under exclusive federal control contributed to its efficiency and the ability of the Trudeau Liberals to keep the work focused through the two-pronged policy lens outlined in their 2015 campaign platform.

Consisting of nine experts from various professional backgrounds, the Task Force was mandated to consult with Canadians and their governments in crafting advice to Ottawa on a new legislative and regulatory framework to legalize recreational cannabis. In conducting its work, the Task Force noted the discussion paper "proved to be a valuable resource in framing our early thinking, questions, and deliberations, as well as a stimulus for the thoughtful input we sought and received." While explicitly acknowledging that the paper identified nine public policy objectives, the Task force conscientiously narrowed its focus to the top two that reproduce the election platform wording: "Chief among these are keeping cannabis out of the hands of children and youth and keeping profits out of the hands of organized crime" (Health Canada 2016, 2).

The Task Force report informed the Trudeau government's approach to legalization, as it decided to divide its reforms into two companion pieces of legislation, both introduced in April 2017. The Cannabis Act (Bill C-45) contained the public health elements, including making it permissible for people over the age of 18 to legally purchase, grow, and consume limited amounts of cannabis in certain, non-edible forms. Each province and territory would be given latitude in terms of raising this minimum age (e.g., to match their liquor laws). Further federal rules restricted public possession and gifting to 30 grams of fresh or dried cannabis or equivalent. Cannabis oils could also be sold and consumed, permitting adults to make cannabis-containing food and drinks at home. Edible and drinkable cannabis products were not made available for legal sale until the following year at the earliest (fall 2019). The Act set forth further restrictions on how cannabis could be commercially produced, promoted, packaged, displayed, sold, and distributed, with a particular focus on limiting appeals to youth. Penalties for contravening the Act ranged from criminal charges to ticketing and fines. The most serious offences, including providing cannabis to youth, carried with them maximum penalties of fourteen years in jail. The second piece of federal legislation, an Act to Amend the Criminal Code (Bill C-46) contained provisions to promote public safety. This included a crackdown on impaired driving, involving much stronger penalties and increased police powers to conduct roadside testing.

## 10.3 OF OUTCOMES AND OUTPUTS

All told, it took the Trudeau Liberals three years to transform the recreational cannabis regime in Canada from one of prohibition to a patchwork of provincial/territorial systems where it can be grown, distributed, sold, and consumed in a variety of ways. Like most massive efforts at policy reform, full legalization was less likely to take place under longer timelines. In Canada, few prime ministers are bold or prescient enough to predict they will be around to shepherd the process through a second mandate. This said, the combination of speed and decentralization carries with it certain risks to achieving the broader policy objectives beyond the initial outputs achieved in the first government mandate.

First and foremost, critics hold that the federal government did not allow enough time for licensed producers to cultivate enough supply to meet the demand in the newly legalized market (Sen and Wyonch 2018). While industry and Health Canada attribute the problem to localized "supply chain issues" rather than a systemic shortage of licensed producers (Thomson 2018), the lack of legal supply at the point of sale has created a scenario where less-risk-averse consumers may choose to purchase recreational cannabis from the illicit market. While few projections indicate that illegal operations, including organized crime, will end up further ahead as a result of legalization, and while law enforcement resources are set to shift from the pursuit of possession charges to a crackdown on illegal production and sales, the shortages in the legal market contradict the Trudeau Liberals' stated objective to remove cannabis profits from the pockets of illicit sellers. On the eve of legalization in 2018, even the most optimistic policymakers felt that governments could only make a dent in the black market, the size of which remains exceedingly difficult to measure (Ivison 2018). Six months into legalization, this nebulous target remains even more in doubt, given the inability of government and legal private retailers to access enough supply to federally approved cannabis and the incapacity of provincial/territorial governments to expand retail operations to meet consumer demand.

Legalization also came before law enforcement officials had reliable means of enforcing the stiffer impaired driving laws. Science remains unable to bridge the gap between detecting the consumption of cannabis (e.g., THC in one's blood or saliva) and the level of intoxication and impairment. Unlike roadside breathalyzer tests, which rely on scientifically proven and court-tested evidence based on blood-alcohol levels, no such tests exist for measuring cannabis-impaired driving. Traditional sobriety tests may provide a stopgap measure, but as police begin experimenting with THC-detection devices, those charged under the new federal laws have begun challenging their reliability in court. Previous backlogs attributable to simple cannabis possession charges noted in the Liberals' 2012 policy resolution and 2017 Task Force report may well be replaced by those caused by challenges under the new impaired driving legislation, at least in the short term. Perceptions of these challenges could discourage law enforcement and justice officials from pursuing drug-impaired charges to the full extent of the law, especially given the perceived severity of the new fourteen-year sentences. Together with the supply challenges, this places the Liberals' public safety objectives at risk.

Second, in handing off the implementation of large parts of the legalization regime to their provincial/territorial partners, the Trudeau Liberals have relinquished significant control when it comes to defining and meeting their broader policy objectives. While all federal/provincial/ territorial governments have been onside with the federal government's approach at the level of directional policy (i.e., they have not opposed the concept of legalization itself, nor the broad public health and public policy objectives attached to it), they have disagreed with the Trudeau Liberals at the strategic and operational policy levels (Wesley 2018). In addition to opposing the tight timelines involved with the policy, premiers contested the Trudeau government's initial proposal to share the proceeds of a 10% federal excise tax with the provinces and territories on a 50/50 basis. Within weeks, the premiers secured a temporary concession; for the first two years of legalization, three-quarters of all federal excise tax revenues would flow to the provinces and territories to cover anticipated costs associated with policing and health care. However, this deal must be revisited after the 2019 federal election, opening up the prospect of heated federal/provincial/territorial negotiations.

Aside from these looming resource tensions, a number of provincial governments have made operational policy decisions that run contrary to the Trudeau Liberals' approach. For example, Quebec and Manitoba were among the least enthusiastic supporters of legalization, with both prohib- iting home growing and increasing the minimum age of consumption above those in their respective liquor laws. The Trudeau government has indicated a willingness to challenge the first provisions in court, arguing that the federal Cannabis Act allows all Canadians to grow a limited number of plants in their homes (subject to certain restrictions like landlord-tenant agreements). Trudeau, himself, publicly criticized Quebec Premier François Legault for his decision to increase Quebec's minimum age of cannabis consumption from 19 to 25 following the 2018 provincial election. "If we eliminate the segment of the population between 18 to 19 and 21 years, which is a population often in university, often in areas where they'll try to consume, we're keeping an important segment of potential consumers for the black market," Trudeau remarked (Marquis 2018). Conservative governments in other parts of the country may make similar moves in the future, particularly if implementation of cannabis legalization is contested in their jurisdictions. These provide prime examples of the principal-agent problem in federations like Canada, where an initial policy direction can become distorted as it passes from the principal policymaker (Ottawa) to the agents charged with implementing it (provinces and territories).

## CONCLUSION

This chapter traced the evolution of the Liberal Party's policy on recreational cannabis over recent decades, with a particular focus on the period since its support for legalization in 2012. As with most election promises, the transition from campaign to government resulted in key adjustments to the party's approach. This was particularly evident in terms of its overall framing of the issue (from social justice to public health and safety) and its approach to intergovernmental collaboration. These strategic decisions enabled the Liberal government to meet the letter, if not the entire spirit, of its campaign commitment within the first three years of its mandate. In doing so, Trudeau achieved one of the most complex feats of policy reform in recent Canadian history. Beyond convening a cross-country consultation and passing two signature pieces of legislation, the government convinced its provincial and territorial partners to construct their own regulatory regimes, creating a patchwork of legal frameworks that, together, made Canada the first member of the G7 to legalize the production, distribution, sale, and consumption of recreational cannabis. The longer-term success of the legalization process will define a core component of the Prime Minister's legacy.

REFERENCES

Bryden, Joan. 2012. "Mulcair clarifies stand on marijuana in time for 4/20 'pot holiday'," *The Globe and Mail*, April 20, 2012.
CBC News. 2015. "Mulcair pledges NDP will decriminalize pot 'the minute we form government'," *CBC News*, August 21, 2015.

Health Canada. 2016. *A Framework for the Legalization and Regulation of Cannabis in Canada: The Final Report of the Task Force on Cannabis Legalization and Regulation.* Ottawa: Minister of Health. https://www.canada.ca/content/dam/hc-sc/healthy-canadians/migration/task-force-marijuana-groupe-etude/framework-cadre/alt/framework-cadre-eng.pdf

Ivison, John. 2018. "Keep calm, and legislate on: Bill Blair is arguably the reason Canada is on the cusp of cannabis legalization," *National Post*, June 14, 2018.

Janus, Andrea. 2013. "Trudeau makes headlines for calls to legalize marijuana," *CTV News*, July 25, 2013.

Liberal Party of Canada. 2012. "Ottawa 2012—Liberal Biennial Convention—Priority Policy Resolutions." Liberal Party of Canada. https://www.liberal.ca/wp-content/uploads/2013/01/Ottawa-2012_Adopted-Policy-Resolutions.pdf.

Liberal Party of Canada. 2015. *Real Change: A New Plan for a Strong Middle Class.* https://www.liberal.ca/wp-content/uploads/2015/10/New-plan-for-a-strong-middle-class.pdf.

Marquis, Melanie. 2018. "Quebec government's cannabis plan could leave opening for organized crime, Trudeau says," *The Globe and Mail*, October 14, 2018.

Mcknight, Zoe. 2013. "Trueau calls for legalization of pot; 'It's more difficult for young people to get their hands on cigarettes' than weed," *The Vancouver Sun*, July 13, 2013.

Raj, Althia. 2013. "Justin Trudeau Smoked Marijuana After Becoming MP," *Huffington Post*, August 22, 2013.

Raphael, Mitchel. 2013. "Mitchel Raphael on what Justin learned from his Whistler days and a Helena homage," *Macleans*, May 6, 2010. https://www.macleans.ca/general/mitchel-raphael-on-what-justin-learned-from-his-whistler-days-and-a-helena-homage/.

Sen, Anindya, and Rosalie Wyonch. 2018. *Cannabis Countdown: Estimating the Size of Illegal Markets and Lost Tax Revenue Post-Legalization.* Toronto: C.D. Howe Institute.

Task Force on Marijuana Legalization and Regulation. 2016. *Toward the Legalization, Regulation, and Restriction of Access to Marijuana: Discussion Paper.* Ottawa: Government of Canada.

Thomson, Aly. 2018. "Expect no quick end to Canada-wide cannabis shortages, producers warn," *Financial Post*, November 14, 2018.

Wesley, Jared J. 2018. "Huddling or Muddling? Intergovernmental Relations and Cannabis Legalization in Canada," Annual Meeting of the Canadian Association of Programs in Public Administration, Regina, SK, May 31, 2018.

# Chapter 11
## Federal Interventionism in Health Policy: Back to the Future?

AMÉLIE QUESNEL-VALLÉE, RACHEL MCKAY,
AND ANTONIA MAIONI

C anada's "Fathers of Confederation" were men of their time, which is why, among other things, "health" was not seen as a primary responsibility for governments, and certainly not the Dominion government (Maioni and Smith 2003). This is not surprising, given that at the time, medical care was not particularly effective nor sought after, and health and social matters were of a local nature, to be addressed by family, charity, and religious communities. How surprised these men would have been to learn that, a century and a half after Confederation, health care had become such a powerful political symbol, a salient electoral issue, and a lightning rod for federal-provincial-territorial tension. It is little wonder, then, that health care was again a top-of-mind issue for Canadian voters, and for political candidates, in the 2015 election campaign.

The Liberal Party of Canada, which has long had a crucial role in the politics of health care, indeed made health-related promises a leitmotif of their electoral campaign. In this chapter, we analyze the fulfillment of the Liberal government's electoral promises in the areas of population health and health services, henceforth referred to as "health policy." We also took into consideration actions taken by the government while in power that moved up on the government's agenda either from previous legacies or because of current events. However, we should note from the outset that two areas of critical importance in this government's health policy portfolio, namely the creation of Indigenous Services Canada and the legalization of cannabis, are not part of this chapter, but rather respectively of chapters 10 and 13. Electoral promises related to older adults and early childhood are covered in Chapter 9 on social policy.

This chapter begins with a review of the context pertinent to health policy in 2015. We then analyze the electoral promises made in the federal election campaign and assess their fulfillment. Next, we review select issues that arose on the political agenda, not necessarily in relation to electoral promises.

Broadly speaking, we find that the Liberal government's actions in health policy have demonstrated a return to a more interventionist stance by the federal government, one that involves a more deliberate steering of provincial/territorial health and social services delivery through spending and performance assessment. This marks a significant shift from previous Conservative governments. In even starker contrast, the Liberal government's rhetoric appears to seek to extend the purview of the Canada Health Act to the new areas of home care, mental health, and pharmacare. Finally, action on many of these items is closely monitored through pan-Canadian harmonized performance indicator development, in line with this government's commitment to "deliverology" with the transparency—and visibility—it offers.

## 11.1 HEALTH POLICY CONTEXT IN 2015

From the wording of the Constitution Act in 1867, and the evolution of responsibilities since then, health care organization and delivery fall on the provinces and territories. The federal government mainly exercises its role in health policy through financial support of provincial health care systems through the Canada Health Transfer (CHT), which is the current designation for the fiscal transfer of federal funds to support provincial health care services. Liberal governments fashioned the federal funding of health care starting with the 1957 Hospital Insurance and Diagnostic Services Act, followed by Saskatchewan's universal, medical plan in 1962, which inspired the federal plan 1966 known as the Medical Care Insurance Act and, finally, the Canada Health Act (CHA) of 1984. They outline the terms and conditions of funding through five broad principles (public administration, comprehensiveness, universality, portability, accessibility) that define the contours of provincial health care systems (Canada 1985). In addition, the federal government is responsible for service delivery for specific populations (i.e., First Nations people living on reserves, Inuit, serving members of Canadian Forces and eligible veterans, some groups of refugee claimants, and federal inmates). Over time, the federal government developed a considerable role in health protection, health promotion, disease prevention, and education, as well as providing funding for health research (Braën 2002).

This division of powers, overlaid with intricate fiscal relationships, has set the stage for a classic political game that has played out between provinces/territories (P/T) and the federal government for over a half-century (see Chapter 3 on federal-provincial-territorial relations). This has involved, on one side, provinces/territories clamoring for more generous federal handouts to address ever-increasing health costs, and on the other, the federal government seeking more oversight into the allocation of its spending or cutting back that spending, sometimes at the same time. A dramatic example is the change in the funding arrangements in the mid-1990s that led to significant decreases in federal transfers to the provinces. The re-investment that would follow through the 2004 Health Accord, an agreement between the federal government and the P/T to provide stable health funding on a ten-year basis, aligned priorities nationwide around reducing wait times and improving patient care (Health Canada 2004). Both the cuts in funding and the reinvestment in health care were the actions of Liberal governments.

As the Health Accord was due to expire in 2014, Stephen Harper's Conservative government announced in 2011 that annual health transfer funding increases of 6% per year would be extended until 2017, followed by 3% increases per year thereafter, but these transfers were no longer associated with specific federal priorities to direct health spending as in prior governments (Scoffield 2011). This lack of priority-setting led critics to argue that the Harper government eschewed its leadership role with respect to health and health policy when they came to power in 2006, thus undermining the goals of the 2004 Health Accord (Kates 2014). Where the Harper government prioritized provincial autonomy over national policies, as we shall see, the Trudeau Liberals favoured pan-Canadian health policy goals and initiatives, with provincial variations in delivery.

The rhetoric and actions of the Liberal government since 2015 in health policy therefore mark a sharp contrast with that of the previous government. It has indeed taken more of an intervention approach to this portfolio, with policy direction aimed at addressing the impact of social determinants of health, increasing access to services where it is within their jurisdiction to do so, and using their spending power to shape priorities otherwise.

## 11.2 LIBERAL PARTY 2015 ELECTORAL PROMISES

In 2015, 18 promises in the Liberal Party's electoral agenda, as recorded by the Polimetre, specifically focused on health policy matters. Ten promises address traditional federal policy areas such as tobacco control, food inspection and regulations, and health care funding, while eight others expand the federal role in health policy matters. Table 11.1 presents the key Liberal promises in health care and flags the five most important ones in bold based on their potential social impact as new policy initiatives, their potential budget impact (costs and cost-savings), or both.

TABLE 11-1 – Key Promises in Health Policy in Traditional
and New Health Policy Areas

| # | PROMISE | VERDICT |
|---|---------|---------|
| **Promises in <u>Traditional</u> Federal Health Policy Areas (Medicare and Public Health)** | | |
| **12.03** | **We will negotiate a new Health Accord with provinces and territories, including a long-term agreement on funding.** | **Kept in part/ In the works** |
| 4.08 | We will develop a pan-Canadian collaboration on health innovation. | Kept |
| 12.12 | We will introduce new restrictions on the commercial marketing of unhealthy food and beverages to children, similar to those now in place in Quebec. | Kept in part/ In the works |
| 12.14 | We will bring in tougher regulations to eliminate trans fats, similar to those in the U.S., and to reduce salt in processed foods. | Kept |
| 12.34 | We will introduce plain packaging requirements for tobacco products, similar to those in Australia and the United Kingdom. | Kept |
| 12.16 | Working together with experts and advocates, we will develop and implement a comprehensive federal gender violence strategy and action plan, aligned with existing provincial strategies. | Kept |
| **Promises in <u>New</u> Federal Health Policy Areas** | | |
| **12.26** | **We will make high-quality mental health services more available to Canadians who need them, including our veterans and first responders.** | **Kept in part/ In the works** |
| **6.03** | **We will invest $3 billion, over the next four years, to deliver more and better home care services for all Canadians. This includes more access to high quality in-home caregivers, financial supports for family care, and, when necessary, palliative care.** | **Kept in part/ In the works** |

| # | PROMISE | VERDICT |
|---|---------|---------|
| 12.25 | We will work with the provinces and territories to develop a coordinated national action plan on post-traumatic stress disorder, which disproportionately affects public safety officers. | Kept |
| 12.23 | **We will improve access to necessary prescription medications.** | **Kept in part/ In the works** |
| 12.24 | **We will join with provincial and territorial governments to buy drugs in bulk, reducing the cost Canadian governments pay for these drugs, and making them more affordable for Canadians.** | **Kept in part/ In the works** |
| 12.10 | To eliminate systemic barriers and deliver equality of opportunity to all Canadians living with disabilities, we will consult with provinces, territories, and other stakeholders to introduce a National Disabilities Act. | Kept in part/ In the works |

\* Source: Trudeau Polimetre and Liberal Party of Canada platform
\*\* The most important pledges are in **bold.**

Table 11-1 acknowledges the largely successful policy work that the Liberal government promised and carried out in the areas of health protection, prevention, and promotion.

## 11.3 INCREASING PUBLIC COVERAGE FOR SERVICES FALLING OUTSIDE THE CANADA HEALTH ACT

In their 2015 election platform, the Liberals pledged to increase public coverage for health and social services falling outside the Canada Health Act (CHA), which marks a sharp break with the previous government's less interventionist stance. The Liberals promised to improve access to home care and palliative care, mental health services, and prescription drugs. These services have indeed historically been only partially covered through provincial public programs, notably because home care services are designated as extended health care services in the Act, outside the formal realm of insured health services, while the others are not referred to at all (Parliament of Canada 1985). As a result, significant variation in public coverage and access exists both within and across the provinces.

However, the Liberal government's commitment to transparency (and likely, the desire to increase visibility) led to a firm stance on separating the proposed new funding from the Canada Health Transfer (CHT) (as the latter flows into provinces' general budget, making accountability to federal investments more difficult) (Marchildon 2016). Operationally, the Liberal government maintained the previous Conservative government's scheduled halving of the CHT escalator from 6% to 3% in 2017 and used that leverage to compel provinces into this new targeted health financing agreement. The negotiations between the federal and P/T governments were arduous, with the provinces/territories fixed on seeing the CHT escalator remain at least at 5.2%. After many months of negotiations, all provinces and territories finally signed on to bilateral agreements in which they agreed (under various terms and conditions) to improve access to mental health and home care. Ultimately, the final amounts negotiated through the bilateral agreements add up to the 5.2% increase sought by the provinces, but the Liberal government did succeed in carving out some of that increase toward earmarked spending to be administered separately so that it can be better monitored for accountability (Picard 2017).

It also succeeded in bringing the provincial and territorial governments (except Quebec, which agreed to an asymmetrical arrangement) to agree to the Common Statement of Principles on Shared Health Priorities, released in 2017 (Health Canada 2017). This statement declared priority areas of home and community care and mental health and addictions as targets for federal funding, as well as a commitment to performance measurement through a focused set of indicators to be developed in collaboration with the Canadian Institute for Health Information (CIHI 2018). It is expected that CIHI will begin annual reporting on these selected indicators in 2019; they include wait times, early intervention, understanding of services available, access to effective care, self-injury awareness, appropriate care settings, caregiver experiences, and end-of-life care (CIHI 2018).

### 11.3.1  Home Care

The Liberals promised an investment of $3 billion over four years to improve access to home care, including access to high-quality in-home caregivers, financial supports for family care, and palliative care. This pledge was reiterated in the mandate letter sent in 2015 to Jane Philpott, the new Minister of Health, with the expectation that this commitment would result in a new Health Accord (Trudeau 2015). Despite home care services being outside the scope of insured services in the Canada Health Act (CHA), the government used their spending power to fulfill this promise: Budget 2017 (Department of Finance 2017) confirmed investments of $6 billion over ten years for home care to flow through the bilateral targeted funding agreements with the provinces and territories. While this is an important attempt at harmonizing coverage across Canada, a gap will likely remain between this increased federal output and outcomes for Canadians, which will depend on the scope and depth of P/T's service delivery, and may be amplified further by the bilateral nature of the agreement. Hence, much as there is interprovincial variation in other components of the health care basket that are covered under the CHA, we should not expect that this additional targeted funding will completely smooth out the substantial existing variations in home care coverage between provinces/territories.

### 11.3.2 Mental Health

Mental health has been a persistent issue for governments—both federal and provincial—in the health policy arena. In 2007, the Conservative government created the Mental Health Commission of Canada to work toward a comprehensive, national mental health strategy without any significant investment of money into the delivery of services. In 2015, the Liberal Party made promises to increase access to mental health services, albeit largely limited to populations (Indigenous people and veterans) already under their service delivery responsibility.

Indigenous Services Canada has now taken on the mandate of mental health, addictions, and Indigenous health (see Chapter 13). Many of the promises to veterans have also materialized. In 2016, the government allocated funding to the Mood Disorders Society of Canada to provide employment assistance services to vulnerable veterans; established a virtual Centre for Excellence on PTSD and other related Mental Health Conditions at the Royal Ottawa Hospital, with investments committed for research and education; and addressed the election promise to implement the Auditor General's recommendations regarding mental health services for veterans by opening a satellite clinic for operational stress injury services.

Finally, improvements in access to mental health may also be afoot for the general population, as the 2017 budget also allocated $5 billion over ten years to support provincial mental health initiatives through the same targeted funding mechanism used for home care initiatives (Department of Finance 2017).

### 11.3.3 Pharmacare

Pharmacare (i.e., a publicly funded universal program for prescription drugs) was not explicitly discussed in the party's platform, but the Liberals did campaign on a promise to improve access to necessary prescription medications (Liberal Party of Canada 2015). Two important developments have contributed to moving it forward on the policy agenda in recent decades. Indeed, while the lack of universal drug coverage has long been noted as a problem in several high-level policy discussions (such as the Romanow Commission in 2002), these discussions lacked the robust body of empirical evidence on the cost efficiency and greater equity of universal coverage that is now at our disposal (Morgan et al. 2015). Finally, the reduction — or threats thereof — of coverage for older adults in many provinces, coupled with the demographic and political weight of this age group in an aging population, has led groups such as the Canadian Association for Retired Persons (CARP) to take up this issue in their lobbying efforts. This issue now appears to have risen to the forefront of the policy agenda, ostensibly in preparation for the 2019 election.

Many steps have been taken toward an improved, affordable pharmacare. In 2016, the federal government joined the Pan-Canadian Pharmaceutical Alliance, which was established in 2010 as a mechanism to leverage purchasing power by coordinating provincial and territorial bulk buying of prescription drugs. The Liberal government's Budget 2017 pledged to improve access to prescription drugs by an outlay of $140.3 million over five years, with $18.2 million per year for Health Canada, the Patented Medicine Prices Review Board, and the Canadian Agency for Drugs and Technologies in Health (Morneau 2017). Amendments to the Patented Medicines Regulations aiming to lower the prices for patented medicines in Canada came into effect on January 1, 2019 (Government of Canada 2017a).

In April 2018, the House of Commons Standing Committee on Health released a report to Parliament called "Pharmacare Now: Prescription Medicine Coverage for All Canadians." It asserts that "the best way to move forward in establishing a universal single payer public prescription drug coverage program is by expanding the Canada Health Act to include prescription drugs dispensed outside of hospitals as an insured service under the Act" (Casey 2018, 2). The report provided 18 recommendations toward the implementation of a national public pharmacare program and commissioned a costing analysis by the Parliamentary Budget Office (PBO). The PBO found a net savings of $4.2 billion per year based on a framework of Quebec's current program and list of insured medicines (Office of the Parliamentary Budget Officer 2017).

Meanwhile, the last two budgets of this government spelled out concrete investments, suggesting the Liberal government has moved past considerations of desirability and feasibility and is deliberately and purposefully progressing toward policy formulation. As such, Budget 2018 announced the creation of an Advisory Council on the Implementation of National Pharmacare. While the Council's report was only due in late spring 2019, an interim report was released within days of Budget 2019 (Hoskins 2019). This interim report provided the foundational principles for the investments announced on March 19, 2019, namely the creation of a new Canadian Drug Agency, a pan-Canadian formulary, and a national strategy for high-cost drugs for rare diseases (Morneau 2019). The stated goals of these initiatives are to harmonize coverage nationally and increase cost efficiency of coverage through economies of scale and bargaining power.

Thus, it appears the government will present a national pharmacare strategy as an electoral promise in the 2019 campaign. Considering the support from influential lobby groups and the work accomplished to date in laying out the policy options, they would then be in a good position to fulfill these promises should they win a second mandate.

## 11.4 ISSUES THAT AROSE ON THE AGENDA

Along with electoral promises made in the 2015 campaign, the Liberal government has had to address delicate, controversial issues arising from political legacies, such as the medical assistance in dying, which moved to the front burner of the policy agenda very early in their term. With the emerging issue of the opioid crisis, it has had to wrestle with a difficult issue that falls within the federal mandate in health protection.

### 11.4.1 Medical Assistance in Dying

A significant policy that the Liberal government finalized during its tenure is medical assistance in dying. On February 6, 2015, eight months before the elections, the Supreme Court decision in *Carter v. Canada* struck down the federal prohibition on medically assisted dying, arguing this violated the Canadian Charter of Rights and Freedoms, and gave the government one year to adjust. Following consultations, Trudeau's team proposed Bill C-14 (adopted June 2016), legalizing assisted dying and laying out rules for how it could be accessed (Health Canada 2016).

Interestingly, the 2015 platform was silent on this controversial issue despite the fact that it would obviously rise to the policy agenda during the next government's tenure. Thus, it was not part of the 2015 electoral promises. However, as this new law is already under judicial contestation because of the conditions limiting access to assisted dying to cases where death is foreseeable (Bryden 2019), it will persist as an issue on this and the next government's policy agenda.

### 11.4.2  Responding to the Opioids Crisis in Canada

The opioids crisis is a major issue, which emerged since 2015. Harm reduction guides the Liberal government's public health-oriented response to the issue (Government of Canada 2017b). This is in stark contrast to the previous Conservative government's "tough on drugs" stance.

The federal government has implemented legislative and regulatory supports and has participated in international discussions aiming to reduce the flow of harmful substances. It has enshrined the harm reduction approach in a new Canadian Drugs and Substances Strategy and has committed federal money ($100 million over five years and $22.7 million ongoing) to address the problem (Government of Canada 2017b). Legislative and regulation changes include the streamlining and support for supervised drug consumption sites across Canada and the passing of the Good Samaritan Drug Overdose Act (as a private Member's bill) in May 2017, which provides some legal protection for anyone reporting a potential overdose to first responders.

## CONCLUSION

For more than half a century, health care has been a persistent and salient electoral issue and often, this has worked to the benefit of the Liberal Party (Blais et al. 2002). Indeed, successive Liberal governments have played an important role in the evolution of health policy in Canada. It was no surprise then that the Liberal Party would showcase health issues in its 2015 electoral platform and that once in power, health matters would feature prominently in this government's attention to promise keeping.

The overarching goal of the 2015 health policy platform was to increase access to health care services, particularly with respect to a more equitable distribution by reaching out to underserved groups and decreasing financial barriers. Thus, the Liberal Party focused on investments in mental health and home care services—two areas that exist largely outside the Canada Health Act definition of insured services. When it came to power, the Liberal government fulfilled these promises by leveraging financial incentives to compel provinces to address these as priority areas. As for pharmacare, population aging and the steady public debate about the costs of prescription drugs have meant that the Liberal government has had to address the issue in a more comprehensive way than had been suggested in the 2015 electoral campaign. With the recommendations from the Standing Committee on Health to change the CHA's definition of publicly insured services to include prescription drugs, the stage may be set for even bolder electoral promises in the future.

The 2015 Liberal platform attempted to place its health care promises simultaneously within both the party's agenda for specific populations and in its appeal to a broader electoral constituency. The Liberal government's actions in health policy have thus been within the purview of its responsibilities toward Indigenous peoples and veterans, as well as its commitment to families, older adults, and the "middle class." Since opinion polls consistently show wait times and shortages as irritants in public satisfaction, the Liberal government also remained focused on improving service delivery with performance measurement and reporting.

Health policy is, essentially, the most universal of issues for Canadian voters since it affects everyone in some way and since all taxpayers contribute to its financing. Even though most health care services are delivered through provincial and territorial programs, health has come to be seen as a quintessential marker of how Canadian governments "care" for their citizens and, accordingly, how they respond to voter concerns. The Canada Health Act has long embodied the federal role in health care. In both its promises and its realizations, this Liberal government has flexed its muscle to expand the scope of publicly insured services across the provinces and lead the way in providing better coverage of some of the same services for the populations under its responsibility. However, while bolstering its financial commitment to Medicare is a necessary step forward, it is not likely to be a sufficient condition to ensure the kind of lasting structural impact on Canadians' access to care that a more formal expansion of the definition of insured services would achieve.

## References

Advisory Council on the Implementation of National Pharmacare. 2018. "National Pharmacare Online Consultation | Let's Talk Health," September 17, 2018. https://www.letstalkhealth.ca/pharmacare.

Braën, André. 2002. "Health and the Distribution of Powers in Canada." Discussion Paper No. 2. University of Ottawa. https://doi.org/10.3138/978144 2681392-004.

Casey, Bill. 2018. "Pharmacare Now: Prescription Medicine Coverage for All Canadians—Report of the Standing Committee on Health." Ottawa: House of Commons.

CIHI. 2018. "A Canadian First: CIHI to Measure Access to Mental Health and Addictions Services and to Home and Community Care." Canadian Institute for Health Information. July 3, 2018. https://www.cihi.ca/en/a-canadian-first-cihi-to-measure-access-to-mental-health-and-addictions-services-and-to-home-and.

Department of Finance Canada. 2017. *Building a Strong Middle Class*. Ottawa: Department of Finance. https://www.budget.gc.ca/2017/docs/plan/budget-2017-en.pdf.

Department of Finance Canada. 2019. "Investing in the Middle Class." Ottawa: Department of Finance. https://www.budget.gc.ca/2019/docs/plan/budget-2019-en.pdf

Government of Canada. 2017a. "Regulations Amending the Patented Medicines Regulations," *Canada Gazette*. http://www.gazette.gc.ca/rp-pr/p1/2017/2017-12-02/html/reg2-eng.html.

Governement of Canada. 2017b. "Government of Canada Actions on Opioids 2016 and 2017". Ottawa: Governement of Canada. https://www.canada.ca/content/dam/hc-sc/documents/services/publications/healthy-living/actions-opioids-2016-2017/Opioids-Response-Report-EN-FINAL.pdf.

Governement of Canada. 2018. "Towards Implementation of National Pharmacare: Discussion Paper". Ottawa: Governement of Canada. https://www.canada.ca/content/dam/hc-sc/documents/corporate/publications/council_on_pharmacare_EN.PDF.

Health Canada. 2016. "Medical Assistance in Dying." Ottawa: Health Canada. https://www.canada.ca/en/health-canada/services/medical-assistance-dying.html.

Health Canada. 2017. "A Common Statement of Principles on Shared Health Priorities." Ottawa: Health Canada. https://www.canada.ca/en/health-canada/corporate/transparency/health-agreements/principles-shared-health-priorities.html.

Hoskins, Eric. 2019. "Interim Report of the Advisory Council on the Implementation of National Pharmacare." Advisory Council on the Implementation of National Pharmacare. https://www.canada.ca/content/dam/hc-sc/documents/corporate/about-health-canada/public-engagement/external-advisory-bodies/implementation-national-pharmacare/interim-report/interim-report.pdf.

Kates, David. 2014. "As Accord Expires, Ottawa Takes a Back Seat on Health Care Policy," *O.Canada.Com*, May 16, 2014. https://o.canada.com/health-2/as-accord-expires-ottawa-takes-a-back-seat-on-health-care-policy.

Liberal Party of Canada. 2015. *Real Change: A New Plan for a Strong Middle Class*. https://www.liberal.ca/wp-content/uploads/2015/10/New-plan-for-a-strong-middle-class.pdf.

Maioni, Antonia, and Miriam Smith. 2003. "Health Care and Canadian Federalism." In *New Trends in Canadian Federalism*, François Rocher and Miriam Smith (eds.), Second edition: 295–312. Peterborough: Broadview Press.

Marchildon, Greg. 2016. "Bilateral Health Agreements between the Federal and Provincial/Territorial Governments in Canada," 13. *IRPP Insight.* http://irpp.org/research-studies/insight-no13/.

Office of the Parliamentary Budget Officer. 2017. "Federal Cost of a National Pharmacare Program." http://www.pbo-dpb.gc.ca/web/default/files/Documents/Reports/2017/Pharmacare/Pharmacare_EN_2017_11_07.pdf.

Parliament of Canada. 1985. *Canada Health Act.* http://laws-lois.justice.gc.ca/PDF/C-6.pdf.

Picard, André. 2017. "Provinces Get Their Cash, but Do We Get Better Health Care?," *The Globe and Mail*, March 13, 2017, sec. Opinion. https://www.theglobeandmail.com/opinion/provinces-get-their-cash-but-do-we-get-better-health-care/article34283737/.

Scoffield, Heather. 2011. "Ottawa's Health-Care Role about Measurement, Not Money, Aglukkaq Says," *The Globe and Mail*, December 29, 2011. https://www.theglobeandmail.com/news/politics/ottawas-health-care-role-about-measurement-not-money-aglukkaq-says/article4085704/.

Trudeau, Justin. 2015. "Minister of Health Mandate Letter (November 12, 2015)," November 12, 2015. https://pm.gc.ca/eng/minister-health-mandate-letter_2015.

# Chapter 12
# Gender Equality, Diversity, and Inclusion: Between Real Change and Branding

Karen Bird

The 2015 federal election returned a self-proclaimed feminist prime minister who appointed Canada's first gender-balanced cabinet, and assigned portfolios comprised of priority policy files to women, Indigenous, and visible minority ministers. Over the following four years, Trudeau's government has implemented a host of policy initiatives related to gender equality, diversity and inclusion. The fact that many of these appeared nowhere on the Liberal Party campaign platform raises questions about the traditional promissory principle of representation, which concerns "the normative duty to keep promises made in the authorizing election" (Mansbridge 2003, 516). Of course, governments are often faced with issues that were not foreseen, and for which they could not seek prior authorization by the voters. This chapter considers whether the policy developments on the gender, diversity, and inclusion front were propelled by a configuration of external events and forces that could not have been predicted during the 2015 campaign. It also weighs the possibility that the diverse and strong female representation in Trudeau's cabinet is a key contributor to the expansion of this legislative agenda.

## 12.1 DIVERSITY AND INCLUSION: PLATFORM PROMISES AND NEW INITIATIVES

The Liberal platform contained more than 60 pledges addressing principles of diversity and inclusion. Most of these targeted Indigenous people, immigrants, and refugees. Fewer than one-third addressed women and gender issues, while a handful of others concerned official language minorities, northern residents, and those with disabilities. As immigrant, refugee, and Indigenous-related platform promises are addressed in other chapters, the focus here is on diversity and inclusion pledges for "other" groups (Table 12-1) and gender-focused initiatives (Table 12-2).

TABLE 12-1 – Promises and Verdicts Concerning "Other" Groups*

| # | PROMISE | VERDICT |
|---|---------|---------|
| 8.02 | We will develop a new official languages plan to support English and French linguistic minorities. | Kept |
| 8.03 | We will establish a free, online service for learning and retaining English and French as second languages. | Kept in part |
| **9.14** | **We will reinstate the Court Challenges Program of Canada cut by Stephen Harper.** | **Kept** |
| **10.01** | **We will ensure that all federal services are delivered in full compliance with the Official Languages Act.** | **Kept in part** |
| 10.10 | To help northern residents and to help our northern economies grow, we will increase the residency component of the Northern Residents Deduction by 33 percent to a maximum of $22 per day [and] index this benefit so that it keeps pace with inflation. | Kept |
| 12.10 | To eliminate systemic barriers and deliver equality of opportunity to all Canadians living with disabilities, we will consult with provinces, territories, and other stakeholders to introduce a National Disabilities Act. | Kept |
| 12.21 | We will prioritize investments in affordable housing and seniors' facilities. | Kept in part |

\* Source: Trudeau Polimetre and Liberal Party of Canada platform
\*\* The most important pledges are in **bold**.

### 12.1.1 The Court Challenges Program

Amongst the diversity and inclusion pledges, a significant marker of promise fulfillment is the reinstatement of the federal Court Challenges Program (CCP) (promise 9.14). This was one of Trudeau's main campaign promises. The CCP was created in 1978 under Prime Minister Pierre Trudeau to assist official language minorities (Francophones outside Quebec and Anglophones inside Quebec) to challenge provincial legislation that might violate the Constitution Act of 1867. Following implementation of the Charter of Rights, it was expanded to provide support for challenges to federal laws based on Charter sections 15 (equality rights) and 28 (gender equality rights). With a budget of less than $3 million annually, the program provided modest funding to minority and women's groups for pursuing litigation, some of which resulted in major Supreme Court rulings in areas ranging from voting rights for prisoners, to same-sex marriage, to access to education in minority official languages. However, this program became a source of contention among leading conservative thinkers who linked the CCP to suspicions of increasing judicial activism and the erosion of traditional democratic processes (Brodie 2001; Morton and Knopff 2000). Stephen Harper's Conservative government canceled the CCP in 2006 as one of its first acts, though it restored funding partially in 2008.

In addition to returning funding, the Liberal government extended the program to subsidize claims based on a broader range of rights, including those rooted in sections 2, 3, and 7 of the Charter (protecting, respectively, freedom of religion, expression, and association; the right to vote; and life, liberty, and security of the person). The modernized CCP has subsequently supported lawsuits against the federal government's use of solitary confinement in prison and may yet be used to challenge Quebec's ability to ban public employees from wearing religious symbols in the workplace. The reforms also established an independent governance structure that oversees which applicants receive funding, addressing critics' concerns that the program historically favoured some kinds of test cases over others.

While these changes have been widely applauded in legal circles, some substantive concerns remain. One is that claims based on Charter section 35 and section 25 (Aboriginal and Treaty) rights are not eligible for funding. Minority and women's rights advocates have criticized the relaunched program for failing to return the historic mandate to protect substantive equality, meaning that funding may be used to support challenges to some of their hard-fought gains (restrictions on hate speech, LGBTQ rights, women's reproductive choice). The political "spin" of the relaunch also raised some eyebrows. Though the program now covers a broad range of rights, the government has continued to emphasize its protections for linguistic minorities. The main spokesperson on the file was not the Justice Minister, but rather Quebec MP and then-minister of

Heritage Mélanie Joly, who framed the restored CCP almost exclusively in terms of protecting official minority language rights. Some have also marveled at the "uncanny convenience" that the announcement came almost immediately following Trudeau's abandonment of his promised electoral reform (Hays 2017). The rush to deliver on this promise at the right moment may explain why the program was not enshrined in law, as was recommended in the Justice Committee's report (House of Commons 2016). In the case of the CCP, it appears that "deliverology" is as much about sharpening the optics of pledge fulfillment, including the timing and framing of policy delivery, as it is about keeping campaign promises.

### 12.1.2   Official Languages

The CCP reinstatement was part of a bundle of campaign pledges to "renew the federal government's commitment to our official languages" (promises 8.02, 8.03, 10.1) and to CBC/Radio Canada to ensure media in both official languages (promise 2.05), all of which the Liberals argued had been ignored under Stephen Harper. These have been largely fulfilled. Funding for CBC/Radio-Canada has been restored with a cash injection of $625 million over five years (Department of Finance 2016). The government has also developed a new official languages plan, investing $2.5 billion over five years to strengthen the declining population of Canadian Francophonie and support minority English-speaking communities in Quebec (Heritage Canada 2018). Regarding compliance with the Official Languages Act (OLA), it introduced a set of significant amendments to the OLA regulations (Government of Canada 2018). These revisions provide a more expansive method for measuring the minority language population and deeming services in that official language mandatory. More than 600 additional federal offices and services are expected to be newly designated as bilingual under these changes. The amended regulations help address concerns about the erosion of minority French language rights under Conservative governments in Ontario and New Brunswick.

### 12.1.3   Racism and Religious Discrimination Including Islamophobia

The Liberals have pursued initiatives beyond their campaign promises on diversity and inclusion. A symbolic gesture of significant measure came in response to rookie MP Iqra Khalid's motion proposing that the government "recognize the need to quell the increasing public climate of hate and fear" and "condemn Islamophobia and all forms of systemic racism and religious discrimination." Khalid, a Liberal backbencher from the multiculturally diverse riding of Mississauga–Erin Mills, had tabled her non-binding motion M-103 in December 2016. However, it only came up for debate just five days after the January 2017 Quebec City mosque shooting where six Muslim men were killed. It sparked a firestorm of reaction, with opponents painting it as a slippery slope toward limiting freedom of speech and even bringing in Sharia law. In the end, the House voted 201 to 91 in support of the motion, which was then referred to a Standing Committee for further study. The Committee's report made 30 recommendations, several of which were in turn adopted (House of Commons 2018). Notably, the 2018 budget introduced $50 million for new anti-racism and multicultural programming, as well as increased funding for Statistics Canada to better analyze and collect data on diversity and inclusion, including hate crimes. The government also completed a Task Force on Building a Diverse and Inclusive Public Service and rolled out new practices for diverse and equitable hiring and promotion within the federal public service and within academic institutions receiving federal research grants (Treasury Board of Canada Secretariat 2018). However, it declined the Committee's recommendation to make January 29 a national day of remembrance and action on Islamophobia and other forms of religious discrimination.

## 12.2 GENDER EQUALITY: PLATFORM PROMISES AND NEW INITIATIVES

Out of 353 Liberal Party platform promises tracked by the Trudeau Polimetre, just 17 (4.8%) are explicitly gender related (see highlights in Table 12.2). Chief among them are the commitment to gender parity in cabinet (7.47) and to conducting gender-based analysis plus (GBA+) in all federal departments (7.22). A large number of pledges concerned issues of sexual violence and harassment (promises 8.01, 9.01, 9.03, 9.12, 9.13, 9.20, 9.21, 9.22, 12.18). There were also promises addressing homelessness and the need for shelters and transitional housing for those facing domestic violence (12.21, 12.22), as well as maternity and shared-parental leave rules (6.07, 6.08), and support for abortion services as part of international aid (12.11). While commendable in its concern for the pressing issue of sexual harassment and violence—especially as this election took place prior to the viral spread of the #MeToo movement—there were many gender-related issues left off the Liberal Party platform. Missing from the list of campaign pledges was any reference to universal child care, pay equity, Status of Women Canada, or LGBTQ issues.

TABLE 12-2 – Selected Promises and Verdicts Concerning Gender Equality and Women

| Nº | PROMISES | VERDICTS |
|----|----------|----------|
| 6.08 | We will introduce more flexible parental benefits that will make it possible for parents to take a longer leave—up to 18 months when combined with maternity benefits—at a lower benefit level. | Kept |
| 7.23 | **We will also ensure that federal departments are conducting the gender-based impact analyses that have been required of them for the past 20 years.** | Kept |
| 7.48 | **We will include an equal number of women and men in our Cabinet.** | Kept |
| 8.01 | To help those who are new to Canada, we will change the rules so that spouses immigrating to Canada receive immediate permanent residency—rather than a two-year waiting period. | Kept |
| 9.01 | **We will launch a national public inquiry into missing and murdered Indigenous women and girls in Canada, to seek recommendations on concrete actions that governments, law enforcement, and others can take to solve these crimes and prevent future ones.** | Kept |
| 9.13 | We will take action to ensure that Parliament and federal institutions—including the public service, the RCMP, and the Canadian Armed Forces—are workplaces free from harassment and sexual violence. | Kept |
| 9.20 | We will amend the Criminal Code to reverse onus on bail for those with previous convictions of intimate partner violence. | Kept in part |
| 1.14 | **We will ensure that Canada's valuable aid initiative on Maternal, Newborn and Child Health (MNCH) is driven by evidence and outcomes, not ideology. […] We will cover the full range of reproductive health services as part of MNCH initiatives.** | Kept |
| 12.16 | Working together with experts and advocates, we will develop and implement a comprehensive federal gender violence strategy and action plan, aligned with existing provincial strategies. | Kept |
| 12.20 | We will increase investments in growing and maintaining Canada's network of shelters and transition houses, as part of our broader investment in social infrastructure. | Kept |

\* Source: Trudeau Polimetre and Liberal Party of Canada platform
\*\* The most important pledges are in **bold**.

The Liberal government has fulfilled thirteen of its seventeen gender-equality focused promises and partially fulfilled four others. The first and most visible of these was Trudeau's naming of a gender-balanced cabinet. That group of 30 ministers included 15 women, but also two Indigenous members (including in the key post of Justice Minister and Attorney General), five of South Asian descent, two with disabilities, and one who had arrived in Canada as a refugee. The government also conducted Canada's first-ever gender-based analysis of the federal budget (Department of Finance 2017) and passed subsequent legislation, entitled the Canadian Gender Budgeting Act, under budget Bill C-86 enshrining GBA+ in the budgetary and financial management processes. In March 2017, on International Women's Day, it announced a re-orientation of Canada's foreign-aid strategy regarding women's maternal health that ended the previous government's policy of prohibiting Canadian assistance for pregnancy terminations. In October 2018, it passed Bill C-65, "An Act to amend the Canada Labour Code," which requires the RCMP and other federally regulated workplaces such as banks, telecommunications, and transport industries to make substantial changes in how they address workplace violence and harassment. In December 2018, it passed Bill-51, ushering in major reforms under the Criminal Code to protect sexual assault victims from intrusive questioning. It also created a comprehensive federal Strategy to Prevent and Address Gender-Based Violence, backed by $100.9 million in funding over five years, plus $20.7 million per year ongoing to support implementation (Status of Women Canada 2017). And it developed a ten-year, $40 billion National Housing Strategy, in which at least 25% of overall investments are to support projects specifically targeting the needs of women and girls.

Finally, it is noteworthy that while the Liberal government introduced a new parental sharing benefit (allowing five additional weeks of leave for mothers and fathers when they both take time off) and revised maternity benefit rules to offer working women greater flexibility, there is still no formal rule allowing MPs to take baby leave. So, while Democratic Institutions Minister Karina Gould made history as the first federal cabinet minister to take a maternity leave, it was a matter she had to negotiate with the Prime Minister's Office (PMO) and party whip.

Beyond fulfilling these platform promises, the Trudeau government has implemented a dozen other gender-focused legislative reforms during its time in office. In June 2017, it passed Bill C-16 amending the Criminal Code's hate crime provisions and the Canadian Human Rights Act to include gender identity and expression and to increase protections of

LGBTQ2 and gender non-conforming individuals. As part of the October 2018 omnibus budget bill, it upgraded Status of Women Canada to become a full department under the law—the Department for Women and Gender Equality (WAGE)—reestablished its feminist advocacy role, and expanded its mandate for gender equality to include sexual orientation, gender identity, and expression. As an element of its GBA+ initiative, the government created a Gender, Diversity and Inclusion Statistics Hub as well as a whole-of-government Gender Results Framework to track and monitor progress on gender equality. Several reforms were taken to promote gender balance and diversity in the workplace, including in universities and research chairs, STEM (science, technology, engineering, mathematics) fields, business entrepreneurship, and skilled trades. The judicial appointment process was redesigned to stress diversity, which has boosted both the share of female applicants and the appointment rate of women to the bench (Fine 2018). The government also made amendments through Bill C-25 to the Canadian Business Corporations Act, adding "comply or explain" rules to advance diversity on governing boards and in senior management—though the law does not make such policies mandatory and does not define *diversity*. Finally, the government used Canada's G7 presidency over the course of 2018 to elevate gender equality as a priority. As part of that initiative, it adopted a Feminist International Assistance Policy, renewed Canada's Woman, Peace and Security National Action Plan, and created a new Canadian Ambassador for Women, Peace and Security.

These advances are momentous compared to where feminism and women's issues were on the Harper government's agenda (Bird and Rowe 2013). However, the Liberal record is not without its disappointments. Notably the government refused in October 2016 to support NDP MP Kennedy Stewart's private Member's bill to advance gender parity among MPs. Bill C-237, the Candidate Gender Equity Act, proposed to financially penalize parties that run a larger proportion of men than women in a general election. The NDP, which fielded 43% female candidates in the 2015 election, would not have been penalized, but the Liberals, who ran 31% and the Conservatives with 20%, would have taken a financial hit. The proposal met the typical fate of private Members' bills and was defeated by a vote of 68 in favour to 209 opposed. In the free vote, 23 Liberal backbenchers voted for the bill, while the Minister of Status of Women, Patty Hajdu, and the rest of the Liberal cabinet voted against. This posed an optics problem for a government that had made headlines a year earlier for its much-vaunted parity cabinet, and critics argued that it was a lost opportunity to make parity a more deeply institutionalized norm that would apply as governments come and go.

Progressive feminists have also criticized the Trudeau government for pursuing policy that is steeped in the neoliberal discourse of "social investment" in women's access to work and enhanced productivity, but that fails to address the pressing needs of low income women. They point to the Liberals' failure to deliver publicly funded universal child care, a commitment dating back to the Martin government. They also remark that the promised delivery on an 18-month parental leave package comes with no additional spending, but simply extends existing Employment Insurance (EI) benefits by six additional months (CBC 2017; Friendly, Prentice and Ballantyne 2017).

## 12.3 EXPLAINING THE EXPANDING LEGISLATIVE AGENDA ON GENDER EQUALITY, DIVERSITY, AND INCLUSION

The diversity and inclusion policies of the Trudeau Liberals are remarkable for both promise fulfillment and action that transcends the party's campaign platform. That is especially true of the government's gender-focused legislative program, which began tentatively and then picked up steam as the mandate progressed. No doubt, this was propelled by a unique configuration of external events and forces, including the election in November 2016 of U.S. President Donald Trump and the growing momentum of the #MeToo movement. However, theories on the impact of female representation and executive dominance in parliamentary democracies suggest that the strong female representation in Trudeau's cabinet is likely another contributing factor (Atchison 2015). Two of the most powerful women on the Trudeau cabinet have been Foreign Affairs Minister Chrystia Freeland and former Justice Minister Jody Wilson-Raybould. We turn here to briefly weigh their impact.

Canada's feminist foreign policy began tentatively under Foreign Affairs Minister Stéphane Dion, but was advanced more vigorously with Chrystia Freeland at the helm over the last two years of Trudeau's mandate (Ho 2018; Thompson and Asquith 2018). How much of this is due to having a woman in the role is impossible to say with certainty, as circumstances in the world had changed once Freeland took over in February 2017. Yet, comparison of the mandate letters to each minister shows virtually no difference with respect to gender issues, suggesting that much of the change was driven by Freeland and her team. Further evidence can be gleaned from differences between their first major foreign policy speeches. In March 2016, Dion articulated a principle of "responsible conviction" by which he defended, among other things, the Liberals' campaign commitment not to cancel a $15 billion defence contract with Saudi Arabia. In contrast, Freeland's major statement, delivered in June 2017, emphasized the importance of a rules-based international order.

Freeland's first noted accomplishment as Minister was a months-in-planning secret mission that rescued several dozen persecuted gay men from the Russian republic of Chechnya, and granted them asylum in Canada (Ibbitson 2017). A year later, in September 2018, she hosted the first-ever women foreign ministers' meeting and announced the creation of a new Ambassador for Women, Peace and Security. Undoubtedly, Minister Freeland's most significant gendered mark in this portfolio has been her strong stance with respect to women's rights in Saudi Arabia. After a series of orchestrated tweets triggered retaliatory diplomatic and trade sanctions from the Saudi kingdom, Freeland stood firm, proclaiming in August 2018, "We are always going to speak up for human rights; we're always going to speak up for women's rights; and that is not going to change." Her leadership on this file was confirmed in early January 2019, when Canada granted asylum to Rahaf Mohammed, the Saudi teenager who drew worldwide notice on Twitter after fleeing to Thailand to escape male guardianship laws and her abusive family. Commenting on Canada's role in assisting that young woman, Professor Bessma Momani (2019) proclaimed, "This is us finally walking the walk of being a feminist government in the world."

Jody Wilson-Raybould, in her former role as Canada's first Indigenous female Justice Minister and Attorney General, has been equally consequential, though for entirely different reasons. Above and beyond her other major files (assisted dying, legalization of marijuana), Wilson-Raybould led important feminist reforms. Her first act was to withdraw formally the Supreme Court appeal process launched by the Harper government to ban the niqab at citizenship ceremonies. She also introduced important changes including revisions to the Criminal Code to clarify sexual assault and domestic violence offenses, and changes to the judicial appointment process that have improved gender balance on the federal bench. However, it is her resignation from cabinet over allegations of political interference by the PMO with respect to the prosecution of engineering giant SNC-Lavalin that has been most impactful, both in terms of damage to Trudeau's feminist brand and the trust that had been built with Indigenous communities. While the full story cannot be recounted here, one aspect that merits attention is the degree to which the public's sense of Wilson-Raybould's integrity within the corridors of power hinges on her identity as an Indigenous woman (Ball et al. 2019; Green and Starblanket 2019). The notion of Puglaas (her traditional name) speaking truth to power is consistent with perceptions of women's higher moral nature and incorruptibility in politics (Goetz 2007), and with acknowledged tensions between indigeneity and the world of partisan politics (Maddison 2010). Puglaas herself has elaborated on her identity as the source of her convictions about truth, justice, and power. She did so in the closing words of her February 27 testimony to the Justice committee, but also in a much earlier speech made immediately prior to announcing her Liberal candidacy (Wilson-Raybould 2015). Relating her upbringing as a descendant of the Musgamagw-Tsawateineuk/Laich-Kwil-Tach peoples, she described the customary position she held within this matriarchal society:

> In our potlatch the highest-ranking male leaders are called Hamatsa… I am a Hiligaxste', a role always held by women. One of my jobs is to lead my Hamatsa, the chief, into the big house. This role can be translated as one that "corrects the chief's path." We show them the way; a metaphor for life and in the potlatch symbolized in our rituals where now symbolically the power of the Hamatsa is "tamed" and he is ready to be the chief.

The centralization of power in the PMO is not a new feature of Canadian government (Savoie 1999). However, Wilson-Raybould's resignation from cabinet shone a bright light on Trudeau's broken promise to reverse that trend and govern with greater openness and transparency (CBC 2015). It was a clear repudiation of his claim that "government by cabinet is back" (Hall 2015). Her temerity in acting to curb the power at the centre, alongside Chrystia Freeland's leadership in shaping Canada's feminist foreign policy, suggest that the diverse composition of Trudeau's cabinet was not merely of symbolic value, but has had substantive impact.

## CONCLUSION

Finally, what conclusions can we draw about the Trudeau government's promise delivery with respect to gender equality, diversity, and inclusion? First, the government's record of action on this front merits praise. It is not whether Trudeau is a "fake feminist" that should concern us (Kingston 2016), for a lot of feminist work has been done by this government. And, in light of the xenophobia being whipped up by Brexiteers and Trumpians, it is worth pondering that a Conservative government might have steered a very different course. Nevertheless, the slate of actions without promises (as opposed to actions with promises), together with the evident concentration of power in the PMO, raise deep concerns about the chain of promise making, delivery, and accountability as well as the role of backroom operators in this process. "Deliverology," in this sense, seems largely untethered to principles of democratic accountability. Instead, it appears symptomatic of strong, central control that is focused on establishing and maintaining a brand, keeping a prime minister in power, and getting a government re-elected. Still, in light of Puglaas openly challenging that power, it is conceivable that the seeds of democratic transformation may well lie in a cabinet that truly looks like Canada.

REFERENCES

Atchison, Amy. 2015. "The Impact of Female Cabinet Ministers on a Female-Friendly Labor Environment," *Journal of Women, Politics & Policy*, 36 (4): 388–414.

Ball, David P., Jenna Moon, and Kevin Maimann. 2019. "Jody Wilson-Raybould testimony was 'Canada's Indigenous constitution in action,' say experts," *Toronto Star*, February 28, 2019. https://www.thestar.com/news/canada/2019/02/28/jody-wilson-raybould-testimony-was-canadas-indigenous-constitution-in-action-say-experts.html.

Bird, Karen, and Andrea Rowe. 2013. "Women, Feminism and the Harper Conservatives." In *Conservatism in Canada*, Jim Farney and David Rayside (eds): 165-83. Toronto: University of Toronto Press.

Brodie, Ian. 2001. "Interest Group Litigation and the Embedded State: Canada's Court Challenges Program," *Canadian Journal of Political Science*, 34 (2): 357–376.

CBC. 2015. "Justin Trudeau interview with Peter Mansbridge," *CBC News*, September 15, 2015. https://www.cbc.ca/news/politics/canada-election-2015-justin-trudeau-interview-peter-mansbridge-full-transcript-1.3219779.

CBC. 2017. "Liberal's 18-month parental leave a disservice to women, says critic." *The Current*, March 27, 2017. https://www.cbc.ca/radio/thecurrent/the-current-for-march-27-2017-the-current-1.4040102/liberal-s-18-month-parental-leave-a-disservice-to-women-says-critic-1.4040118

Department of Finance. 2016. *Growing the Middle Class*. Ottawa: Department of Finance. https://www.budget.gc.ca/2016/docs/plan/budget2016-en.pdf.

Department of Finance. 2017. *Building a Strong Middle Class*. Ottawa: Department of Finance. https://www.budget.gc.ca/2017/docs/plan/toc-tdm-en.html.

Fine, Sean. 2018. "Ottawa appointing more female judges, but bench still short of gender parity," *The Globe and Mail*, June 18, 2019. https://www.theglobeandmail.com/canada/article-ottawa-appointing-more-female-judges-but-bench-still-short-of-gender/.

Friendly, Martha, Susan Prentice and Morna Ballantyne. 2018. "No Equality Without Universal Childcare." *Policy Options*, March 8, 2018. https://policyoptions.irpp.org/magazines/march-2018/no-equality-without-universal-child-care/

Goetz, Anne Marie. 2007. "Political Cleaners: Women as the New Anti-Corruption Force?," *Development and Change*, 38 (1): 87–105.

Governement of Canada. 2018. *Regulations Amending the Official Languages (Communications with and Services to the Public) Regulations.* Ottawa: Governement of Canada. https://www.canada.ca/en/treasury-board-secretariat/services/values-ethics/official-languages/public-services/regulations-amending-official-languages-communications-services-public-regulations.html.

Green, Joyce, and Gina Starblanket. 2019. "The shameful mistreatment of Jody Wilson-Raybould on full display," *The Globe and Mail*, February 13, 2019. *https://www.theglobeandmail.com/opinion/article-the-shameful-mistreatment-of-jody-wilson-raybould-on-full-display/*.

Hall, Chris. 2015. "Justin Trudeau begins his bold experiment in 'government by cabinet'," *CBC News*, November 5, 2015. https://www.cbc.ca/news/politics/government-cabinet-chris-hall-1.3304812.

Hay, Nicholas. 2017. "Return of the Court Challenges Program: Timely, Critical and Deficient," *TheCourt.ca*, February 13, 2017. http://www.thecourt.ca/the-return-of-the-court-challenges-program-timely-critical-deficient/.

Heritage Canada. 2018. *Action Plan for Official Languages—2018–2023: Investing in Our Future.* Ottawa: Heritage Canada. https://www.canada.ca/content/dam/pch/documents/services/official-languages-bilingualism/official-languages-action-plan/action-plan.pdf.

Ho, Karen H. 2018. "Canada puts its feminist foreign policy to the test," OpenCanada.org special issue: Is the Future of Foreign Policy Feminist? https://www.opencanada.org/indepth/future-foreign-policy-feminist/.

House of Commons. 2016. "Access to Justice, Part I: Court Challenges Program'. Report of the Standing Committee on Justice and Human Rights." https://www.ourcommons.ca/Content/Committee/421/JUST/Reports/RP8377632/justrp04/justrp04-e.pdf.

House of Commons. 2018. "Taking Action Against Systemic Racism and Religious Discrimination Including Islamophobia." Report of the Standing Committee on Canadian Heritage. http://www.ourcommons.ca/Content/Committee/421/CHPC/Reports/RP9315686/chpcrp10/chpcrp10-e.pdf.

Ibbitson, John. 2017. "How Canada has been secretly giving asylum to gay people in Chechnya fleeing persecution," *The Globe and Mail*, September 1, 2017. https://www.theglobeandmail.com/news/canada-chechnya-gay-asylum/article36145997/.

Kingston, Anne. 2016. "Is Justin Trudeau a fake feminist?," *Maclean's*, September 8, 2016. https://www.macleans.ca/politics/ottawa/is-justin-trudeau-a-fake-feminist/.

Maddison, Sarah. 2010. "White Parliament, Black Politics: The Dilemmas of Indigenous Parliamentary Representation," *Australian Journal of Political Science*, 45 (4): 663–680.

Mansbridge, Jane. 2003. "Rethinking Representation," *American Political Science Review*, 97: 515-28.

Momani, Bessma. 2019. "By granting asylum to Saudi woman, Canada shows its moral leadership," *The Globe and Mail*, January 11, 2019. https://www.theglobeandmail.com/opinion/article-by-granting-asylum-to-saudi-woman-canada-shows-its-moral-leadership/.

Morton, F. L., and Rainer Knopff. 2000. *The Charter Revolution and the Court Party*. Peterborough: Broadview Press.

Savoie, Donald. 1999. *Governing from the Centre: The Concentration of Power in Canadian Politics*. Toronto: University of Toronto Press.

Wilson-Raybould, Jody. 2015. "'Power' A presentation by Regional Chief of the BC Assembly of First Nations," at the 25th Annual National Retreat for Women. Inn at Laurel Point, April 17–19, 2015, Victoria, BC.

Status of Women Canada. It's Time: Canada's Strategy to Prevent and Address Gender-Based Violence. Ottawa: Status of Women Canada. https://cfc-swc.gc.ca/violence/strategy-strategie/index-en.html.

Thompson, Lyric, and Christina Asquith. 2018. "One Small Step for Feminist Foreign Policy," *Foreign Policy*, September 20, 2018. https://foreignpolicy.com/2018/09/20/one-small-step-for-feminist-foreign-policy-women-canada/.

Treasury Board of Canada Secretariat. 2018. *Building a Diverse and Inclusive Public Service: Final Report of the Joint Union/Management Task Force on Diversity and Inclusion*. Ottawa: Treasury Board of Canada Secretariat. https://www.canada.ca/en/treasury-board-secretariat/corporate/reports/building-diverse-inclusive-public-service-final-report-joint-union-management-task-force-diversity-inclusion.html#toc12.

# Chapter 13
# Renewing the Relationship with Indigenous Peoples: An Ambitious Discourse, Limited Accomplishments

Thierry Rodon and Martin Papillon

The Trudeau government chose to focus its Indigenous policy on the principle of reconciliation. The rhetoric adopted was generous and the agenda ambitious, in stark contrast to the previous government, which focused on issue management, without really seeking to address the structural foundations of the strained relationship between Indigenous peoples and the federal government. By choosing reconciliation as the central theme, and especially by making the implementation of the Truth and Reconciliation Commission's (TRC) 94 calls to action a mandate priority, the new government was setting the bar very high when it came to Canada's relationships with Indigenous peoples. In fact, expectations were so high that the government, despite unprecedented activism on Indigenous issues, could not help but disappoint observers. Some controversial decisions, such as the approval of the Trans Mountain pipeline despite opposition from several Indigenous nations, only reinforced the cynicism of those who believed for a while that the Trudeau government would truly transform the relationship between Indigenous Peoples and the Canadian government.

Institutions that are 150 years old cannot be changed in a matter of months. The legal-administrative system that governs relations between Indigenous peoples and the settler state, more particularly the Indian Act, has deep historical roots. It has created a well-entrenched bureaucratic culture and a set of practices and expectations that are hard to transform (Ladner and Orsini 2003; Morden 2016).

Even if relationships with Indigenous peoples were genuinely a top priority early in the mandate, other political and economic interests outweighed them eventually as the electoral cycle closed. Geopolitical and economic priorities (such as Alberta's oil, for example) took precedence over the reconciliation agenda. This is hardly surprising given Indigenous peoples only represent 4.9% of the Canadian population (Statistics Canada 2017) and tend to vote in lower proportions than other Canadians (Dabin et al. 2019). In addition, a recent survey by Angus Reid (2018) shows that public opinion remains divided on Indigenous issues. Sixty-six percent of Canadians believe that Indigenous peoples should accept integration into Canadian society and that we should stop apologizing for assimilation policies such as residential schools. Ironically, this survey shows that 60% of respondents also believe that the Canadian government neglects Indigenous peoples. As a result, political gains are not that obvious for a government seeking re-election. With the next election being imminent, it is not surprising that the government is now trying to lower expectations. That being said, as we will see in this chapter, the government's record on Indigenous issues is not entirely negative.

## 13.1 PROMISES TO IMPROVE THE RELATIONSHIP WITH INDIGENOUS PEOPLES

Federal programs for First Nations and other Indigenous communities have long faced chronic underfunding in comparison with equivalent programs addressed to other Canadian citizens through provincial and territorial authorities. This underfunding is well documented. The Auditor General of Canada (2011) notes that "structural impediments severely limit the delivery of public services to First Nations communities and hinder improvements of the living conditions on reserves." In a recent decision, the Canadian Human Rights Tribunal (2016) concludes that this underfunding is a form of discrimination based on ethnicity. Systemic discrimination, high rates of incarceration, and the victimization of Indigenous women are other symptoms of a deep social crisis that is increasingly difficult to ignore. The Idle No More movement, which began in 2012 in reaction to the Harper government's policies, reminded Canadians that Indigenous peoples' patience, especially within the younger generations, has its limits.

The 2015 Liberal platform therefore clearly distinguished itself from the previous government's policies by proposing an ambitious policy agenda based on reconciliation. The 25 Indigenous-related promises of the 2015 Liberal platform listed for the Polimetre clearly highlight two main themes, namely reinvestment in services and relationship renewal (respectively, 52% and 48% of these promises were oriented toward these Indigenous issues). Table 13.1 shows some of the most important election promises in this regard. The verdicts are based on a quantitative and qualitative analysis of policy outputs as of December 31, 2018. There are obviously some limitations to such an analysis, particularly with respect to structural reforms to the relationship, whose effects will only be felt in the medium or long term. It should also be noted that several proposals are still in the works at the time of writing. In that respect, a true final assessment of the proposed reforms will have to wait.

TABLE 13-1 – Most Important Promises for Reconciliation
with Indigenous Peoples and Their Verdicts

| # | PROMISE | VERDICT |
|---|---------|---------|
| **Reinvestment in Services to Indigenous Peoples** | | |
| 10.06 | We will ensure that the Kelowna Accord— and the spirit of reconciliation that drove it— is embraced, and its objectives implemented in a manner that meets today's challenges. | Kept in part |
| 10.03 | As part of this new fiscal relationship, we will also make sure that all First Nations receive equitable funding for child and family services provided on reserves. | Kept in part |
| 4.04 | We will invest $50 million in additional annual funding to the Post-Secondary Student Support Program, which supports Indigenous students attending post-secondary education, ensuring the program will keep up with growing demand. | Kept |
| 4.05 | We will also invest an additional $500 million over the next three years for building and refurbishing First Nations schools. | Kept |
| 10.05 | We will provide new funding to help Indigenous communities promote and preserve Indigenous languages and cultures. | In the works |
| 10.04 | We will immediately lift the two percent cap on funding for First Nations programs and work to establish a new fiscal relationship that gives First Nations communities sufficient, predictable, and sustained funding. | Kept in part |

| # | PROMISE | VERDICT |
|---|---------|---------|
| **Renewing the Relationship** | | |
| **10.08** | **We will immediately re-engage in a renewed nation-to-nation process with Indigenous Peoples to make progress on the issues most important to First Nations, the Métis Nation, and Inuit communities.** | Kept in part |
| **10.09** | **We will work alongside provinces and territories, and with First Nations, the Métis Nation, and Inuit, to enact the recommendations of the Truth and Reconciliation Commission.** | Kept in part |
| 7.43 | We recognize the relationship between Indigenous Peoples and the land, and will respect legal traditions and perspectives on environmental stewardship. | Kept in part |
| **7.44** | **We will undertake, in full partnership and consultation with First Nations, Inuit, and the Métis Nation, a full review of laws, policies, and operational practices.** | Kept in part |
| 10.22 | We will work, on a nation-to-nation basis, with the Métis Nation to advance reconciliation and renew the relationship, based on cooperation, respect for rights, our international obligations, and a commitment to end the status quo. | In the works |
| **9.01** | **We will launch a national public inquiry into missing and murdered Indigenous women and girls in Canada, to seek recommendations on concrete actions that governments, law enforcement, and others can take to solve these crimes and prevent future ones.** | Kept |
| 10.07 | As Prime Minister, Justin Trudeau will meet with First Nations, Métis Nation, and Inuit leaders each and every year of a Liberal government mandate. | Kept |

\* Source: Trudeau Polimetre and Liberal Party of Canada platform

\*\* The most important pledges are in **bold**.

Considering the promises made during the election campaign, the government's record of accomplishment appears positive, although several of these initiatives are still works-in-progress. However, a proper assessment of the government's performance should also include the more substantial commitments made *after* the election campaign, in ministerial mandate letters and following the tabling of the final report of the Truth and Reconciliation Commission (TRC) in December 2015.

The first mandate letter of then minister of Indigenous and Northern Affairs Carolyn Bennett announced the government's ambitions. The Prime Minister set considerable expectations by stating that "no relationship is more important to me and to Canada than the one with Indigenous peoples." He added that, "[...] the primary objective will be to build a nation-to-nation relationship with Indigenous peoples based on recognition, rights, respect, co-operation and collaboration." The Prime Minister also wanted to prioritize reinvestments in housing, health care, child welfare, and education. He reiterated his commitment to create an inquiry on missing and murdered Indigenous women and girls and finally urged the Minister to work with her colleagues to "act on the recommendations of the Truth and Reconciliation Commission, starting with the implementation of the United Nations Declaration on the Rights of Indigenous Peoples" (PMO 2015).

Without doing an exhaustive analysis of all measures taken since 2015, we assess in the following pages the government's performance in light of both its electoral promises and its early mandate commitments. We suggest that while some achievements are significant, the government ultimately failed to engage in real transformative change to Canada's relationship with Indigenous peoples.

## 13.2 SIGNIFICANT REINVESTMENT IN INDIGENOUS SERVICES

The new government committed to implement the Kelowna Accord, which the Martin government and the representatives of Indigenous organizations (promise 10.06) signed in 2005. It included investments of $5.1 billion over five years in various Indigenous services. The Harper government had refused to endorse the agreement and a reinvestment was long overdue.

The 2016 budget announced an additional funding of $8.4 billion over five years for Indigenous programs and services, primarily in education, health services, support to Indigenous children and families, languages, housing, and access to clean water (Department of Finance 2016). The 2017 budget provided additional funding of $3.4 billion over five years, primarily for infrastructure (Department of Finance 2017). The 2018 budget injected $4.7 billion in new funding for Indigenous infrastructure and services (Department of Finance 2018). The 2019 budget added 4.7 billion in new funding in similar areas while adding funds to create a National Council for Reconciliation and to reimburse or cancel all loans for comprehensive claims negotiations.

By adding up the last three Trudeau government budgets, we obtain a total of $21 billion in new funding over eight years. This may seem like a lot, but most of these investments are spread out over many years, well beyond the current mandate. Furthermore, as some commentators have pointed out, the money will barely meet the needs, which have become quite colossal after years of neglect (Blackstock 2019). For example, while it is recognized as an urgent infrastructure crisis, access to safe drinking water is still a problem on some remote reserves, as highlighted by the Parliamentary Budget Officer (PBO 2017). Despite some significant long-term challenges, we can nonetheless conclude that the Trudeau government has delivered on its promises to reinvest in Indigenous communities' services and infrastructure (promises 10.03, 10.05, 4.04, and 4.06).

## 13.3 A NECESSARY BUT CONTROVERSIAL COMMISSION OF INQUIRY

One of the Liberals' key promises was to establish a commission of inquiry into the disturbing number of missing and murdered Indigenous women and girls in Canada (promise 7.42), an issue put forward by many Indigenous organizations as well as by the United Nations Special Rapporteur on the rights of Indigenous peoples (Anaya 2014). This promise allowed the Liberals to distinguish themselves from the Harper government, which had refused such a commission, claiming that it was an individual criminality problem and not a societal one.

The commission of inquiry was quickly set up after the election. However, the organization experienced a chaotic start due to an ill-defined mandate and a workforce management problem. It quickly became stretched to the limit and was faced with too short of a timeframe. In response to numerous criticisms, including those from Indigenous organizations, the Trudeau government refused to prolong the mandate of the commission beyond 2019. The Commission tabled its final report in May 2019 with 231 calls to justice and a call to recognize a colonial genocide. It remains to be seen whether this report's impact will be similar to that of the TRC report.

## 13.4 IMPLEMENTATION OF THE TRC CALLS TO ACTION

The Trudeau government quickly endorsed the recommendations of the Truth and Reconciliation Commission (promise 10.09), which tabled its final report a few months after the 2015 election (TRC 2015). The

TRC's 94 calls to action go beyond federal jurisdiction. Many of these recommendations require long-term transformations that cannot be achieved in a single mandate. However, it is possible to review what has been accomplished so far. CBC News has created a web interface tracking all 94 calls to action. As of April 29, 2019, the website reports that to date, only 10 calls to action are fulfilled, 56 are announced or in the works, while 28 remain ignored (CBC 2019).

Fulfilled or in-progress calls to action include reforms to the child welfare system, reinvestments in education, better protection and promotion of Indigenous languages, the establishment of the Commission on Missing and Murdered Indigenous Women and Girls, funding for the National Centre for Truth and Reconciliation, and measures to implement the United Nations Declaration on the Rights of Indigenous Peoples.

The results are less promising for calls to actions touching on the structural foundations of the relationship. The TRC called for a comprehensive reform of the legal framework and institutions governing Indigenous-Crown relations, in particular through a new Royal Procla-mation reaffirming the principle of nation-to-nation relationships. As we will see in the next section, some measures were put forward to transform the relationship; however, the government ultimately failed in its attempt to achieve substantive changes.

## 13.5 RENEWING THE RELATIONSHIP BETWEEN THE CANADIAN GOVERNMENT AND INDIGENOUS PEOPLES

The institutional transformation of the relationship is undoubtedly the most ambitious aspect of the Trudeau government's Indigenous policy agenda (promises 10.07, 10.08, 10.16). This transformation is also at the heart of the TRC's calls to action. Admittedly, the government has brought forward an impressive number of reforms to that effect. While it is not possible to conduct a detailed review (see King and Pasternak 2018), we draw attention to those we consider most significant.

### 13.5.1 Crown/Indigenous Tables

Improving the relationship starts with better collaboration with the main actors concerned. Learning from past failures in this area, the Trudeau government established a series of bilateral and multilateral mechanisms to facilitate dialogue and jointly develop new policies and bills. In addition to an annual cabinet meeting with key Indigenous organizations, bilateral mechanisms were created with Inuit, Métis, and First Nations, alongside numerous sectoral tables, including education, health, child welfare, treaty implementation, self-government funding, and justice reforms (CIRNAC 2018a).

This model of collaborative policy development is certainly more consistent with a nation-to-nation view of the relationship, but the real test remains the Indigenous representatives' ability to influence government decisions. Some of these discussion tables resulted in a real policy co-development process, including policy on funding for self-governing, Indigenous governments, while others remained more contentious. This is particularly true of the proposed Recognition and Implementation of Indigenous Rights Framework. In some cases, such as the new Indigenous languages legislation and child and family welfare reforms, the federal government chose to go ahead despite a lack of consensus among Indigenous representatives (Kirkup 2019).

A comprehensive review of these "nation-to-nation" tables would be required to assess further their impact and the true influence of the Indigenous organizations that participated in these processes. The fact remains that the multiplication of processes also resulted in the dispersion of resources and energies, not only within the government machinery, but also and especially within the Indigenous organizations that must prioritize these many tables at the expense of other issues.

### 13.5.2 The Division of the Department of Indigenous Affairs

The division of the Department of Indigenous and Northern Affairs into two separate departments is part of the same drive for structural reforms aiming to change the very nature of the relationship with Indigenous peoples. Indigenous Services Canada (ISC), with a budget of $9.3 billion, is now responsible for delivering services to Indigenous communities. Crown-Indigenous Relations and Northern Affairs Canada (CIRNAC), with a budget of $2.2 billion, has the mandate to "renew the nation-to-nation/ government-to-government relationship between Canada and the First Nations, Inuit and Métis peoples, and to modernize Canadian government structures in support of self-government" (PMO 2017). Paradoxically, this institutional transformation took place without consultation with Indigenous organizations.

The long-term goal is to make ISC obsolete by fostering Indigenous control over programs and services currently managed by Ottawa. Instead, agreements modeled on transfers to provinces and territories would be used to ensure funding and the quality of services. It is again too early to judge the success of this initiative, as the government has not yet completed the separation of the department at the administrative level. Moreover, it is not clear whether the planned change in culture will take place. It should be noted, however, that from now on, Indigenous issues will have two spokespersons in the cabinet.

### 13.5.3  Implementation of the United Nations Declaration on the Rights of Indigenous Peoples

This was a key promise of the new government and a core recommendation of the TRC. In May 2016, the Canadian government announced with great fanfare its "full" adherence to the United Nations Declaration on the Rights of Indigenous Peoples (UNDRIP) and pledged to review its policies and laws to ensure that they are consistent with the principles it sets out. An interdepartmental committee was established to conduct this review. The government also chose to support Bill C-262, introduced by New Democratic Party MP Romeo Saganash. The Bill's aim is to ensure the consistency of Canada's laws and policies with the UNDRIP. At the time of writing, the Bill was still debated in the Senate. It is difficult to say whether such implementing legislation will have an impact since the UNDRIP establishes general principles that leave room for interpretation.

### 13.5.4  Recognition and Implementation of Indigenous Rights Framework

In July 2017, the government released a policy statement outlining ten principles to guide government action on relations with Indigenous peoples (Department of Justice 2017). According to the statement, the government's actions must be consistent with respect for the inherent rights of Indigenous peoples and the principles set out in the UNDRIP, including the principle of Indigenous peoples' free, prior, and informed consent (FPIC) to government actions that may affect the exercise of their rights.

These ten principles set the stage for what remains to this day the most ambitious and complex initiative of the Trudeau government: to put into place a policy and legislative framework that facilitates the recognition and implementation of Indigenous peoples' rights (PMO 2018). The purpose of this framework is primarily to define the parameters by which Indigenous nations could exercise their rights and jurisdictions in a manner consistent with their own laws and traditions. This would allow First Nations wishing to do so to move beyond the rigid framework of the Indian Act without going through the court system to have their rights recognized or through the lengthy process of negotiating the terms of their self-government.

However, this ambitious proposal has come up against criticism from a number of Indigenous organizations and intellectuals. Some groups demanded a "reset" of the process in light of its lack of transparency. Others argued the proposed framework did not truly propose a break with the existing model of delegated autonomy and, therefore, did not constitute a true nation-to-nation relationship based on the recognition of Indigenous peoples' inherent jurisdiction (King and Pasternak 2018). When the Assembly of First Nations asked the government to rethink the current process, the government decided to defer the introduction of legislation until after the next election.

### 13.5.5  Other Legislative and Policy Initiatives

While the ambitious plan to overhaul the legal framework defining the exercise of Indigenous rights is now stalled, a number of initiatives continue to remain works-in-progress. The government reports that 70 negotiation tables on governance and services' funding in various sectors are currently active (CIRNAC 2018b). These sectoral negotiations do not replace the recognition of true legislative authority, but they can nonetheless allow communities to exercise greater influence in programs and services management. Reforms to taxation and self-government financing, the land claims process and treaty negotiations, a bill on Indigenous languages recognition and a bill on child and family services were at various stages of the legislative process at writing time.

Finally, Bill C-69, a public bill to reform the environmental impact assessment process for projects under federal jurisdiction, is still in the legislative process (promise 7.43). This bill contains measures to better integrate Indigenous knowledge into the impact assessment process and better define the obligations of government agencies with respect to Indigenous consultation. For many, however, the bill does not go far enough, particularly with respect to the implementation of the principle of free, prior, and informed consent (Papillon 2018).

### 13.5.6  Natural Resource Development: A Challenge for Reconciliation

The reconciliation agenda ultimately hit a roadblock in the context of conflicts surrounding the authorization of natural resource development and energy transportation projects. In particular, the government faced difficult choices when it came to deciding between its commitments to

Indigenous peoples and the economic and political interests behind various pipeline projects.

The conflict surrounding the Trans Mountain pipeline project illustrates the government's difficult position. Despite a clear lack of consent from some Indigenous nations directly affected by this project, the Trudeau government chose to approve the pipeline in 2016, arguing that First Nations did not have a veto over development projects. In response, six Indigenous nations challenged this decision in court, and the Federal Court of Appeal ruled in their favour, overturning the government's authorization and forcing the National Energy Board to resume the project assessment process, partly due to inadequate consultations with affected Indigenous nations (*Tsleil-Waututh Nation v. Canada* 2018).

Another example is the conflict over the Coastal GasLink project, a gas pipeline projected to go through Wet'suwet'en ancestral territory without the consent of the Nation's hereditary chiefs. Following an injunction, an RCMP tactical unit intervened in January 2019 to remove a roadblock and arrest several protesters. This highly publicized intervention was seen by many as a violation of Wet'suwet'en jurisdiction and title, contrary both to Canadian law and Canada's UNDRIP commitments (Papillon 2019).

These two examples illustrate the fragility of the reconciliation process when broader economic and political interests collide with the rights and interests of Indigenous peoples.

## CONCLUSION

The Liberals set a very ambitious Indigenous policy agenda with a plethora of promises. It is in all fairness still too early to draw any definitive conclusions on the many reforms that have been undertaken. It is possible that a few years from now, the Trudeau era will be seen as a golden age in terms of Indigenous policies, as it sits in stark contrast with previous governments. Whether one considers the refinancing of services to Indigenous peoples, the division of the Department of Indigenous Affairs or the multiple reforms still underway, changes have been numerous, and their long-term impacts could well be significant.

Nevertheless, the Trudeau government faced both internal and external institutional resistance when it came to more radical changes in the very architecture of Canada's relationship with Indigenous peoples. The failure of the Recognition and Implementation of Indigenous Rights

Framework is perhaps the most representative case in this regard. Despite the generous speeches about rights recognition, the government quickly fell back into old patterns when it came time to prioritizing energy projects over Indigenous rights.

As cynicism sets in among Indigenous communities, who were expecting much more from the Trudeau government, we also note a certain disengagement from Indigenous issues within the government itself as the election cycle is closing in. The January 2019 cabinet shuffle is indicative of this shift in priority. Jody Wilson-Raybould, the first Indigenous woman to hold the prestigious position of Minister of Justice, was transferred to the much less visible position of Minister of Veterans Affairs. She resigned a few weeks later following the SNC-Lavalin affair.

A few months later, she declared that she encountered strong resistance from the Cabinet and the government bureaucracy while trying to implement her mandate on reconciliation with the goal of transforming the law and policy to put an end to injustice (Canadian Press 2019). As Karen Bird points out in her chapter, it is clear that Jody Wilson-Raybould's resignation further erodes the sympathy of Indigenous peoples for a government that promised a lot, yet could only deliver so much. Time will tell whether this government was a tipping point or a missed opportunity in the long struggle to decolonize the relationship between Indigenous peoples and the Canadian state.

## References

Anaya, James. 2014. *Report of the Special Rapporteur on the Rights of Indigenous Peoples. The Situation of Indigenous Peoples in Canada*. Human Rights Council. A/HRC/27/52/Add.2.

Blackstock, Cindy. 2019. "For Indigenous kids' welfare, our government knows better; it just needs to do better," *The Globe and Mail*, January 16, 2019. https://www.theglobeandmail.com/opinion/article-for-indigenous-kids-welfare-our-government-knows-better-they-just/.

Canadian Broadcasting Corporation (CBC). 2019. *Beyond 94. Truth and Reconciliation in Canada*. https://newsinteractives.cbc.ca/longform-single/beyond-94?&cta=1.

The Canadian Press. 2019. Feds not interested in Indigenous reconciliation, Wilson-Raybould says. https://bc.ctvnews.ca/feds-not-interested-in-indigenous-reconciliation-wilson-raybould-says-1.4393866.

Crown-Indigenous Relations and Northern Affairs Canada (CIRNAC). 2018a. New permanent bilateral mechanisms. Ottawa: Crown-Indigenous Relations and Northern Affairs Canada. https://www.rcaanc-cirnac.gc.ca/eng/14997119 68320/1529105436687.

Crown-Indigenous Relations and Northern Affairs Canada (CIRNAC). 2018b. *About Recognition of Indigenous Rights and Self-Determination discussion tables.* Ottawa: Crown-Indigenous Relations and Northern Affairs Canada. https:// www.rcaanc-cirnac.gc.ca/eng/1511969222951/1529103469169.

Dabin, Simon, Jean-François Daoust and Martin Papillon. 2019. "Indigenous Peoples and Affinity Voting in Canada," *Canadian Journal of Political Science,* 51(1): 39-53.

Department of Finance Canada. 2016. Growing the Middle Class. Ottawa: DepartmentofFinance.https://www.budget.gc.ca/2016/docs/plan/budget2016-en.pdf.

Department of Finance Canada. 2017. *Building a Strong Middle Class.* Ottawa: Department of Finance. https://www.budget.gc.ca/2017/docs/plan/budget-2017-en.pdf.

Department of Finance Canada. 2018. *Equality Growth. A strong Middle Class.* Ottawa: Department of Finance. https://www.budget.gc.ca/2018/docs/plan/budget-2018-en.pdf.

Department of Finance Canada. 2019. *Investing in the Middle Class.* Ottawa: Department of Finance. https://www.budget.gc.ca/2019/docs/plan/budget-2019-en.pdf.

Department of Justice. 2017. *Principles respecting the Government of Canada's relationship with Indigenous peoples.* Ottawa: *Department of Justice.* https:// www.justice.gc.ca/eng/csj-sjc/principles-principes.html.

King, Hayden and Shiri Pasternak. 2018. *Canada's Emerging Indigenous Rights Framework: A Critical Analysis.* Yellowhead Institute. https://yellowheadins-titute.org/wp-content/uploads/2018/06/yi-rights-report-june-2018-final-5.4.pdf.

Kirkup, Kristy. 2019. "Trudeau Liberals face pushback on Indigenous child welfare legislation," *Toronto Star,* February 8, 2019. https://www.thestar.com/ news/canada/2019/02/08/trudeau-liberals-face-pushback-on-indigenous-child-welfare-legislation.html.

Ladner, Kiera and Michael Orsini. 2004. "De l'infériorité négociée à l'inutilité de négocier: la Loi sur la gouvernance des Premières Nations et le maintien de la politique coloniale," Politique *et Sociétés,* 23(1): 59-87.

Liberal Party of Canada. 2015. Real Change: *A New Plan for a Strong Middle Class.* https://www.liberal.ca/wp-content/uploads/2015/10/New-plan-for-a-strong-middle-class.pdf.

Morden, Michael. 2016. "Theorizing the resilience of the Indian Act," *Canadian Public Administration,* 59 (1): 113–133.

Office of the Auditor General of Canada. 2011. "Programs for First Nations on Reserves." Status Report of the Auditor General of Canada. http://www.oag-bvg.gc.ca/internet/English/parl_oag_201106_04_e_35372.html.

Office of the Parliamentary Budget Officer (PBO). 2017. *Budget Sufficiency for First Nations Water and Wastewater Infrastructure.* Ottawa: Office of the Parliamentary Budget Officer (PBO). https://www.pbo-dpb.gc.ca/en/blog/news/FN_Water_Infrastructure.

Papillon, Martin. 2018. "Collaborative nation-to-nation decision-making is the wayforward,"*PolicyOptions.* http://policyoptions.irpp.org/magazines/collaborative-nation-nation-decision-making-way-forward/.

Papillon, Martin. 2019. "Les oléoducs de la discorde," *Le Devoir,* January 16, 2019. https://www.ledevoir.com/opinion/idees/545596/environnement-les-oleoducs-de-la-discorde.

Prime Minister's Office (PMO). 2015. *Minister of Indigenous and Northern Affairs MandateLetter,* November 12, 2015. https://pm.gc.ca/eng/minister-indigenous-and-northern-affairs-mandate-letter_2015.

Prime Minister's Office (PMO). 2017. *Minister of Crown-Indigenous Relations and Northern Affairs Mandate Letter,* October 2, 2017. https://pm.gc.ca/eng/minister-crown-indigenous-relations-and-northern-affairs-mandate-letter.

Prime Minister's Office (PMO). 2018. *Government of Canada to create Recognition and Implementation of Rights Framework.* https://pm.gc.ca/eng/news/2018/02/14/government-canada-create-recognition-and-implementation-rights-framework.

Statistics Canada. 2017. *Focus on Geography Series, 2016 Census.* Product n° 98-404-X2016001. *First Nations Child and Family Caring Society of Canada et al. v. Attorney General of Canada (Representing the Minister of Indian Affairs and Northern Development Canada)* [2016] TCDP 16. https://decisions.chrt-tcdp.gc.ca/chrt-tcdp/ decisions/en/109981/1/document.do.

Truth and Reconciliation Commission's (TRC). 2015. *Honouring the Truth, Reconciling for the Future. Final Report of the Truth and Reconciliation of Canada,* National Centre for Truth and Reconciliation. https://nctr.ca/reports2.php.

*Tsleil-Waututh Nation v. Canada.* [2018] CAF 153. https://decisia.lexum.com/fca-caf/decisions/en/343511/1/document.do.

# Chapter 14
# Reconciling Environment and Economy: Promises Kept, but Gamble Lost

Pierre-Olivier Pineau

I n its 2015 election platform, the Liberal Party of Canada (LPC) made a total of 48 environmental promises (Trudeau Polimetre 2018). Its two major rivals, the Conservative Party of Canada (CPC) and the New Democratic Party (NDP), made far fewer promises in this area with just 2 by the CPC (CPC 2015, 163) and 19 by the NDP (NDP 2015, 23–24, 54–57). At the other end of the spectrum, the Green Party of Canada (GPC) made more than 100 environmental and climate change promises (GPC 2015, 53–103).

Most of the LPC's environmental promises can be found in Chapter 3 of its electoral platform: "A Clean Environment and a Strong Economy." The title of this chapter explicitly states the Trudeau government's position on its environmental choices: they would not be made at the expense of the economy. In fact, the introduction to this chapter claims that in the LPC's view, at least, it would be possible to "protect the environment and grow the economy," leaving no doubt that both goals could be achieved simultaneously. Yet, the very next sentence reverses the order of those objectives, revealing that when it comes to choosing between the environment and the economy, the priorities of the Trudeau government might not be so clear: "Our plan will deliver the economic growth and jobs Canadians need, and leave to our children and grandchildren a country even more beautiful, more sustainable, and more prosperous" (Liberal Party of Canada 2015, 39). Would environmental concerns take precedence over economic issues during the Liberal government's first mandate?

Striking a balance between these two concerns, or rather the imbalance largely perceived at the end of its first mandate, characterized many of the actions taken by the Trudeau government. The federal government's purchase of the Trans Mountain pipeline and its expansion project targeting the exploitation and export of Canadian oil clearly illustrates the paradox inherent in the government's approach. While aiming to position Canada as a key international player in the fight against climate change, the Trudeau government purchased a pipeline to facilitate the exploitation of the Alberta tar sands, an energy source denounced by environmental groups because of the greenhouse gas (GHG) emissions linked to its production.

This chapter begins with an explanation of the LPC's environmental promises and their fulfillment. It then discusses three major environmental issues marking the Trudeau government's first mandate and concludes that, during its four years in power, although it has kept its promises, the Liberal government has not managed to reconcile environmental protection with economic growth as it announced. On the contrary, no matter which government is elected in October 2019, the actions of the Trudeau government have ignited conflicts that will be difficult to resolve in the coming years.

## 14.1 ENVIRONMENTAL AND CLIMATE CHANGE PROMISES

With its 48 separate promises, the LPC made far more environmental commitments in 2015 than did its two principal rivals, the CPC and the NDP. While it is not possible to detail all these promises in this chapter, we can identify the most important ones (see Table 14-1) and the major categories into which they fall (see Table 14-2).

TABLE 14-1 – Most Important Environmental Promises*

| # | PROMISE | VERDICT |
|---|---------|---------|
| **Environmental Assessment and Water (Modernization of the National Energy Board)** | | |
| 5.01 | We will provide ways for Canadians to express their views and opportunities for experts to meaningfully participate (in environmental assessment processes). | Kept in part |
| 5.05 | We will ensure that decisions (for environmental assessments) are based on science, facts, and evidence, and serve the public's interest. | Kept in part |
| 5.06 | We will ensure that environmental assessments include an analysis of upstream impacts and greenhouse gas emissions resulting from projects under review. | Kept in part |
| 5.07 | We will restore robust oversight and thorough environmental assessments of areas under federal jurisdiction, while also working with provinces and territories to avoid duplication. | Kept in part |
| 5.22 | We will do more to protect Canada's endangered species. We will respond more quickly to the advice and requests of scientists, and will complete robust species-at-risk recovery plans. | Kept in part |
| **5.24** | **We will modernize the National Energy Board, ensuring that its composition reflects regional views and has sufficient expertise in fields like environmental science, community development, and Indigenous traditional knowledge.** | **Kept in part** |
| 5.43 | We will deliver more robust and credible environmental assessments for all projects that could impact our freshwater and oceans. | Kept |
| **Climate Change, Green Jobs, and Greener Communities (Energy Transition Measures)** | | |
| 5.04 | With the provinces and territories, we will create a Low Carbon Economy Trust that will provide funding to projects that materially reduce carbon emissions under the new pan-Canadian framework. We will endow the Low Carbon Economy Trust with $2 billion. | Kept |
| **5.17** | **We will fulfill our G20 commitment and phase out subsidies for the fossil fuel industry over the medium-term.** | **Broken** |
| 5.18 | We will work together [the provinces and territories] to establish national emissions-reduction targets. | Kept in part |
| **5.19** | **Within 90 days formally, we will meet [with provincial and territorial leaders] to establish a pan-Canadian framework for combatting climate change.** | **Kept** |
| 5.26 | We will work with the United States and Mexico to develop a continent-wide clean energy and environment agreement. | Kept |

| # | PROMISE | VERDICT |
|---|---------|---------|
| 5.23 | We will improve energy efficiency standards for consumer and commercial products. | Kept |
| 5.25 | We will work closely with the provinces and territories to develop a Canadian Energy Strategy to protect Canada's energy security; encourage energy conservation; and bring cleaner, renewable energy onto the electricity grid. | Kept in part |
| 5.28 | We will deliver a better quality of life for all Canadians by working with the provinces to set stronger air quality standards, monitor emissions, and provide incentives for investments that lead to cleaner air and healthier communities. | Kept in part |
| 5.31 | We will boost investment in green infrastructure by nearly $6 billion over the next four years, and almost $20 billion over ten years. | Kept in part |

* Source: Trudeau Polimetre and Liberal Party of Canada platform
** The most important pledges are in **bold**.

The most important environmental promises fall into two categories. The first are related to environmental assessments (5.01, 5.05, 5.06, 5.07, 5.22, 5.24, and 5.43), culminating in the key promise to "modernize the National Energy Board" (5.24, in bold in Table 8-1.) This commitment synthesizes all promises related to environmental assessments since they could not be kept without modernizing the National Energy Board. All the promises in this category have been kept in part or are in the works.

The second category relates to climate change (5.04, 5.17, 5.18, 5.19, 5.26), green jobs (5.23, 5.25, 5.28), and green communities (5.31) and are linked to the energy transition needed to reduce GHG emissions. Once again, most of these promises have either been kept or are in the works. Promise 5.17 (in bold in Table 14-1) to phase out subsidies for the fossil fuel industry has clearly been broken, however. The lack of tax changes in this industry indicates that nothing has been done in this regard. On the contrary, the government has significantly increased its monetary assistance to this industry, not just once but twice. By buying the Trans Mountain pipeline, the government rescued a project that would otherwise have been scrapped. Then, by announcing $1.6 billion in preferential loans for the oil and gas industry, the government facilitated its access to credit, thereby granting it an indirect subsidy. Promise 5.17 is critical since it provides concrete evidence of the government's commitment (or lack thereof) to ensuring the coherence of its environmental and economic initiatives.

The other main promise in this second group concerns the establishment of a pan-Canadian framework for combatting climate change (promise 5.19, in bold in Table 14-1). This promise represents the federal government's commitment to developing a national approach to reducing GHG, an approach that has been sorely lacking in Canadian efforts to reduce GHG emissions.

In addition to the 16 promises shown in Table 14-1, Chapter 3 of the Liberal platform outlined 32 other environmental promises, for a total of 48, which can be divided into nine categories. As shown in Table 14-2, thirteen promises concerned green jobs, nine concerned environmental assessments, eight concerned national parks, seven concerned climate change, and seven concerned water. Four other "environmental" promises can be found elsewhere in the Liberal platform, and these have been categorized as environmental.

In terms of green jobs, the LPC committed to taking various steps to support investments in clean technology, innovation, and energy efficiency. Of the thirteen promises related to green jobs, seven have been kept and six others either have been kept in part or are in the works.

Of the seven promises related to climate change, potentially the most significant was to establish a pan-Canadian framework for combatting climate change in the first 90 days of the LPC's mandate (5.19). Despite its tight deadline, this promise was kept, as were four others. Just one of these seven promises was kept only partially. However, the promise to end subsidies to the fossil fuel industry (5.17) was broken.

Several promises aimed to restore the credibility of environmental assessments in the eyes of both those who have opposed major projects subject to environmental assessments (such as the Energy East and Trans Mountain pipelines) and those who support those projects and related industries. The goal of those promises was to demonstrate, on the one hand, that the voices of all interested parties would be heard and all facts would be considered and, on the other, that the National Energy Board (NEB) would be modernized. To avoid duplication of effort, the government also promised to combine procedures with similar objectives. It is in this environmental sub-category that the LPC has fared the worst, having kept just one of its nine promises. Seven promises have been kept in part or are in the works, and one has not yet been rated. The major commitment of this group, to modernize the NEB (5.24), is now in the works through Bill C-69, which we discuss in greater detail below.

Of the eight promises related to national parks and the seven related to water, more than half have been kept and none have been broken. Finally, of the four promises made elsewhere in the LPC platform, two have been kept and two are in the works. Overall, as shown in Table 14.2, the LPC has done an impressive job keeping its environmental and climate change promises, with half kept and 46% in the works. Just one (5.17) has been broken, but that is a significant failure since the government did the exact opposite of what it promised, granting additional subsidies to the fossil fuel industry.

## 14.2 MAJOR INITIATIVES

Despite the Trudeau government's excellent track record in terms of keeping these promises, some of its environmental policies have been highly controversial, regularly making headlines and dealing a blow to its gamble to simultaneously "protect the environment and grow the economy."

### 14.2.1 Pan-Canadian Framework for Combatting Climate Change and Carbon Pricing

Within the first 90 days of taking office, the Trudeau government sought to distinguish itself from the Harper government, which had not made significant headway in this area, by launching federal-provincial-territorial discussions on the subject. These led to the pan-Canadian framework for combatting climate change, made public in late 2016 that included carbon pricing. The agreement was signed by the three territories and eight of the ten provinces — only Manitoba and Saskatchewan refused to endorse it. The 2018 election of Doug Ford in Ontario added another voice of dissent, and Alberta and New Brunswick also expressed reservations in 2018. Saskatchewan and Ontario both mounted legal challenges to the federal government's authority to impose this framework onto the provinces.

If the provinces win their case, the efforts of the Trudeau government could be destroyed, but if the courts find in favour of the federal government, climate change will be recognized as a matter of national concern falling within federal jurisdiction. So, while the Trudeau government kept its promise to develop a pan-Canadian framework to combat climate change, the complexity and diversity of provincial/

territorial concerns made it impossible to achieve coast-to-coast support for it (see François Rocher's chapter 3 on federal-provincial-territorial relations).

## 14.2.2 Modernization of the National Energy Board

While environmental assessments of projects designed to expand Canada's capacity to ship oil from Alberta's oil sands to the east (Trans-Canada's Energy East pipeline) and west (Enbridge's Northern Gateway pipeline and Kinder Morgan's Trans Mountain pipeline) have been marked by endless controversy and long delays, the Trudeau government has attempted to lend credibility to the assessment process. Its major achievement in this area has been Bill C-69 (An Act to enact the Impact Assessment Act and the Canadian Energy Regulator Act, to amend the Navigation Protection Act and to make consequential amendments to other Acts), which aims to make environmental assessments more independent from the organization that regulates such projects once they have been approved. Currently, the National Energy Board handles both aspects of this process.

Once Bill C-69 is adopted, the new Impact Assessment Agency of Canada will assess major new energy projects, and the new Canadian Energy Regulator (CER) will regulate them, thereby replacing the National Energy Board. Bill C-69 is supported by several environmental groups, including the West Coast Environmental Law Association, Nature Canada, Ecojustice, Environmental Defence Canada, the Canadian Freshwater Alliance, and the *Centre québécois du droit de l'environnement*. These groups see the creation of these new bodies as a significant improvement to the environmental assessment and consultation process (West Coast Environmental Law Association 2018). Support for these changes is nevertheless far from unanimous in the oil and gas industry. The Canadian Association of Petroleum Producers (CAPP) believes this legislation complicates the .project approval process and creates more opportunities for the public to participate in the process, thereby adding to the uncertainty (CAPP 2018). In short, CAPP sees this legislation as being counter to the country's economic interests, clearly not keeping the Trudeau government's promise to reconcile environmental and economic interests.

TABLE 14-2 – Environmental Promises by Category* and Their Verdicts**

| DOMAIN | NOT YET RATED | KEPT IN PART/IN THE WORKS | KEPT | BROKEN | TOTAL |
|---|---|---|---|---|---|
| Agriculture (p. 16) | | 1 | | | 1 |
| Greener Communities (p. 13) | | | 1 | | 1 |
| Water | | 3 | 4 | | 7 |
| Green Jobs | | 6 | 7 | | 13 |
| New Building Canada Fund (p. 14) | | | 1 | | 1 |
| National Parks | | 3 | 5 | | 8 |
| Environmental Assessments | 1 | 7 | 1 | | 9 |
| Tax Policy (p. 89) | | 1 | | | 1 |
| Climate Change | | 1 | 5 | 1 | 7 |
| **General Total** | **1** | **22** | **25** | **1** | **48** |

\* See Chapter 3 of the Liberal Party of Canada platform unless a page reference indicates otherwise.
\*\* Source of verdicts: Polimetre Trudeau as updated December 2018

## 14.2.3  Purchase of Kinder Morgan's Trans Mountain Pipeline

The pan-Canadian framework for combatting climate change and Bill C-69 no doubt had the potential to satisfy the demands of many Canadians for government action to protect the environment. The May 2018 announcement that the federal government would purchase Kinder Morgan's Trans Mountain pipeline and complete its expansion project had the opposite effect (CBC 2018).

Presented by the Trudeau government as a boon to the Canadian economy, this direct support of the oil and gas industry—one of the biggest sources of GHG emissions in Canada and around the world—can also be viewed as an attack on environmental protection. With this purchase, designed to save a project in which no private company was willing to invest because of the huge opposition and uncertainty it faced, the Trudeau government violated the spirit of its own promise to "phase out subsidies for the fossil fuel industry" (5.17). In fact, purchasing this pipeline with the goal of completing its expansion project provided strong support for that industry. It was an indirect subsidy, without which the project would have been abandoned.

## 14.3 DISCUSSION

While the Trudeau government aimed to reconcile environmental protection and economic growth, it managed to alienate both environmentalists on the one hand and powerful stakeholders in the hydrocarbon sector on the other. Environmental groups were infuriated by the purchase of the Trans Mountain pipeline and the $1.6 billion boost to Canada's oil and gas industry in December 2018. Moreover, many powerful economic interests in Alberta and Saskatchewan opposed both the pan-Canadian framework for combatting climate change and Bill C-69. The government thus found itself in the paradoxical situation of having kept almost all its environmental promises while, at the same time, incurring the wrath of many Canadians—sometimes for opposing reasons!

Was the Trudeau government's gamble based on a delicate balance or a contradiction? It is hard to say. On the surface, the government's promise appeared to be contradictory: to support an industry while tightening its regulatory framework and taxing its products more heavily to discourage their use. However, these appearances can also be interpreted in another way: the government aimed to hold producers accountable for their actions and reduce consumption while removing certain constraints on their production (insufficient pipeline capacity) so as not to penalize them on international markets. This strategy makes sense insofar as most emissions are tied to consumption, not production, and insofar as producers face international competition.

By adopting this approach, the Trudeau government gambled on fighting climate change by reducing oil consumption without directly penalizing Canadian producers, the majority of whose international competitors do not face such pipeline constraints. If consumption had fallen while Canadian producers had remained financially healthy, the government might have won its gamble, achieving environmental benefits without damaging the economy. Canada would have been seen as a responsible producer and a low oil consumer. This is the approach adopted by Norway: limited questioning of hydrocarbon production with tough GHG reduction policies. The oil industry expansion debate has been largely, although not totally, successful in achieving buy-in from Norwegians (see Hornmoen 2018). One factor that no doubt facilitated this process is the people's inherent trust in public institutions and the fact that the Norwegian state is the majority shareholder in Equinor (formerly Statoil), the country's largest petroleum company. As a result, Norwegians may feel that their own prosperity is closely linked to the success of this economic sector, knowing that its profits do not solely benefit private owners.

Norway's position and the attempt to become a sustainable producer and consumer are not immediately clear to all, however. They involve limiting consumption by imposing high taxes on energy, a policy that is not readily accepted by Canadians, as has been seen with efforts to impose a carbon tax. The strategy developed by Trudeau's Liberals was not likely to silence critics and easily rally Canadians around a common vision.

## CONCLUSION

The Trudeau government kept the majority of its environmental promises. It is in the process of fulfilling most of the others. Viewed against a backdrop of increased environmental protection and economic growth, we would therefore expect its environmental record to be positive. However, given the strident protests against the major initiatives arising from those promises, it is hard to draw that conclusion. The pan-Canadian framework for combatting climate change, the carbon pricing scheme, Bill C-69, and the purchase of the Trans Mountain pipeline have all been condemned strongly by stakeholders whose positions are diametrically opposed. So, while the LPC can boast of having kept its environmental promises, it has nevertheless lost its gamble to reconcile economic growth and environmental protection.

REFERENCES

CAPP. 2018. Bill C-69 Impact Assessment, Canadian Association of Petroleum Producers.

CBC. 2018. "Liberals to buy Trans Mountain pipeline for $4.5B to ensure expansion is built," May 29, 2018. https://www.cbc.ca/news/politics/liberals-trans-mountain-pipeline-kinder-morgan-1.4681911.

Conservative Party of Canada. 2015. *Protect our economy — Our Conservative Plan to Protect the Economy.*

Green Party of Canada. 2015. *Vision green 2015.*

Hornmoen H. 2018. "Environmentally Friendly Oil and Gas Production: Analyzing Governmental Argumentation and Press Deliberation on Oil Policy," *Environmental Communication*, 12 (2): 232–246.

Liberal Party of Canada. 2015. *Real Change: A New Plan for a Strong Middle Class.* https://www.liberal.ca/wp-content/uploads/2015/10/New-plan-for-a-strong-middle-class.pdf.

New Democratic Party. 2015. *Building the country of our dreams: Tom Mulcair's plan to bring change to Ottawa.*

Trudeau Polimetre. 2018. https://www.poltext.org/en/trudeau-polimeter.

West Coast Environmental Law Association. 2018. "Oil industry, Notley opposition to Bill C-69 'wildly inaccurate', environmental groups say." https://www.wcel.org/media-release/oil-industry-notley-opposition-bill-c-69-wildly-inaccurate-environmental-groups-say.

# Chapter 15
## From "Sunny Ways" to Stormy Weather: Trudeau's Record on Foreign and Defence Policy

Julien Lauzon Chiasson and Stéphane Paquin

This chapter presents and analyzes the record of the Liberal Party of Canada's foreign policy promises. Government action is analyzed from the perspective of delivering on election platform promises, but also in response to unforeseen international events such as the renegotiation of the North American Free Trade Agreement (NAFTA). The promises chosen for analysis were the most significant to the Liberal government because they set Trudeau's policy direction on defence, trade, and development assistance.

Justin Trudeau's election sparked a wave of hope on the international stage. Following Stephen Harper's Conservative government, the Liberal government promised a return to the glorious days of multilateralism and international cooperation. Betting on this hope, Prime Minister Justin Trudeau even affirmed that "Canada is back" on the international stage (National Post 2015). Whether it was trade, the military, international aid, or international policy, through its "sunny ways," the new government promised to do things differently from the Harper government. Liberal voters could dream of a more diplomatic and peaceful Canada focused on human rights, feminism, peace missions, development assistance, and humanitarian aid. After 11 years of Harper's government, the Trudeau government promised to review the previous policy, and reorient foreign and defence policies to rebuild Canada's international reputation.

The world in which the Liberal government found itself, however, was very different from the one when the Liberals were in power from 1993 to 2006. The Liberal work of reviewing and reorienting the previous Conservative government's policies would unfold in a highly transformed international context. Canada was engaged in military conflicts in Ukraine and Syria, its weight in international politics was diminished by the rise of China and emerging countries, and climate change demanded a radical shift in energy production patterns (Blank and Gattinger 2018). Last, but not least, the new government's attempts to return to Liberal idealism were disrupted by the rise of populist and nationalist currents in the United States and Europe.

The Liberal mandate to change foreign policy unfolded in two phases. First came the heydays of the idyll with U.S. President Obama, and then a tumultuous period in association with Donald Trump's presidency. In this context, the Trudeau government attempted to pursue its Liberal internationalism agenda, emphasizing multilateralism, free trade, environmental protection, democracy, human rights, multiculturalism, and feminism.

## 15.1 LIBERAL PROMISES

The Liberal platform proposed 43 promises directly related to international affairs and defence, of which 18 (42%) have been fulfilled, 19 (44%) partially fulfilled, 1 (2%) broken, and 5 (12%) on hold. Table 15.1 presents the top 15 promises. The five promises in bold print indicate the key promises, either because they signal a change in direction from the Harper government or because they have a significant economic or budgetary impact. The Liberal platform also proposed 12 promises that were fulfilled or in the works in March 2019 in connection with the new national security legislation, which restores the balance between security and civil rights, and the creation of a parliamentary committee to oversee the operations of national security departments and agencies.

TABLE 15-1 – Most Important Promises in International Affairs and Defence

| # | PROMISE | VERDICT |
|---|---------|---------|
| | **International Trade** | |
| **3.21** | **We will carefully consider all trade opportunities currently open to Canada, and explore deeper trade relationships with emerging and established markets, including China and India.** | Kept in part |
| 1.26 | We commit to rescheduling and hosting a new trilateral leaders' summit with the United States and Mexico. | Kept |
| 7.22 | To underscore the importance of the United States to Canada, we will create a Cabinet committee to oversee and manage our relationship. | Kept |
| 5.26 | We will work with the United States and Mexico to develop a continent-wide clean energy and environment agreement. | Kept |
| | **Multilateralism** | |
| **1.33** | **We will recommit to supporting international peace operations with the United Nations, and will make our specialized capabilities—from mobile medical teams to engineering support to aircraft that can carry supplies and personnel—available [...]** | Kept |
| **1.11** | **We will end Canada's combat mission in Iraq.** | **Kept** |
| 1.12 | We will refocus Canada's military contribution in the region (of Iraq) on the training of local forces, while providing more humanitarian support. | Kept |
| 1.25 | We will remain fully committed to Canada's existing military contributions in Central and Eastern Europe: participation in NATO assurance measures (Operation REASSURANCE) and the training mission in Ukraine (Operation UNIFIER). | Kept |
| **1.28** | **We will consult with Canadian and international aid organizations to review current policies and funding frameworks that will refocus our aid priorities on poverty reduction.** | **Kept** |
| | **Security and Defence** | |
| 1.10 | We will not buy the F-35 stealth fighter-bomber. | Not yet rated |
| 1.06 | We will immediately launch an open and transparent competition to replace the CF-18 fighter aircraft. | Kept in part |
| 1.07 | We will reduce the procurement budget for replacing the CF-18s, and will instead purchase one of the many, lower-priced options that better match Canada's defence needs. | Kept in part |
| **1.01** | **We will maintain current National Defence spending levels, including current planned increases.** | **Broken** |

| # | PROMISE | VERDICT |
|---|---------|---------|
| 1.03 | We will develop the Canadian Armed Forces into an agile, responsive, and well-equipped military force that can effectively defend Canada and North America; provide support during natural disasters, humanitarian support missions, and peace operations [...] | Kept in part |
| 1.05 | We will review current programs and capabilities, and lay out a realistic plan to strengthen Canada's Armed Forces. | Kept |

\* Source: Trudeau Polimetre and Liberal Party of Canada platform
\*\* The most important pledges are in **bold**.

## 15.2 ECONOMIC RELATIONSHIPS AND INTERNATIONAL TRADE

In 2015, the Liberal Party committed to rebuilding relationships with the United States and Mexico and to diversifying and deepening trade relationships with other established and emerging economies. Justin Trudeau made good use of his "bromance" with President Obama to deliver on three relatively simple election promises: hosting a new summit with the United States and Mexico (7.21); finalizing a North American clean energy and environment agreement (5.26); and canceling the Mexican visa requirement (1.25).

However, Canadian hopes to deepen relationships with the United States faded after Donald Trump was elected to the U.S. presidency. In his inaugural address, Donald Trump trumpeted his protectionist "America First" doctrine. This doctrine's application to international trade has meant systematic American obstruction of the multilateral system and regional agreements with the objective of crippling the World Trade Organization's dispute settlement mechanism, withdrawing from the Trans-Pacific Partnership (TPP), and forcing the renegotiation of NAFTA on a more favourable basis for the United States.

The protectionist and uncompromising attitude of the U.S. government meant that the renegotiation of NAFTA and trade disputes with the U.S. would largely dominate the Trudeau government's trade agenda for the remainder of its mandate. In April 2017, the U.S. President imposed new countervailing and punitive tariffs of 20% on Canadian lumber, triggering the fifth dispute cycle since 1982. In May 2018, he struck again by imposing countervailing tariffs of 25% on steel and 10% on aluminum (Government of Canada 2019). His tweets targeted the dairy and automotive sectors while scorching Justin Trudeau. President Trump threatened to impose tariffs on the automotive industry on national security grounds and to withdraw completely from NAFTA if he did not win his case and gain more market access for U.S. exports (Lilly 2018). Under such conditions, it was becoming increasingly difficult for Canada to rebuild the bridges with the United States as promised.

After seven rounds of tripartite negotiations since August 2017, during several weeks starting in August 2018, the United States and Mexico renegotiated NAFTA without Canada's presence, which was perceived as a major humiliation for Canada. Canada was under colossal pressure and negotiated intensively with the United States and Mexico in order to reach a trilateral agreement. In October 2018, Canada, the United States and Mexico announced an agreement in principle that created the Canada-United States-Mexico Agreement (CUSMA). On the one hand, several analysts believe that Canada succeeded in maintaining protections for culture, reducing the threat of tariffs against the automotive industry, maintaining protection for culture, and conserving the dispute settlement mechanism for antidumping and countervailing duties (a priority for the softwood lumber sector). On the other hand, they noted that the Trudeau government had to make two main concessions to achieve these results: (1) open up markets under supply management, including 3.6% access to the dairy market that would have to dismantle the classes 6 and 7 (milk powder) which reduced the price for diafiltered milk in Canada; and (2) increase the duration of authors' copyright and patent protection for pharmaceuticals. The Trudeau government was also criticized for its inability to obtain an exemption from American duties on steel and aluminum under CUSMA.

The promise to explore the potential of trade relationships with established and emerging markets builds on the Harper government's policy of diversifying Canada's export markets with one main exception—adding a progressive vision to promote inclusion, gender equality, and other Canadian values. The government concluded negotiations that were already initiated by the previous government for the new Comprehensive and Progressive Agreement for Trans-Pacific Partnership (CPTPP), the Canada-European Union Comprehensive Economic and Trade Agreement (CETA). It modernized the agreement with Chile to include, among others, a chapter on gender equality, and it opened a trade negotiation process with Mercosur countries (Brazil, Argentina, Uruguay, Paraguay) and the countries of the Pacific Alliance (Chile, Colombia, Mexico and Peru). The Trudeau government also tried to reactivate trade negotiations with India and began exploratory discussions with China, the countries of the Association of Southeast Asian Nations (ASEAN), the Philippines and Thailand. However, official visits to China and India have resulted in diplomatic and media storms. According to the Polimètre's rules based on CPPG guidelines, without these trade initiatives, the promise (3.22) to explore deeper trade relationships with emerging and established markets would be broken instead of kept in part, although weakly so because of the difficulties encountered in relations with China and India, the most important emerging economies.

Despite the initial honeymoon, the Chinese-Canadian relationship deteriorated with each new incident of political wrangling. In 2017, during Canada's official visit to China, the Canadian delegation found itself in the middle of a first media storm due to its "progressive" speeches on human rights and trade. This, alongside a deep misunderstanding of the scope of a potential trade agreement, explains why the visit was unsuccessful (Vanderklippe 2017). The Canada-China diplomatic relationship became tense in May 2018 when Canada invoked national security reasons to block the Chinese takeover of Aecon, a Canadian infrastructure company. In December 2018, relations became more complicated following the arrest of Meng Wanzhou, the chief financial officer of China's telecommunications multinational Huawei, by Canadian authorities at the request of U.S. authorities for bypassing the U.S. sanctions against Iran and trade-secret theft (Proctor 2018). In March 2019, China decided to block Canadian canola exports by some Canadian companies, which Canada saw as a retaliatory act to the Huawei case.

The desire to deepen relationships with India goes back to Stephen Harper's Conservative Party in 2010, which had committed previously to concluding a free trade agreement with India. When the Liberals came to power in 2015, trade negotiations with India were in their ninth round. In 2017–2018, the tenth round of negotiations exposed numerous barriers regarding trade negotiation approaches as well as disagreements on the scope of the agreement between the two countries, market access, the investment agreement, labour mobility, technology transfers, services, and Canada's "progressive trade strategy" to include agreements on gender, environment, labour, and human rights (Hemmadi 2018).

These stumbling blocks in negotiations were amplified by a diplomatic and media fiasco during Justin Trudeau's visit to India in February 2018. In addition to the fuss over the Prime Minister and his family wearing traditional Indian clothes, the presence of Jaspal Atwal, a Canadian of Sikh origin, who was convicted previously for the attempted murder of an Indian minister and described in the Indian and Canadian media as a "Khalistani terrorist," triggered the new National Security and Intelligence

Committee of Parliamentarians' first investigation into the security screening process (Dutt 2018; Russel 2018; The Times of India 2018). On this official visit, Prime Minister Trudeau seemed caught between two objectives which were to build diplomatic and commercial relations with India's political class and to please the part of his electoral base in Canada that is of Indian origin and Sikh confession. In trying to accomplish these two contradictory objectives, he succeeded in achieving one—namely showing solidarity with the Sikh community, to the detriment of political and commercial relations between Canada and India. This may be why, on December 16, 2018, in an interview with CTV's Evan Solomon, Trudeau admitted that his biggest regret concerning that year was this infamous trip to India. He also said that if he had to do it all over again, he would do things differently.

The conclusion of a new free trade agreement with the United States and Mexico is definitely good news in itself, considering Canada's dependence on the American economy. The same applies to the efforts to diversify international trade with partners who are more receptive to a progressive and feminist trade agenda. However, the difficulties encountered when attempting to liberalize trade with India, and especially China, probably marks a long-lasting halt in Canada's efforts to include these countries in a trade agreement with the same terms as Western countries.

## 15.3 MILITARY OPERATIONS, MULTILATERALISM, AND FEMINISM

### 15.3.1 Realignment of the Mission in Iraq

The Liberal Party included several elements in its electoral platform that were supposed to distinguish them from the Conservative government from a military standpoint. The two key points were a change in the Canadian mission in Iraq (promise 1.11) and a return to United Nations' peacekeeping operations (promise 1.31). As promised, the Liberals ended the Royal Canadian Air Force strikes in Iraq. While the air strike mission was scheduled to end by the end of March, the Liberal government moved up the end of the mission to February 22, 2016 (Bellavance 2016). In return, Trudeau promised to refocus Canada's contribution on training local forces and humanitarian aid (1.12). This commitment was fulfilled in February 2016 when the government announced $1.1 billion over three years for refugee assistance and basic services and an increase in troops in Iraq (650 to 830), mainly to focus on training activities (Buzzetti 2016). In July 2018, Canada assumed command of the North Atlantic Treaty

Organization's (NATO) training mission in Iraq for one year, until summer 2019 (Le Devoir 2018).

This realignment of the Canadian Armed Forces' (CAF) objectives was consistent with Justin Trudeau's Liberal vision. The Prime Minister wished to strengthen the role of the special operations forces and develop the local security forces' abilities, all while remaining reluctant to engage the CAF in combat missions (Rice and Hlatky 2018). Canada's new defence policy is focused on anticipating and adapting to conflicts, by engaging early on in crises, and thus delivers on a promise (1.05) (Department of National Defence 2017). The government's priority shifted therefore to deploying resources to intervene before a crisis escalates rather than deploying combat forces in advanced stages of armed conflict.

### 15.3.2  Maintaining Commitments in Eastern Europe

This vision is also consistent with Canada's military commitments in Eastern Europe. Indeed, Canada is providing training to security forces in Ukraine. Ukraine is caught in a conflict with Russia that caused the separation, orchestrated by Moscow, of two Ukrainian provinces. In Latvia, Canada is taking part in a display of solidarity among NATO members in their deterrence effort against Russia. This type of mission is consistent with the Trudeau government's approach to military support of local forces. That is how the Liberals promised to maintain Canada's commitment to military operations in Central and Eastern Europe during the election (promise 1.24). On March 6, 2017, the government kept its promise by extending Operation UNIFIER (Ukraine) until March 2019 (Department of National Defence 2018b). On July 10, 2018, it extended Operation REASSURANCE (Latvia) until March 2023, while increasing its strength (Department of National Defence November 2018a).

### 15.3.3  UN Operations: Slowness and Gaps between Will and Actions

A similar approach was ultimately applied to peacekeeping operations. The Liberal platform promised to renew Canada's commitment to the United Nations (UN) and to increase Canada's participation in peacekeeping operations (promise 1.31). On March 19, 2018, the government delivered on this promise as it confirmed the deployment of 250 CAF troops to Mali as part of the United Nations Multidimensional Integrated Stabilization Mission in Mali (MINUSMA) for one year (Marquis 2018). Called Operation PRESENCE- Mali, the CAF's primary mission was to provide air medical evacuation of UN forces.

However, it took almost three years before that promise was fulfilled. In addition, deployment was limited in number and duration compared to what was originally planned. Although it is a fulfilled promise and a support that the UN appreciates, the Liberals promised a much broader re-engagement. As such, in 2016, a plan was put into place for Canada to assume command of MINUSMA and deploy 600 troops to Mali (Coulon 2018). The Chief of the Defence Staff, cabinet ministers, and the UN Secretary-General's office were just waiting for the Prime Minister's confirmation to launch the operation. However, it was the Prime Minister's Office in December 2016 that decided to postpone the final decision in order to examine further the various scenarios. However, with the replacement of Stéphane Dion with Chrystia Freeland at Foreign Affairs in January 2017, a change in direction occurred and peacekeeping missions were no longer a priority. It is at this moment that the original, more ambitious plan was abandoned and replaced by the current, much more modest mission. When the United Nations asked for an extension of this mission from July to October 2019, Minister Freeland declined the proposal by stating that Canada had fulfilled its commitment and suggested replacing the Canadian Forces with private services. As a result, the Trudeau government moved Canada's re-engagement in peacekeeping missions to a lower priority on its agenda. Certainly, there would be a political cost to a more ambitious mission if ever Mali's situation went wrong. Given these risks, did the Trudeau government calculate that this mission would not be a decisive factor in its support?

### 15.3.4  Defence Budgets and the F-35 Saga

Despite its promise to maintain defence budget levels and planned increases (promise 1.01), the first two Liberal years were marked by a decrease in this budget. In fact, the previous government concluded its mandate in 2015 with a defence budget of $20.4 billion. At the end of the 2016 fiscal year, the first year under the Liberal government, this budget was cut to $20 billion. In 2017, it came down to $19.8 billion. By the end of the 2017–2018 fiscal year, budget growth had recovered to around 4%, or a budget of $20.6 billion (Department of National Defence 2019). This return to increasing budgets was announced in 2017 in the government's new defence policy, which calls for a stable increase in funding through 2026–2027 to achieve a total budget growth of 70%, unprecedented in peacetime! (Department of National Defence 2017, 43)

This government's back and forth when it comes to the defence budget is at odds with its campaign promise. However, this trend reversal is attributable to pressure from the U.S. administration, which made it clear to its NATO allies that it was demanding an increase in their defence budgets to reach the previously set target of 2% of their GDP (France 24 2017). The Canadian defence policy objective is therefore to increase spending from 1.16% of GDP (2016–2017) to 1.4% of GDP (2024–2025). Most of this spending is directed toward military equipment, primarily in the aerospace and naval sectors. The government anticipates that these investments will modernize the Canadian military.

The F-35 saga is one of those investment files that have had many twists and turns. It was an election promise (1.10) designed to distinguish the Liberal style of management from the Conservative one. By promising an open and transparent competition (1.06), the Liberals acknowledged the Auditor General's criticism that the Harper government had broken the rules, underestimated costs, and failed to provide all the necessary information on its F-35 acquisition plan (Office of the Auditor General 2012). However, the new government soon discovered that it was easier to promise not to buy than to pursue a firm order. This decision did not change the fact that Canada's aging CF-18 fleet will have to be replaced. As a temporary solution to the Air Force's needs (promise 1.07), the government acquired used F-18s from Australia. However, the Auditor General came back and criticized the Liberal government's temporary plan. According to his report, while future defence aircraft will not be operational until 2032, the CAF does not have the appropriate workforce to operate and maintain the F-18s purchased from Australia (Office of the Auditor General 2018). Canada's air defence needs will not be met or modernized until 2032.

### 15.3.5  Feminist Development Assistance Policy

The Liberal Party made two firm promises on international aid that would lead to a break and a major reorientation from the Harper era (12.11, 12.33). These promises resulted in Canada's Feminist International Assistance Policy (Global Affairs Canada 2017). The main objective of this new policy is gender equality and the empowerment of women and girls (see Karen Bird's chapter). According to this policy, this objective would be the most effective way to reduce poverty in the world.

However, it should also be noted that the main limitation of this new policy is its small budget. A report by the Organisation for Economic Co-operation and Development (OECD) made a disappointing observation about Canada's financial contribution. Indeed, the government budget for official development assistance (ODA) fell as a percentage of

GDP between 2012 and 2017, from 0.31% of GDP to 0.26% (OECD September 2018). In 2016 alone, the first Trudeau budget reduced ODA by 4.4% (Langlois 2017). This means that the previous Conservative government of Stephen Harper allocated a larger share of its budget to ODA in comparison to the current Liberal government. Acknowledging these criticisms, the Trudeau government included in its 2018 budget an ODA investment of $2 billion over five years (Canadian Council for International Cooperation 2018). This meant significant growth of 9% for the 2018–2019 fiscal year. However, the growth rate will sharply drop in the following years to reach around 3%. By the end of these five years of investment, Canada's share of ODA with respect to the GDP will have remained relatively flat and is expected to hover at around 0.26%.

The Trudeau government's feminist approach to international aid most likely reflects the Prime Minister's deep personal convictions. In addition, it responds well to his election promises and represents a real change in philosophy from the Conservative government's approach. However, the real impact of this new policy, in the absence of a supplementary budget, remains to be seen. Considering that the average ODA/GDP ratio of OECD countries remains at around 0.31% (OECD April 2018), is the Canadian contribution sufficiently important to say that Canada is truly back?

## CONCLUSION

Justin Trudeau began his mandate with an ambitious foreign policy agenda. Surprisingly, despite a rather mixed record, 36 of 43 (84%) foreign and defence policy promises were fully or partially fulfilled, which is certainly attributable to the fact that their achievement was relatively easy in many cases. In addition, some international issues — such as the renegotiation of NAFTA — could not be promised as these events were impossible to predict in 2015.

In Trudeau's defence, there is no doubt that Canada has faced a changing international environment that has been particularly hostile to it. While some of the Trudeau government's difficulties can be explained by this change, others arose from misguided Liberal policies. While Justin Trudeau claimed that Canada was back on the world stage, we must recognize that Canada's return was not as glorious as promised. Relations are now difficult with the United States, but also with Saudi Arabia, China, India, and Russia.

From a trade negotiation perspective, Minister Freeland has instilled a progressive and feminist foreign policy vision. While the military engagement and development assistance philosophy has changed significantly, military re-engagement in peacekeeping operations has fallen short of promises, and Canadian aid has received little in the way of additional funding. The Liberal government has stayed the course with the Conservatives by continuing to escalate tensions with Russia in Eastern Europe.

Minister Freeland contributed to the conclusion of the Comprehensive Economic and Trade Agreement (CETA) thanks to her marathon of negotiations with the European Union and Wallonia, as well as the negotiation of the new Comprehensive and Progressive Agreement for Trans-Pacific Partnership (CPTPP) that replaced the TPP after the United States' withdrawal, and a Canada-Chile agreement, the first that includes a chapter on gender equality in such a trade agreement. While the new trade agreements offering the greatest economic potential for Canada (TPP as a precursor to the CPTPP as well as CETA) were largely driven by the previous government, the new economic agreement with the United States and Mexico (CUSMA) is certainly the main outcome to be claimed by the Trudeau government.

## REFERENCES

Bellavance, Joël-Denis. 2016. "EI: le Canada mettra fin aux frappes aériennes," *La Presse,* February 8, 2016. https://www.lapresse.ca/actualites/politique/politique-canadienne/201602/08/01-4948346-ei-le-canada-mettra-fin-aux-frappes-aeriennes.php.

Blank, Stephen and Monica Gattinger. 2018. "Canada-U.S. Relations Under President Trump: Stop Reading the Tweets and Look to the Future." In *Justin Trudeau and Canadian Foreign Policy*, Hillmer, Norman and Philippe Lagassé (eds.), 1ᵗ ed.: 83–102. Cham: Palgrave Mcmillan.

Buzzetti, Hélène. 2016. "Le Canada retire ses avions de Syrie… mais gonfle ses troupes," *Le Devoir,* February 9, 2016. https://www.ledevoir.com/politique/canada/462495/le-canada-retire-ses-avions-de-syrie-mais-gonfle-ses-troupes.

Coulon, Jocelyn. 2018. *Un selfie avec Justin Trudeau: Regard critique sur la diplomatie du premier ministre,* 1ˢᵗ ed., Montréal: Québec Amérique.

Dutt, Barkha. 2018. "Trudeau's India trip is a total disaster—and he has only himself to blame," *Washington Post,* February 22, 2018. https://www.washingtonpost.com/news/global-opinions/wp/2018/02/22/trudeaus-india-trip-is-a-total-disaster-and-he-has-himself-to-blame/?noredirect=on&utm_term=.e986964a9fb8.

France 24. 2017. "Au sommet de l'Otan, Donald Trump fait la leçon aux 'mauvais payeurs' de l'Alliance," April 25, 2017. https://www.france24.com/fr/20170525-sommet-otan-trump-fait-lecon-mauvais-payeurs-alliance-budget-militaire.

Global Affairs Canada. 2015. *Canada-India Free Trade Agreement Negotiations.* Ottawa: Global Affairs Canada. https://international.gc.ca/trade-commerce/trade-agreements-accords-commerciaux/agr-acc/india-inde/fta-ale/info.aspx?lang=eng.

Global Affairs Canada. 2017. *Canada's Feminist International Assistance Policy.* Ottawa: Global Affairs Canada. https://international.gc.ca/world-monde/issues_development-enjeux_developpement/priorities-priorites/policy-politique.aspx?lang=eng.

Government of Canada. 2019. *Steel and aluminum.* Ottawa: Government of Canada. https://international.gc.ca/trade-commerce/controls-controles/steel_alum-acier_alum.aspx?lang=eng.

Hemmadi, Murad. 2018. "Canada and India can't seem to make a trade deal. Here's why," *MacLean's*, February 21, 2018. https://www.macleans.ca/politics/ottawa/canada-and-india-cant-seem-to-make-a-trade-deal-heres-why/.

Langlois, Sophie. 2017. "Aide humanitaire: le Canada moins généreux sous Trudeau que sous Harper," *Radio-Canada*, April 13, 2017. https://ici.radio-canada.ca/nouvelle/1027991/aide-humanitaire-canada-trudeau-harper.

Le Devoir. 2018. "Le Canada commandera une mission de formation en Irak," July 12, 2018. https://www.ledevoir.com/politique/canada/532178/le-canada-commandera-une-nouvelle-mission-de-formation-en-irak.

Liberal Party of Canada. 2015. *Real Change: A New Plan for a Strong Middle Class.* https://www.liberal.ca/wp-content/uploads/2015/10/New-plan-for-a-strong-middle-class.pdf.

Lilly, Meredith B. 2018. "International Trade: The Rhetoric and Reality of the Trudeau Government's Progressive Trade Agenda." In *Justin Trudeau and Canadian Foreign Policy*, Hillmer, Norman and Philippe Lagassé (eds.), 1<sup>st</sup>ed.: 125–144. Cham: Palgrave Mcmillan.

Marquis, Mélanie. 2018. "Les Casques bleus canadiens seront déployés au Mali pendant au moins un an," *Le Devoir*, March 19, 2018. https://www.ledevoir.com/politique/canada/523091/les-casques-bleus-canadiens-seront-deployes-au-mali-pendant-au-moins-un-an.

National Defence. 2017. *Strong, Secure, Engaged: Canada's Defence Policy.* Ottawa: National Defence. http://dgpaapp.forces.gc.ca/en/canada-defence-policy/docs/canada-defence-policy-report.pdf.

National Defence. 2018a. *Operation REASSURANCE.* Ottawa: National Defence. https://www.canada.ca/en/department-national-defence/services/operations/military-operations/current-operations/operation-reassurance.html.

National Defence. 2018b. *Operation UNIFIER.* Ottawa: National Defence. https://www.canada.ca/en/department-national-defence/services/operations/military-operations/current-operations/operation-unifier.html.

National Defence. 2019. *2015 to 2018 Quarterly Financial Reports (QFR) for National Defence,* see Table 2. Ottawa: National Defence. https://www.canada.ca/en/department-national-defence/corporate/reports-publications/quarterly-financial.html.

National Post. 2015. "We're back', Justin Trudeau says in message to Canada's allies abroad," October 20, 2015. https://nationalpost.com/news/politics/were-back-justin-trudeau-says-in-message-to-canadas-allies-abroad.

Office of the Auditor General of Canada. 2012. "Chapter 2 — Replacing Canada's Fighter Jets." In *2012 Spring Report of the Auditor General of Canada..* http://www.oag-bvg.gc.ca/internet/English/parl_oag_201204_02_e_36466.html.

Office of the Auditor General of Canada. 2018. "Report 3 — Canada's Fighter Force — National Defence." In *2018 Fall Reports of the Auditor General of Canada to the Parliament of Canada.* http://www.oag-bvg.gc.ca/internet/English/parl_oag_201811_03_e_43201.html.

Organisation for Economic Cooperation and Development. 2018. *Development aid stable in 2017 with more sent to poorest countries,* Press release. April 9, 2018. http://www.oecd.org/development/financing-sustainable-development/development-finance-data/ODA-2017-detailed-summary.pdf.

Organisation for Economic Cooperation and Development. 2018. *Canada needs to increase foreign aid flows in line with its renewed engagement.* OECD Publishing. http://www.oecd.org/canada/canada-needs-to-increase-foreign-aid-flows-in-line-with-its-renewed-engagement.htm.

Proctor, Jason. 2018. "Everything you need to know about Huawei, Meng Wanzhou and her possible extradition," *CBC,* December 12, 2018. https://www.cbc.ca/news/canada/british-columbia/huawei-meng-extradition-questions-fraud-1.4943162.

Rice, Jeffrey and Von Hlatky, Stéfanie. 2018. "Trudeau the Reluctant Warrior? Canada and International Military Operations." In *Justin Trudeau and Canadian Foreign Policy,* Hillmer, Norman and Philippe Lagassé (dir.), 1ˢᵗed.: 285–302. Cham: Palgrave Mcmillan.

Russel, Andrew. 2018. "Security report on Justin Trudeau's India trip finds serious 'gaps' in vetting process," *Global News,* December 3, 2019. https://globalnews.ca/news/4724222/security-report-on-trudeaus-india-trip-finds-serious-gaps-in-vetting/.

The Times of India. 2018. "Justin Trudeau mocked for his 'Bollywood adventure' in India," February 24, 2018. https://timesofindia.indiatimes.com/india/justin-trudeau-mocked-for-his-bollywood-adventure-in-india/articleshow/63054437.cms.

Vanderklippe, Nathan. 2017. "On Trudeau's rocky China trip, Communist newspaper lashes out at Canadian media," *The Globe and Mail,* December 6, 2017. https://www.theglobeandmail.com/news/world/on-trudeaus-rocky-china-trip-communist-newspaper-lashes-out-at-canadian-media/article37220194/.

# Conclusion
## Overview and Election Perspectives

Lisa Birch and François Pétry

This book has taken you on a journey into the period between two federal elections to scrutinize the performance of the Trudeau Liberal government from 2015 to 2019. On this journey, we explored the meaning of a mandate, the promise-keeping record of the Trudeau government, and its actions on matters about which it made no promises. The Trudeau government began its mandate in a spirit of optimism claiming that it would bring forward an agenda for real change using sunny ways to deliver both its 353 election promises to strengthen the middle class and a general promise to govern according to progressive values in an open, honest, and transparent way. Clearly, Trudeau saw his mandate in two ways: an imperative mandate to fulfill Liberal promises and an independent mandate to govern on all matters according to the Liberal vision and values. His government implemented the "deliverology" model of governance to enhance its results as it began changing policies from the Harper Conservative government to bring Canada back to core Liberal values.

### 16.1 REAL CHANGE AGENDA

The Trudeau government fared well in delivering real change through implementing its promises by fulfilling in whole or in part 90% of its 353 specific election promises. Of the 353 specific election promises, our policy experts flagged 45 pledges as ones of utmost importance. These pledges stood out because they embodied policy transformation, offered a potential social impact of significance, expanded the federal role in a policy domain, shifted policy away from those of the Harper Conservatives, occupied a central place in the Liberal vision, and implied a significant economic and budget impact either for new costs or cost savings. These 45 promises, which were flagged by our collaborators, are at the heart of the real change agenda. Thus, the question: How were the 45 most important promises of change fulfilled in comparison to all the other promises identified by the Polimetre team? Figure 16-1 answers this question by comparing the pledge fulfillment rates for the two types of promises.

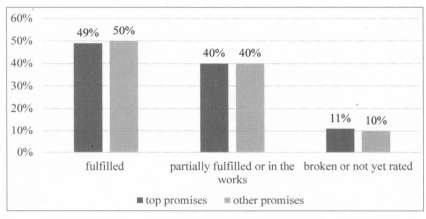

FIGURE 16-1 – Fulfillment of the Top Promises (n=45)
Compared to All Other Promises (n=292)

Whereas the Trudeau government fulfilled entirely or in part 90% of its other pledges, it fulfilled entirely or in part 89% of its top promises, a difference that is too small to claim that the top promises were not fulfilled at the same rhythm as other promises. Let us review in some detail the top promises starting with the two broken budget promises, namely the promise to create a small deficit and the one to return to a balanced budget in 2019 (See Chapter 4 by Geneviève Tellier and Cheick Alassane Traoré, and Chapter 5 by Marcelin Joanis and Stéphanie Lapierre). The decision to break these two promises, however, enabled the Trudeau government to fulfill other promises destined to implement the Liberal vision of a diverse and inclusive Canada with a reinforced middle class.

As promised, the Trudeau government invested in social infrastructure for affordable housing and in an intergovernmental framework agreement with the provinces and territories on early learning and child care. It also invested in public transit, innovation incubators and networks for businesses. It has increased support for families through the Canada

Child Benefit and for seniors through the Guaranteed Income Supplement to reduce poverty (see Daniel Béland and Michael J. Prince's chapter). It has adjusted the immigration rules to facilitate access to permanent residence and citizenship for international students and to reduce the cost of hiring caregivers recruited from abroad. It reinstated access to temporary health services for refugees and hosted Syrian refugees (see the chapter by Mireille Paquet). It has implemented policies for gender equality and against gender-based violence (see Karen Bird's chapter). In the health care sector, in addition to renewing the Health Accord with the provinces and territories, it has taken steps to improve access to and reduce the cost of mental health services. It has also engaged in a new area of federal health policy for prescription drugs and lower drug costs (see the chapter by Amélie Quesnel-Vallée, Rachel McKay, and Antonia Maioni). It legalized and regulated recreational cannabis, moving Canada away from a prohibition-based drug policy (see Jared Wesley's chapter).

At the international level (see the chapter by Julien Lauzon Chiasson and Stéphane Paquin), the Trudeau government put an end to Canada's military operations in Iraq and reoriented foreign policy toward multilateralism and peacekeeping operations. It has refocused international aid on reducing poverty and improving maternal health in developing countries. However, it has broken its promise to maintain military budgets, which may have partly limited its ability to re-engage more quickly and more widely in UN missions. Efforts to diversify Canada's trading partners while promoting a progressive trade policy have been partially achieved, with some initiatives being successful, while those with China and India have failed.

As promised, the Trudeau government increased its use of green technologies and launched a federal-provincial-territorial process to create a pan-Canadian climate change framework and modernize the environmental assessment process. However, it did not eliminate subsidies to the fossil fuel industry as it had committed to do. Opposition from some provinces and territories to climate change and carbon tax policies in this regard has complicated the task of the Liberal government. In addition, the decision to buy the Trans Mountain pipeline seems to contradict the Liberal commitment to reconcile the environment and the economy through an energy transition (see the chapter by Pierre-Olivier Pineau).

As promised, the Trudeau government has taken concrete steps toward reconciliation with Indigenous peoples by, for example, initiating the implementation of the 94 recommendations of the Truth and Reconciliation Commission, including the inquiry into missing and murdered

Indigenous women and girls (see the chapter by Karen Bird and the chapter by Thierry Rodon and Martin Papillon). It has allocated resources for the implementation of the Kelowna Accord. From the beginning of its term of office, the Trudeau government sought to establish nation-to-nation relations with Indigenous leaders, but by acquiring the Trans Mountain pipeline, it compromised its promise to recognize the legal rights and land and environmental management traditions of the Indigenous peoples even though Bill C-69 offers some recognition.

Other important promises of change relate to electoral issues, party financing, and the modification of the electoral system to introduce a form of proportional representation. As promised, a parliamentary committee was created to study electoral reform, but the Liberal government broke its promise to replace the first-past-the-post system with a more proportional system, preferring the status quo to a real change in the electoral system (see the chapter by Henry Milner). The Liberal government has also introduced new rules in the electoral law that limit party funding and third-party interventions in elections, encourage education and voter participation, and seek to prevent foreign interference in elections via social media. It also created an independent auditing system to ensure non-partisan government advertising, reduced public spending on advertising, and nominated former governor general David Johnston as Canada's first independent commissioner responsible for organizing leadership debates in elections (see Alex Marland and Vincent Raynauld's chapter).

Many important promises of change have been fulfilled only in part or are still underway. Several factors come into play to explain why these promises are not fully kept at the end of the mandate. First, as François Rocher explained in Chapter 3, Canadian federalism and the dynamics between the federal government and those of the provinces and territories have a decisive influence on the fulfillment of promises in areas of shared jurisdiction. When the interests and ideology of some provincial premiers are at odds with those of the federal government, it is sometimes difficult to advance on issues such as the fight against climate change, the solution of which requires transformational change at all levels of government. At times, the Liberal Party has been sufficiently cautious in its commitment to work with the provinces and territories so as not to guarantee results in writing. This last observation can also be generalized to certain promises in international relations, which do not explicitly guarantee results since their fulfillment is partly beyond the control of the Canadian government.

Another explanatory factor is that many promises imply both government action in the short term (policy output) and the results of policy action in the long term (policy outcomes), which are difficult to disentangle. Such promises often lead to the fulfillment verdict "kept in part or in the works." Consequently, the impact of the changes introduced by Justin Trudeau through his economic policy to reinforce the middle class was limited because of global economic conditions that account for the lack of progress in middle class salaries over the last three years (see Chapter 5 by Marcelin Joanis and Stéphanie Lapierre). In April 2019, the OCED acknowledged this global trend and called for government action to help the middle class as it released its study entitled *Under Pressure: The Squeezed Middle Class*. In the same vein, some ambitious promises have resulted in limited changes that have fallen short of expectations. This is the case for the attempt at reconciliation with Indigenous peoples. What the Liberal government has accomplished in four years is obviously not enough to reverse 150 years of colonial history and policy toward Indigenous peoples and close the gap in quality and living conditions.

## 16.2 VOTERS AND ELECTION PROSPECTS

What is the link between keeping election promises and voting? Do voters reward elected politicians for their ability to keep their election promises? According to the conventional interpretation of an imperative mandate presented in Chapter 1, citizens hold the government accountable for carrying out campaign promises. If the conventional interpretation is correct, we should expect Canadians to reward Justin Trudeau's government by maintaining (if not increasing) their support for the Liberal Party in the year leading up to the election.

As shown in Figure 16-2, the Liberal government enjoyed an increase in popular support in its first year, but this honeymoon only lasted until September 2016. After that, Liberal voting intentions decreased more or less regularly to the point that in March 2019, seven months before the next election, they went from 39.5% of the vote in the 2015 election to 32.5%. This is significantly lower than the intended Conservative vote, suggesting the possibility of a victory for the Conservative Party led by Andrew Sheer in the 2019 elections.

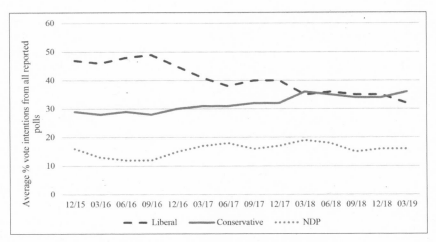

FIGURE 16-2 – Voter Intentions, December 2015–March 2019
Source: 338Canada.com

How can we explain the apparent paradox of declining popular support for the Liberals despite their good record of keeping campaign promises? The first possible explanation brings us back to the 2015 election results. The Liberal Party of Canada formed a majority government with 184 (54%) of the seats in Parliament, but only 39.5% of the popular vote. Thus, 60.5% of Canadians already preferred another party. Naturally then, the more the Liberal government fulfills its promises, the more it pleases its own electoral base, and the more it is likely to displease other voters for a panoply of reasons. For supporters of the Conservative Party, the government is not far enough to the right; for those of the New Democrats, it is not enough to the left; and for Green Party supporters, it is not green enough.

A second explanation lies in the fact that citizens perceive the government's performance in part on the pledge-keeping record; however, their perception of pledge-keeping is not the same as that of experts. As Thomas Mulcair noted in the foreword, the Polimetre verdicts can be interpreted as meaning that 90% of the promises were kept at least in part (this is the interpretation we adopted in this book). Alternatively, they can be interpreted as indicating that only 50% of the promised were kept fully. Furthermore, according to negative stereotypes that are well anchored in Canadian society, though not founded in fact, political parties "break their promises". Given the negativity bias that characterises popular evaluations of the ability of politicians to keep their promises, it seems inevitable that many Canadians lean at best toward the second interpretation when they assess the degree to which the government fulfills its promises and in the worst case, toward the stereotyped interpretation.

This difference of interpretation between citizens and experts is linked in part to the distinction between government-action promises (*policy output*), which in principle are to be fulfilled in the more or less short term, and the results of policy action (*policy outcomes*) in the longer term. This distinction is paramount in the case of the many liberal promises of change whose effects on society and the economy will only materialize in the medium and long term. This distinction has often led the Polimetre team to award a verdict of "promises in the works" to promises involving a result. However, it seems that many Canadians do not always distinguish between promises of action and promises of results. This lack of distinction is likely to affect negatively their perceptions of promise fulfillment especially if citizens seek results while governing parties can only produce policy decisions whose effects will materialize over time.

It is interesting to note that the three moments of declining voter intentions in Figure 16.1 tend to coincide with a deterioration in the tone of political coverage by the Canadian media portraying Justin Trudeau in an unfavourable light. At the beginning of January 2017, a first decline in support for the Trudeau government appeared. This decline in support comes after the controversy surrounding the failure to honour the promise to change the voting system, the approval of pipeline projects in November 2016, Justin Trudeau's official visit to China, and a Trudeau family vacation on a private island. In the winter of 2018, Trudeau's official visit to India provoked a media hurricane and exposed security clearance issues for Canadian delegations (see Chapter 15 by Julien Lauzon Chiasson and Stéphane Paquin).

The media storm surrounding the SNC-Lavalin affair in the winter of 2019 tainted the Trudeau government's record regarding its overall implicit promise of a transparent and accountable government with strong and ethical leadership. The real change agenda of the Liberals projected the image of greater diversity in cabinet and a different approach to governance. Ironically, this seems to be both a success story of the Trudeau government and a factor in its current difficulties. The numerical gender parity and the greater ethnic diversity in the composition of the cabinet of ministers is one thing, but their consequences are of a different order. This has resulted in changes in the way of doing politics. Former Justice minister Jody Wilson-Raybould in her testimony and former minister of Aboriginal

Services Jane Philpott in her letter of resignation both invoked funda-
mental values and ethical principles. Clearly, from a moral standpoint,
these former senior cabinet members have placed loyalty to the values,
principles, and people who defend them above loyalty to the prime
minister, cabinet, and party.

The SNC-Lavalin case raises important issues. Should potential job
losses and their potential economic impact be considered as a criterion for
concluding a deferred prosecution agreement? Is it appropriate for the
Prime Minister and his closest advisers to raise such criteria, and does that
interfere with the independence of the judiciary? Do Deferred Prosecution
Agreements undermine the rule of law? Should the roles of the Attorney
General and the Minister of Justice be separated to protect the rule of law
and the independence of the judiciary? Is it appropriate to record a conversation without the knowledge of an interlocutor and make it public? How
much can, or should, a prime minister "do politics differently" by allowing
an exception to the rules of confidentiality of cabinet discussions and by
relaxing party discipline in our parliamentary system? The resignations of
these high-level ministers, as well as Gerald Butts, principal secretary to the
Prime Minister, and clerk of the Privy Council, Michael Wernick, have
eroded the Liberal brand, raised questions about Justin Trudeau's leadership,
and provoked internal quarrels in the Liberal caucus. Since the beginning
of this affair, voting intentions favourable to the Liberals have dropped
considerably. It may be that for the Canadian electorate, the explicit Liberal
commitment to govern responsibly and lead the country in the right
direction is paramount before any other criteria. Thus, while the Trudeau
Liberals have excelled in fulfilling their campaign promises with results
superior to those of any government since 1993, public perceptions may
well be influenced by a change in branding optics following the
SNC-Lavalin affair.

In the end, many voters are probably more concerned with outcomes
such as the economic conditions in their area or the perceptible changes in
policies that produce observable effects for them in their daily lives. Yet in
a four-year term, in many cases, the best a government can do is to make
decisions and produce policy outputs that may create the desired social
and economic changes over the long term.

Are the results of these analyses unique to Justin Trudeau's Liberal
government? Is the link between the Liberal performance in office and the
evolution of their popular support comparable to links observed for
previous governments? To answer these questions, the Table 16-1 presents

the data on the performance of recent federal governments compared to their popular support. More precisely, Table 16-1 situates changes in the vote for the incumbent party from one election to the other (first column) relative to the percentage of promises kept at least in part (second column) and the real GDP growth rate for the year of the election (third column). The last two variables are adjusted to take into consideration the pheno- menon of attrition of the popular vote for the governing party. In fact, recent research (Thomas 2015; Achen and Bartels 2016) shows that parties who held mandates consecutively are not as successful at the polls compared to political parties that are on their first mandate (see the appendix for a description of the adjustment method).

TABLE 16-1 – Promise Keeping, GDP Growth and Popular Support, 1993-2015

| GOVERNMENTS | VOTE CHANGE SINCE THE LAST EÉLECTION (%) | ADJUSTED KEPT PROMISES (%) | ADJUSTED REAL GDP GROWTH RATE IN THE ELECTION YEAR (%) |
|---|---|---|---|
| Chrétien (1993-1997) | -2.9 | 53 | 4.3 |
| Chrétien (1997-2000) | +2.4 | 59 | 4.7 |
| Chrétien (2000-2004) | -4.1 | 62 | 2.5 |
| Martin (2004-2006) | -6.5 | 50 | 1.8 |
| Harper (2006-2008) | +1.4 | 68 | 1.0 |
| Harper (2008-2011) | +2.0 | 56 | 2.8 |
| Harper (2011-2015) | -7.7 | 68 | 0.8 |

Sources: Figure 1-1, Chapter 1 for promises; Elections Canada 2019 (various years) for the vote change; World Bank 2019 for real GDP

According to the numbers in the first column of the table, four out of seven of the most recent governments "lost feathers" from one election to the other.[1] Therefore, the expected drop in popularity for the Liberal Party of Justin Trudeau is not an exceptional phenomenon in Canada. The comparison of numbers in the second column reveal the absence of a clear relationship between promise keeping and change in popular support. The scatter plot shown in Figure 16-3 illustrates this absence of a relationship in a graph. The linear regression line indicates a positive correlation that is not significant statistically (R=0.04). In other words, even if the data

---

1. The drop in electoral support for the incumbent party between two elections is not unique to Canada. This disadvantage effect for the governing party has been observed in many countries (Strøm 1990, Nannestad et Paldam 2002).

suggest that the governments which kept their promises better lost less popular support than the others, the relationship is not robust enough to draw a conclusion one way or the other. The lesson to retain here is that promise keeping probably has little influence on voting, at least in Canada. We will thus resist the temptation to extrapolate from the trend line in Figure 16-3 the estimated value of the change in popular vote for Justin Trudeau and the Liberal Party that would correspond to their promise keeping score of 90%.

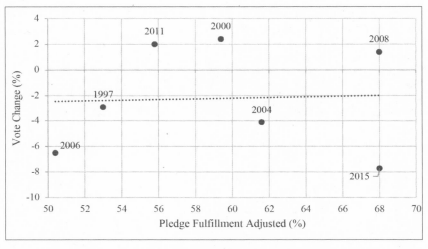

FIGURE 16-3 – Scatter Plot of the Change in Votes and Promise Keeping

By contrast, the comparison of the numbers in the third column indicate a relationship that is significantly positive between the change in popular support and the real GDP growth rate during the election year, which is confirmed by the scatter plot and the linear regression line in the Figure 16-4 (R=0.58). Thus, contrary to promise keeping, the GDP growth rate seems to have a real influence on the popular vote, at least in Canada. Given that the World Bank predicts a growth rate of 1.2% in Canada in 2019, by extrapolating from the trend line in Figure 16-4, we estimate the value of the change in the popular vote for Justin Trudeau's Liberals in the 2019 elections to be at -5.8%, which corresponds to a vote score of 33.7% (with a confidence interval of plus or minus 4%).

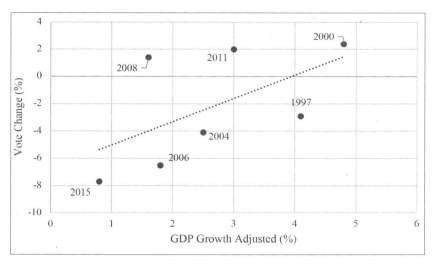

FIGURE 16-4 – Scatter Plot of the Change in Votes and GDP Growth

Next October, voters will have the final say on the assessment of the Trudeau government's mandate for real change. What will be their evaluation criteria? The government's record of promises kept in full or in part relative to those that were broken (its imperative mandate)? Their perceptions of the capacity of Justin Trudeau and the Liberal Party to govern well (its independent mandate), the Liberal Party's image and brand? The economic conditions in their region or the overall GDP growth rate? The government's performance on critical issues for them such as climate change, health care of the federal deficit? The election promises of all parties and their credibility regarding the most important issues? Alternatively, will they vote by opposition to minimise the chances of the political party they like the least of winning the elections? Whatever criteria citizens retain when they are in the voting booth, this book reveals just how important it is to know the election platform of each political party because it provides a sampling of how each party's ideology translates into public policies. Moreover, it will become the priorities of the new government, which will seek to fulfill its election promises, and it will guide the government of Canada for the next four years.

## APPENDIX – ADJUSTING THE DATA FOR THE LENGTH OF PARTY TENURE IN OFFICE

Research has shown that incumbent parties that have been in power consecutively over more than one term do not fare as well electorally as first-term incumbent parties (Thomas 2015; Achen and Bartels 2016). This phenomenon of attrition associated with a party's tenure in office is measured here by the number of years since the last change of party in power. It is expected that the longer a party has been in power on a continuous basis, the greater the attrition and the greater its negative impact on the popular support for the party. These results lead us to adjust the values of our explanatory variables in the model of change in popular support to account for the length of party tenure in office.

To measure the impact of attrition, we regress the change in popular support for each party on the number of terms the party has been in power, the percentage of pledges fulfilled at least in part and the rate of real GDP growth during the election year. The regression estimates indicate that each additional term in office reduces the incumbent party's popular support by 10 percentage points of pledges fulfilled and of the GDP growth rate. We calculate adjusted pledge fulfillment rates and GDP growth rates by subtracting 10% for each additional term in office from the actual rate of pledge fulfillment.

REFERENCES

Achen, Cristopher, and Larry Bartels. 2016. *Democracy for Realists. Why elections do not produce responsive government.* Princeton: Princeton University Press.

Elections Canada. 2019. *General Election—October 19, 2015.* https://www.elections.ca/content.aspx?section=ele&document=index&dir=pas/42ge&lang=e.

Nannestad, Peter, and Martin Paldam. 2002. "The Cost of Ruling", dans *Economic Voting*, Han Dorussen and Michael Taylor (dir.). London: Routledge, 17-44.

OECD. 2019. *Under Pressure: The Squeezed Middle Class.* https://read.oecd-ilibrary.org/social-issues-migration-health/under-pressure-the-squeezed-middle-class_689afed1-en#page1Qc125--Canada—Sondages. Sondages pour la 43e élection fédérale canadienne http://canada.qc125.com/sondages.htm.

338Canada.com. Electoral Projection for 43rd Canadian General Election. http://338canada.com/index.htm

Strøm, Kaare. 1990. "A Behavioral Theory of Competitive Political Parties". *American Journal of Political Science* 34 (2): 565-598.

Thomas, Jason J. 2015. *Party Duration: Examining the effect of incumbent party tenure on electoral outcome*. Doctoral Dissertation. Iowa City: University of Iowa.

World Bank. 2019. *GDP per capita Annual Growth Rate*. https://data.worldbank. org/indicator/NY.GDP.PCAP.KD.ZG

# Authors' Biographies

**ANTOINE BABY-BOUCHARD** is completing his integrated baccalaureat degree in philosophy and political science, for which he was the program representative from fall 2015 to fall 2018. Since January 2017, he works as a research assistant at the Center for Public Policy Analysis where he participates actively in research and content analysis activities linked to the production, updating, and closing of Polimetres. He was also a tutorial leader in the course entitled Public Administration and Public Policy in the winter 2019.

**DANIEL BÉLAND** was recently appointed Director of the McGill Institute for the Study of Canada. He is also a James McGill Professor in the Department of Political Science at McGill University. Previously, he held the Canada Research Chair in Public Policy (Tier 1) at the Johnson-Shoyama Graduate School of Public Policy, University of Saskatchewan. Professor Béland has published more than 15 books and 130 articles in peer-reviewed journals. He specializes in social policy.

**LISA BIRCH** is Executive Director of the Center for Public Policy Analysis, Associate Professor (Université Laval), and Professor (Champlain St. Lawrence College). Her expertise focuses on public management and public policy, textual analysis, and the fulfillment of campaign promises, including the methodology of the Polimetre, of which she is a co-founder.

**KAREN BIRD** is Professor and Chair in the Department of Political Science, McMaster University. Her work focuses on ethnic and gender diversity, intersectionality, and the political representation of women, Indigenous groups, and immigrant-origin and ethnic minorities in parliaments. In 2015, she was the winner of the Canadian Political Science Association Jill Vickers Prize for the best conference paper on gender and politics.

**STEVE JACOB** is Professor of Political Science at Université Laval and Director of the Center for Public Policy Analysis. His research interests include policy evaluation, public administration ethics, and result-based management.

**MARCELIN JOANIS** is Professor in the Research Group on Globalization and Management of Technology at Polytechnique Montréal. He is the Vice-President for Research of the Center for Interuniversity Research and Analysis of Organizations (CIRANO) where he has published seven volumes of the *Québec économique* series that he founded. He is an expert in public economics. His current research centres on infrastructure, public contracts, and public finance.

STÉPHANIE LAPIERRE is a master's level graduate of economics from the University of Sherbrooke and an economist and project director at the Center for Interuniversity Research and Analysis of Organizations (CIRANO). She is interested in public finance, regional development, and education. Since 2013, she is the coordinator of the project *Le Québec économique* at CIRANO.

JULIEN LAUZON CHIASSON is studying in the master of public administration program at École nationale d'administration publique. His thesis concerns the attempted Russian meddling in Western democratic processes. As a research assistant, he has participated in many projects about Canadian foreign and defence policy, Quebec's international relations, trade, and international security. He also works as a military analyst for the reserves of the Canadian Armed Forces.

ANTONIA MAIONI is Professor of Political Science and Dean of the Faculty of Arts at McGill University. She is a past-current President of the Canadian Federation for the Humanities and Social Sciences and a Member of the Board of the Canadian Institute for Advanced Research. Canadian Foundation for Healthcare Improvement. She is an internationally recognized expert in health care. Her book *Health Care in Canada* was recently published by Oxford University Press.

ALEX MARLAND is Full Professor of Political Science, Memorial University of Newfoundland. His research centres on political marketing and communication, public policy, and political elites in Canada. His book *Brand Command: Canadian Politics and Democracy in the Age of Message Control* (UBC Press) won the Donner Prize for best public policy book by a Canadian.

RACHEL MCKAY is a post-doctoral fellow at the McGill Observatory on Health and Social Services Reforms at McGill University. Her post-doctoral training in health services and policy research includes quantitative research using health administrative data and policy analyses of health and social services reforms in Quebec.

HENRY MILNER is a researcher at the Canada Research Chair in Electoral Studies at the Department of political science at the Université de Montréal, and has been a visiting professor or researcher in many universities in Canada and abroad. He was President of the Quebec political science Association (SQSP) from 2003 to 2005. He was invited to testify on the reform of political institutions before committees of the Parliament and Senate of Canada, the National Assembly of Quebec, the legislature of Ontario, and the House of Lords of the United Kingdom.

THE HONOURABLE THOMAS MULCAIR is a Visiting Professor in the Department of Political Science at the Université de Montréal. A lawyer with a degree in civil law and common law from McGill, he worked for the Quebec Ministry of Justice and served as president of the Office des professions du Québec.

Elected three times to the National Assembly, he was the author of the Sustainable Development Act when he was Minister of the Environment. Elected four times to the House of Commons, he was elected leader of the New Democratic Party and leader of the Official Opposition.

**MARTIN PAPILLON** is Associate Professor of Political Science at Université de Montréal and Director of the Research Centre on Public Policy and Social Development. His research focuses on federalism, citizenship, and the rights of Indigenous People in Canada.

**MIREILLE PAQUET** is Associate Professor of Political Science and Director of the Centre for Immigration Policy Evaluation at Concordia University. Her award-winning work focuses on the production of public policies for the selection and integration of immigrants. She recently co-edited *Citizenship as a Regime: Canadian and International Perspectives* (McGill-Queen's University Press).

**STÉPHANE PAQUIN** (Ph.D. Sciences Po Paris) is full professor at the École nationale d'administration publique (ENAP). He is the director of the Groupe d'études et de recherche et sur l'international et le Québec (GERIQ) and research director at the Centre d'études sur l'intégration et la mondialisation (CEIM). He is also the co-director of the collection, "Politique mondiale" at the Presses de l'Université de Montréal. He is authored, coauthored and directed 28 books or scientific journal articles and published over a hundred articles on international and comparative political economy. He obtained numerous prestigious scholarships, including the Canada Research Chair in International and Comparative Political Economy, a Fulbright distinguished Chair in Quebec Studies at the State University of New York, research grants from the SSHRC, the FQRSC and the PIERAN. In 2008, he was recruited to participate in the prestigious International Visitor Leadership Program of the American government.

**FRANÇOIS PÉTRY** is Professor Emeritus of Political Science at Université Laval. In 2013, he created the Polimetre in collaboration with Lisa Birch to track the promises of governments in Canada and Quebec. The Société québécoise de science politique (SQSP) honoured him by creating the annual Jenson-Pétry Award for the author of the best Master's thesis in political science submitted to a Canadian university. In May 2019, he received the SQSP excellence award for his exceptional contributions throughout his career to advancing knowledge in political science.

**PIERRE-OLIVIER PINEAU** is Professor at Hautes études commerciales in Montreal where he holds the Chair in Energy Sector Management. He specializes in energy policies, the electricity market, decision support, and economic development. His current research focuses on the environmental impact of business, electricity, and sustainable energy development in developing countries.

MICHAEL J. PRINCE is Lansdowne Professor of Social Policy at the University of Victoria. In 2012, he was presented the Queen Elizabeth II Diamond Jubilee Medal for his public services. In 2014, he was named Academic of the Year by the Confederation of Faculty Associations of British Columbia. The same year, he was awarded the Donald Smiley Prize by the Canadian Political Science Association for the best book published in the field of government and politics in Canada.

AMÉLIE QUESNEL-VALLÉE is Associate Professor with a joint appointment in the Faculty of Arts (Sociology) and Medicine (Epidemiology, Biostatistics and Occupational Health). She holds the Canada Research Chair in Policies and Health Inequalities and is Director of the McGill Observatory on Health and Social Services Reforms. Her current research examines the contribution of social policies to the development of social inequalities in health.

VINCENT RAYNAULD is Assistant Professor of Communication Studies at Emerson College in Boston. His research activities focus on political communication, social media, online politics, and journalism. In his capacity as a researcher for the Senate of Canada, he submitted a research report on CBC/Radio-Canada's national news bulletins to the CRTC in 2012.

FRANÇOIS ROCHER is Full Professor in the School of Political Studies at the University of Ottawa where he served as Director between 2008 and 2013. He is a founding member of Groupe de recherche sur les sociétés plurinationales. His research focuses on Canadian federalism, nationalism, issues related to citizenship and immigration policies, and management of ethnocultural diversity.

THIERRY RODON is Associate Professor in the Department of Political Science at Université Laval. He holds the Chair of Sustainable Development of the North and is Director of the Centre interuniversitaire d'études et de recherches autochtones (CIERA). His research focuses on northern policy and governance, Indigenous politics, and participatory democracy.

GENEVIÈVE TELLIER is Full Professor in the School of Political Studies at the University of Ottawa. Her research focuses on monetary and fiscal policies, public finances, tax policies, electoral behaviour, and parliamentary organization.

CHEICK ALASSANE TRAORÉ has a master's degree in management and is currently a doctoral candidate in public administration at the University of Ottawa. His research focuses on infrastructure financing in Canada, notably the determinants of public-private partnerships as an instrument (mode, tool, or mechanism) of financing. He is a member and officer for communications and public relations of Centre Africain de recherche pour la paix et le développement durable, an independent group created Montreal in 2018 by different students and researchers from the African diaspora with the goal of promoting exchanges and research.

**JARED WESLEY.** Prior to joining the University of Alberta, where he is Associate
Professor of Political Science, Jared served in various senior management roles
in the Government of Alberta. He is Vice Chair of the Institute of Public
Administration of Canada (IPAC). In 2018, he was awarded IPAC's National
Award of Merit in recognition of the valued personal services contributed to
further the purposes and objectives of IPAC.